POPULATION DYNAMICS

POPULATION DYNAMICS

A New Economic Approach

C. Y. CYRUS CHU

New York   Oxford
Oxford University Press
1998

Oxford University Press

Oxford   New York
Athens   Auckland   Bangkok   Bogotá   Buenos Aires   Calcutta
Cape Town   Chennai   Dar es Salaam   Delhi   Florence   Hong Kong   Istanbul
Karachi   Kuala Lumpur   Madrid   Melbourne   Mexico City   Mumbai
Nairobi   Paris   São Paulo   Singapore   Taipei   Tokyo   Toronto   Warsaw

and associated companies in
Berlin   Ibadan

Published by Oxford University Press, Inc.
198 Madison Avenue, New York, New York 10016

Oxford is a registered trademark of Oxford University Press

Library of Congress Cataloging-in-Publication Data
Chu, C. Y. Cyrus.
Population dynamics : a new economic approach / C. Y. Cyrus Chu.
p.   cm.
Includes bibliographical references and index.
ISBN 0-19-512158-9
1. Family demography.
2. Family size—Economic aspects.
3. Households—Economic aspects.
4. Population—Economic aspects.
I. Title
HQ759.98.C48   1998
304.6—dc21   98-19032

9 8 7 6 5 4 3 2 1
Printed in the United States of America
on acid-free paper

Foreword

A recent survey article described economic demography as "an offshoot of modern labor economics," which is a strange idea indeed. But it is certainly true that much of the best work in economic demography in recent decades has been carried out by labor economists, particularly under the seminal influence of Gary Becker. This literature has focused on aspects of individual and family behavior such as fertility, female labor supply, marriage, divorce, investment in children's health and education, and related micro topics.

Yet much of the substantive interest in economic demography derives from quite different questions, pertaining to population at the macro level. Does rapid population growth in the Third World lead to poverty and prevent development? Does it worsen income distributions? Has high child dependency forestalled growth and depressed saving? Will the costs of supporting growing proportions of elderly, following the demographic transition, impoverish workers and lead to economic stagnation? Is the current global economic-demographic growth trajectory sustainable, or will it encounter natural limits and do lasting damage to the environment? Do industrial populations oscillate about their equilibrium growth paths, as fertility overcompensates for labor market imbalances? Has population growth in the past fueled human progress, stimulating technical progress and facilitating massive investments in social infrastructure?

Many demographers and economic demographers since Malthus have studied these and similar questions. This tradition of research has paid relatively little attention to behavior at the individual level, and instead has developed the macro-economic and macro-demographic sides of the analysis. However, these core questions in economic demography have received less attention in recent decades from micro-oriented economic demographers. This division in substance and methods between the micro and macro orientations may reflect a dichotomy in backgrounds: very few economists actually have deep backgrounds in analytic demography, and very few demographers have deep backgrounds in economics.

Cyrus Chu is an excellent economist who has also mastered some of the most distant reaches of mathematical demography. He gives us here a brilliant and highly original volume with the stated purpose "to fill the gap between the classical supply-side population theory of Malthus and the modern demand-side theory of economic demography." He successfully joins the micro-economic approach to demographic behavior with the macro-demographic study of population dynamics. While it would be impossible to develop every theme, he does provide us with a fresh and original approach to many important problems, focusing particularly on aspects of individual or family behavior which, when aggregated, have interesting consequences for population dynamics or composition.

He typically begins an analysis by developing a model of individual behavior, often reflecting some kind of heterogeneity; and then aggregates to populations, and studies the resulting dynamics and composition, taking account of economic feedback. But he is not content to develop the classical demographic dynamics based on the synchrony of the flow of age and the flow of time. Indeed, he gently chastises demographers for succumbing to the convenience of age-time correspondence, and devoting too much attention to it, while avoiding the more difficult and equally important dynamic analysis of other relevant quantities.

In this volume, he expands the scope of economic demography and mathematical demography in some novel directions, analyzing the dynamics of income distribution, cultural patterns of behavior, occupation, and other variables. As an example of his approach, in one chapter he discusses the classical literature on the extinction of family lines. This is a mathematical literature, which takes the distributions of fertility and mortality as given, and investigates their implications. Chu takes the analysis to another level by considering how families might behaviorally respond to the likelihood of extinction by changing strategies. He views primogeniture as one adaptation to the risk of extinction in a context in which families have multiple goals. He then derives new results for probabilities of extinction under a behavioral regime.

In addition to the original material in this volume, there are also some very clearly organized synthetic and expository chapters, presenting material that will be unfamiliar to most readers. Sometimes these are just starting points for Chu's extensions and clarifications, and sometimes they stand on their own. There are illuminating chapters or sections of this sort on the "two sex problem," self generating population cycles, age in economic growth, age distribution and the politics of public pension systems, and a collection of other topics related to the consequences of the demographic transition.

This fascinating volume is fresh, original, and clearly written, and it breaks important new ground in economic demography and population dynamics. The approach it takes should stimulate work by others along similar lines.

Ronald D. Lee

Preface

The standard new household model of fertility, pioneered by Gary Becker, studied parental demand decisions on the quantity and quality of children. This demand-side approach to family fertility decisions has expanded in scope over the years as people have begun to realize that the decisions in question are usually related to such considerations as female labor supply, timing of marriage, amount of investment in children's education, and size of intergenerational transfers. But as Paul Schultz pointed out, the above-mentioned micro economic model of household behavior has not been extended to a framework suitable for analyzing any aggregate general equilibrium behavior of a population. The purpose of this book is to fill this gap and, more specifically, to find the dynamic macro implications of the various static micro family economic decisions.

The early research focused on the fertility-related decisions of the family, but as the characteristic composition of the macro population is always an aggregate result of some corresponding micro decisions of individuals, the analysis can naturally be extended to other economic decisions. Thus, it is in this framework that I studied the income distribution, attitude composition, occupation structure, and aggregate savings and pensions of the population. I hope that this book will be useful not only to researchers of demography and economics but also to all those who seek to integrate population issues more fully into the science of rational decisions.

I am grateful to many people who have made important contributions to the successful completion of this book. I would especially like to acknowledge the help of Noël Bonneuil, Gregory Chow, Chin-wen Chu, Yaw-Tsong Lee, John Fei, Hui-wen Koo, John Laitner, Ron Lee, Marc Nerlove, Kelly Olds, Hal Varian, Ken Watcher, and Tsong-min Wu, who assisted either at the early stage, when the ideas for some chapters were first developed, or later, when the scattered ideas were compiled into this book.

The research for this volume was partly supported by the National Science Council of Taiwan, the Foundation for the Advancement of Outstanding Scholarship, the Rockefeller Foundation, and the Population Council, to whom I express my sincere gratitude.

This volume integrates and extends work of mine that previously appeared in various journals. I am indebted to the publishers for agreeing to the use of the following:

> "An Existence Theorem on the Stationary State of Income Distribution and Population Growth," *International Economic Review* 31 (1990): 171–185, published by the Economics Department of the University of Pennsylvania and the Osaka University Institute of Social & Economic Research Association.
>
> "Intergenerational Income Group Mobility and Differential Fertility," *American Economic Review* 80 (1990): 1125–1138, published by the American Economic Association.
>
> "Primogeniture," *Journal of Political Economy* 99 (1991): 78–99, published by the University of Chicago Press.
>
> "Oscillatory vs. Stationary Enforcement of Law," *International Review of Law and Economics* 13 (1993): 303–315, published by Elsevier Science.
>
> "Famine, Revolt and the Dynastic Cycle: Population Dynamics in Historic China," *Journal of Population Economics* 7 (1994): 351–378, published by Springer-Verlag.
>
> "Toward a General Analysis of Endogenous Easterlin Cycles," *Journal of Population Economics* 8 (1995): 35–57, published by Springer-Verlag.
>
> "Age Distribution Dynamics During Demographic Transition," *Demography* 34 (1997): 551–563, published by the Population Association of America.

Finally, I owe a great debt to my wife Shiaolee, my son John, and my daughter Efan. I have always believed that the perseverance and concentration of a researcher are in general positively correlated with the love and support of his or her family. This is a proposition that has not been (and cannot be) proven, but is nevertheless true in my case.

Taipei, Taiwan   C. Y. Cyrus Chu
August 1997

Contents

POPULATION DYNAMICS

CHAPTER 1

Introduction

1.1 CLASSICAL AND MODERN POPULATION THEORY

The classical model of Malthus ([1783] 1970) can be described as a *supply-side, dynamic, macro* theory of population. It is a supply-side theory because Malthus did not emphasize the role of individual demand decisions on population-related variables. Individuals in ancient times certainly had their preferences for children and marriage; but Malthus assumed that such preferences would by and large be checked by natural constraints and that only when families had sufficient incomes would their preferences for children and marriage be effectively revealed (Schultz, 1981). In ancient times, when the hygienic environment and medical technology were primitive, and when production technology and administrative capacity changed relatively slowly, the natural checks on human growth and fertility almost always dominated the dynamics of population; the demand-side scenario, which originates from individual preferences, never played a significant role.[1]

The Malthusian theory is mainly a dynamic one because it describes why a population would have an equilibrium size that corresponds to the subsistence level of income and why a population would converge to such an equilibrium. Malthus argued that when a population size is larger than the equilibrium size, the per capita income will fall because of diminishing returns. This fall will be followed by an increase in mortality and a reduction in population growth rate, which in turn will drive the population size down to the equilibrium. When a population size is smaller than the equilibrium, the adjustment mechanism works in the opposite way, and the size increases toward the equilibrium.

The conventional Malthusian model also largely ignores differences in decisions made by individual families; hence a set of macro

3

variables becomes the only focus, thereby making a simple dynamic analysis possible.

As Samuelson (1976) pointed out, although most classical economists, such as Adam Smith, David Ricardo, and John Stuart Mill, considered population analysis part of economics, by the early twentieth century most economists had decided that demographic movements were largely exogenous to the economic system and should be left to sociologists and other noneconomists for discussion.

A more active alternative for economists is to modify the conventional Malthusian theory to allow it to be compatible with contemporary population practices and issues. The continuous advancement of technology in the twentieth century has made the "law" of diminishing returns rather questionable (at least in many developed countries). The ever-improving standard of living, together with continuous advances in hygiene and medical knowledge, has also diminished the role of the previously prevalent natural checks on population. Furthermore, as the role of exogenous environmental checks on fertility supply diminishes, the fertility demand decisions made possible by widespread and effective contraception techniques become more and more important in explaining modern fertility behavior, as well as population changes. It was this background that propelled the so-called demand-side approach to demographic behavior. The most important contribution to the theory of fertility demand was made by Becker (1960) and subsequent followers.

1.2 Gaps Between Malthus and Becker

The standard new household model of fertility, pioneered by Becker (1960), Becker and Lewis (1973), and Willis (1973) emphasized that parental demand decisions about the quantity and quality of children are the key to understanding current fertility behavior, as well as demographic patterns. Research on this demand-side approach to family fertility decisions has gradually expanded with the realization that the female fertility decision within a family is usually related to factors such as female labor supply, timing of marriage, decision to divorce, amount of child-education investment, and size of intergenerational and within-family transfers of income. These ramifications have attracted the attention of most researchers in the area of new household economics and have been developed into the main framework of the demand-side theory of economic demography.[2]

Yet the development of the above-mentioned demand-side theory of economic demography does not constitute a complete counterpart to classical Malthusian theory. One weakness of this literature, as Dasgupta (1995) noted, is that it has mainly focused on decisions made by a single household and has not studied how individual household decisions might lead to outcomes of a collective failure.

Although Dasgupta's criticism is valid, the problem with the demand-side theory of demographic behavior seems to be more than its inability to explain collective failure. In fact, Schultz (1988) pointed out that the micro economic model of household behavior has not been extended to a framework suitable for analyzing any aggregate general equilibrium behavior of a population. From this point of view, the micro static demand-side theory of economic demography seems to contrast significantly with the macro dynamic supply-side Malthusian theory.

There is one exception in the literature that makes possible an accommodation between the micro behavior of individual households and the macro constraints of the society. The welfare analysis of fertility, summarized in Nerlove et al. (1987) and in Razin and Sadka (1995), studied the possible differences between the social and private costs of having children and how the economy as a whole should react to such differences to attain Pareto efficiency. In this way the micro incentives and the macro efficiency can be analyzed together. But outside of this special branch, there are indeed gaps between classical Malthusian theory and modern household-decision models.

1.3 RESTRICTIONS OF AGE-SPECIFIC MODELS

The demand-side theory of economic demography is also weak in that it is very much detached from mainstream (mathematical) demography theory. This traditional demography theory, pioneered by Lotka (1939), Leslie (1945, 1948), Keyfitz (1968), and Coale (1972), segregated the human population into discrete or continuous age groups and discussed the steady state and dynamics of the population growth rate or the distribution of ages. Mathematical biologists called such models *age-classified* or *age-specific* models. In an age-specific model, vital rates are functions of ages only. But since human age is never a decision variable of individuals, very often it is difficult to reconcile the demand-side decision theory of the family with the age-specific demographic models.

In order to combine various family economic decisions with demographic variables, in most cases the researcher has to either search for models other than the Lotka–Leslie age-specific one or find a natural relationship between a household decision and the age of the household decision maker. For decision variables that have a life-cycle context (such as consumption, saving, labor supply, pension payments, and benefits), the age-specific model is clearly suitable for analysis, because the life cycle of an individual is, by definition, related to his or her age profile. But, very often, constructing a connection between age and decision is either unlikely or tortuous. For instance, there is hardly any relation between parents' age and their bequest division decisions. The female fertility decision used to be very age-specific, but once that decision is made in conjunction with the variable of female labor supply, the age-specific connection is weakened. Furthermore, the demand theory of fertility often emphasizes that fertility is affected by the opportunity cost (wage or income) to the female, so fertility is at minimum a function of wage or income, and hence the pure age-specific model cannot be applied directly.

Despite its restrictions in the applications just mentioned, the age-specific demographic model has one unique mathematical feature that is convenient for analysis. When we classify people by their ages, people aged a this year, if they survive, will always be aged $(a + 1)$ next year. Thus, treating age as the state variable, the flow of the state space synchronizes with that of the time space, so that the dynamic state-transition rule across periods is relatively simple, and hence relevant dynamic properties are easy to derive. Conversely, when people are classified according to variables other than age, almost any dynamic transition rule is possible, and hence the analysis will generally be rather difficult. Perhaps we demographic economists are more or less spoiled by the convenience of the age-specific Lotka–Leslie models and hesitate to face the importance of other variables which may be highly relevant to economic decisions. Difficult as it is, the analysis of general demographic models is a research area into which we have to proceed.

1.4 OUTLINE OF THIS BOOK

The purpose of this book is to fill the gap between the classical supply-side population theory of Malthus and the modern demand-side theory of economic demography. Specifically, in most chapters of this book I want to investigate the dynamic macro implications of the various static micro family economic decisions. The general approach to summarizing individual micro decisions into a macro demographic state variable is to apply the Markov branching process. Therefore, in many chapters the mathematical tool of branching processes will be applied, although there are also cases in which the micro–macro connection can be easily established under regular behavioral assumptions.

As to the focus of this research, of course one cannot study all the decisions that a family makes. My approach is rather demographic: I focus on only family decisions that, when aggregated to the macro level, have interesting implications in population growth or population composition. Other family decisions that are not evidently connected with the macro population structure, such as the within-household division of labor or the efficiency argument of family joint decisions, will not be discussed. To the extent possible, I try to provide a balanced discussion of background motivation, theoretical characterization, and empirical evidence. I hope that this effort can help the reader understand my proposed synthesis of microeconomic and macro approaches.

This book is separated into three parts: I, Steady States; II, Cycles and Transitions; and III, Population Dynamics in the Past and in the Future. These are typical topics in demography, and to each part I add the subjectivity of economic decisions. The steady state of a population branching process always has a constant (positive or negative) population growth rate that, as Samuelson (1972) pointed out, is not a very interesting case. Therefore; in various chapters of part I, the steady-state case is just a cornerstone of the analysis, and to the extent possible I broaden the discussion to include the comparative dynamics of the population structure.

The organization of the book is as follows. In chapter 2 I first formulate population dynamics as a multitype Galton–Watson branching process, where the state space (type) may be age or any economic variables. I provide a general analysis for the existence of the steady state. The condition for the existence theorem may have a natural economic interpretation that can be applied to some economically interesting cases.

Chapter 3 analyzes the steady-state and comparative statics of age-specific models with which most demographers are familiar. We summarize the results of Coale (1972), Arthur and McNicoll (1978), and others, which contain interesting economic implications. Chapter 4 changes the type space to general economic variables, which were treated by the new household economists as the critical factors in determining modern fertility behavior. I show how the micro static fertility decision of families can be combined to form a general type-specific stable population theory. When the above-mentioned economic variable refers to family income, I demonstrate how to estimate the state-transition probability matrix empirically. To study comparative dynamics, I review the work of Kalmykov (1962) for the case of Markov processes and extend it to the case of Markov branching processes. I explain the economic implications and applications of the revised Kalmykov condition.

Chapter 5 analyzes the case of a degenerated steady state. The origin of branching process research was the study by an English engineer (Agner Krarup Erlang), who intended to calculate the extinction probability of his mother's rare surname (Krarup). When lineage extinction was a worrisome threat in ancient periods, I show how people could make economic decisions to reduce the extinction probability of their lineage and how these decisions have affected the development of some institutions. I also study how the probability of minimum lineage extinction is affected by exogenous changes.

In chapter 6, I classify people by sex and study the equilibrium of the two-sex model. I analyze how the steady-state sex ratio is affected by parental preference for boys, a preference prevalent in many Oriental countries. The existence of the steady state in macro two-sex models was analyzed by Pollak (1990), and micro parental preferences for boys or girls were studied by Leung (1991). Although traditional wisdom tells us that there is no connection between the equilibrium sex ratio and parents' attempts to have boys, our analysis demonstrates that under reasonable assumptions such a connection does exist.

Part II of this book concerns population cycles and demographic transitions. Chapter 7 starts with a short summary discussion of the cyclical movement of population structure. Chapter 8 considers a simplified 2-type population model. The macro pattern of individual type distribution forms the "custom" of the society, while each micro individual chooses his or her type, taking into account the influence of the existing custom. I derive the formula for dynamic custom evolution and study why there are cyclical movements in such an evolution process.

I follow the classification of Chesnais (1992) and separate the population cycles in human history into pre- and posttransition ones. In chapter 9 I study population waves that respond to natural checks (or natural catastrophes) in pretransitional periods. Human beings react to these checks rationally, but it turns out that the economic decisions of human beings may either weaken or strengthen the original natural cycles. Chapter 10 moves into the discussion of the posttransitional Easterlin cycles that occur in many developed countries. These cycles are connected to an economic institution, the labor market. It is this connection that makes the Easterlin cycle unique. I analyze the existence, amplitude, and stability of these cycles and how these properties relate to the specificities of the labor market.

Chapter 11 deals with demographic transition, which refers to a shift in reproductive behavior from a state of high birth rate–high death rate to a state of low birth rate–low death rate. I analyze how individual decisions on fertility, child-education investment, saving, and voting change during the transition period and how these decisions affect the path of economic growth, the appearance of social security in democratic countries, the deficit of intergenerational transfer account, and the pattern of family income inequality. Because individual reproductive differences do not play a significant role in these macro phenomena, I do not use branching processes to proceed with my analysis in this chapter. In chapter 12 I characterize the formal dynamics of the age structure during the demographic transition process. The age dynamics derived can be viewed as an extension of the comparative static result of Coale (1972) to comparative dynamics. I also propose several indexes related to the tail composition of the age distribution, which have both interesting dynamic contexts and rich economic implications.

Part III is about the general relationship between environmental checks and human responses. I first review the well-known work of previous researchers and discuss whether population size has really "spurred" innovations and the spread of new technology in early human history and whether technological change caused by population pressure could really relieve this pressure. However, it is noted that modern economic growth and technological change have quite a different pattern from the preindustrial world. From Romer (1990) we know that modern technologies are mostly related to the extent of research and development (R&D) activities. In chapter 13 I show what the exact role of population is in the history of economic development.

Chapter 14 studies the relationship between population and environment from a broader perspective. The dynamic interaction between population and environment is in fact the main theme of Malthus's classic work. Currently, however, the Malthusian theory of environmental pressure has to be interpreted differently. In ancient times, fertility was not a decision variable, whereas it is today. In Malthus's time, environmental pressure mainly referred to a scarcity of food in large populations, whereas environmental pressure today refers to the general deterioration of air quality, the degradation of rain forests and the ozone layer, pollution, global warming, and so on. In this chapter I provide a modern version of the Malthusian dynamics on population, taking into account the endogenous changes in environmental deterioration.

The last chapter contains conclusions.

1.5 READERSHIP BACKGROUND

Readers are expected to have some background in elementary calculus and linear algebra, which are normally prerequisites for graduate programs in economics and demography. Although detailed analysis of some topics, such as the comparative dynamics presented in chapter 4, may be intrinsically mathematical, I try to make it accessible for readers with the abovementioned background. Except in particularly intriguing cases, I do not provide proofs for theorems stated in this book. However, clear and detailed references are always given so that readers can easily refer to any literature that interests them for further reading. Beyond the restatement of pure mathematical results, I try to make all analyses and presentations heuristic and intuitive.

This book can be treated either as a research monograph or as a (supplementary) textbook for a graduate course in economic demography. In the latter case, I believe that parts I and II may be more appropriate topics for one or two semesters. Part III contains idiosyncratic topics and needs to be accompanied by related essays to make the coverage comprehensive.

When treated as a research monograph, almost no book can claim to be truly comprehensive. I hope my economic approach to population dynamics will inspire readers to pursue the ideas that have been illuminated by the various chapters of this book. Clearly, the research on population economics would benefit by any further work supplementing this effort.

PART I

Steady States

CHAPTER 2

Demographic Models and Branching Processes

2.1 BACKGROUND

All models describing the dynamic pattern of human population have two common features. First, the human population is usually divided into several types, and second, each type has a type-specific stochastic reproduction rate. The traditional literature of demography has been dominated by the age-specific models of Lotka (1939) and Leslie (1945, 1948), where the type refers to the age of an individual and the type-specific reproduction rates refer to the age-specific vital rates in a life table. It has been shown that, mathematically, these age-specific models can be analyzed in a more general framework, namely, the multitype branching process. Most demography researchers, however, do not bother to pursue properties of the general branching process. They prefer to follow Lotka's (1939) age-specific renewal equation approach in proceeding with their analysis because that renewal equation is technically convenient, whereas the steady-state and dynamic properties of a general branching process are usually much more difficult to derive.

Although the analytical convenience of the age-specific models has facilitated the research on age-related topics, it also tends to obscure the fact that the age-specific model is merely a special kind of branching process. When female fertility becomes a decision variable of the family and the fertility-related family decision problems expand, these age-specific models are often unworkable. Despite the difficulties inherent in applying the traditional age-specific models to these decision dimensions, researchers still hesitate to go back to the general, but more difficult, branching process for solutions. This is perhaps why, as we mentioned in chapter 1, the demand-side theory of demography has not made much progress in describing the macro aggregate pattern of the population.

In this chapter, I separate the discussion into the age-specific branching process and general branching processes. I show that the steady states and ergodic properties of these models can both be established under some regularity conditions. Although the material in this chapter is mostly a reorganization of previously established mathematical results, I believe that my summary is systematic and will be helpful to most readers. All the results summarized will be used in later chapters, but aspects of branching processes that are irrelevant to our purposes will not be discussed. Interested readers can go to Harris (1963), Mode (1971), and Asmussen and Hering (1983) for a more detailed and thorough analysis.

Readers who are not interested in the rigorous foundation of demographic models can skip this chapter and move on to chapter 3. Thus, for non-technical readers, this chapter can be treated as an appendix which provides the (optional) mathematical background for most of the following chapters.

2.2 PRELIMINARIES

2.2.1 Type Transition and Reproduction

A multitype branching process is characterized by the condition that each individual in the population produces a random number of offspring of the various types (Mode, 1971). It is important to note that, in the above sentence, the verb "produce" should not be understood literally as "reproduce." It could refer to females reproducing children; it could also refer to across-period mobility. Specifically, an individual of type i at period t could "move" to type j at period $t + 1$. In this case we say that between period t and period $t + 1$, individual i "produces" one unit of himself in the type-j group.

2.2.2 Time Space and Type Space

The time span for the verb "produce" may either be discrete or continuous. In the former case, we say that the *time space* is discrete, and in the latter case that the time space is continuous. Similarly, the space measuring people's type, called *type space*, may also be discrete (e.g., sex, age, occupation, rural/urban location) or continuous (e.g., wealth, income, age, physical size, weight). Some type criteria, such as income or wealth, may be measured continuously or in discrete units (dollars), depending on its analytical convenience to the researcher. One should also note that, because age and time have the same measurement, when age is the type for classifying people, the state space is usually assumed to be the same as the time space. For the remainder of this book, except in the situation of age-specific models, I will concentrate upon the analysis of discrete time space and type space.[1]

2.3 Evolution of the Type Distribution

As mentioned above, we classify people by types, and the space of people's possible types belongs to a bounded subset $\mathbf{B}$ in the Euclidean l-space $\mathcal{R}^l$. Let $\mathcal{N}$ be the set of nonnegative integers, and let

$$\mathbf{Z} \equiv \left(b_1, N_1;\ b_2, N_2; \cdots; b_n, N_n \right), \quad b_i \in \mathbf{B},\ N_i \in \mathcal{N},\ i = 1,\, 2, \cdots,\, n,$$

where n can be any nonnegative integer. We shall interpret $\mathbf{Z}$ as a set of N_1 people of type $b_1, \cdots$, and N_n people of type b_n. $n = 0$ corresponds to the absence of any object. $\mathbf{Z}$ defined above is called a *point distribution* on $\mathbf{B}$.

The development of a branching process can be described by a sequence of point distributions $\mathbf{Z}_t$, $t \in \{0, 1, 2, \cdots\}$, where $\mathbf{Z}_t$ represents the objects in the tth period; $\mathbf{Z}_t = (b_1, N_{t,1}; \cdots; b_n, N_{t,n})$ means that there are $N_{t,1}$ people of type $b_1, \cdots$, and $N_{t,n}$ people of type b_n in the tth period. We let $Z_t(A)$ be the total number of people belonging to the set A in the tth period: $Z_t(A) = \Sigma_{b_i \in A}\, N_{t,i}$.

For an individual of type b in period 0, there are two kinds of uncertainties involved in the evolution of the point distribution of his offspring. First, the number of offspring an individual can produce in future periods is random, and second, his offspring may transit to become other types in the future. These uncertainties make the evolution of the sequence $\mathbf{Z}_t$, $t \in \{0, 1, 2, \cdots\}$, a stochastic process.

We shall suppose that (i) the information contained in $\mathbf{Z}_t$ is complete enough so that if we know the point distribution $\mathbf{Z}_t$, then the knowledge of previous generations adds nothing to our ability to predict the future; and (ii) the decision of a person to procreate is not affected by the presence of other people. Supposition (i) corresponds to the mathematical assumption that the sequence $\mathbf{Z}_t$, $t \in \{0, 1, 2, \cdots\}$, is a Markov process of which the state space is a point distribution. Supposition (ii) makes our Markov process a *branching process*, or a *Galton–Watson process*.[2] These two suppositions are assumed to be satisfied unless otherwise specified.

2.4 Projection Matrices and Functions

Let $Q(A, b) \equiv Q_1(A, b) \equiv E_b Z_1(A)$, which is the expected number of period-1 offspring in the set A produced by a person of type b at period 0, where E_b denotes the conditional expectation operator given b. Let $Q_t(A, b)$ be the expected number of period-t offspring in the set A produced by a period-0 person of type b. Evidently, a person with type b at period 0 will have a type-a period-t offspring if and only if he produces some descendants in period 1, who in turn produce a type-a offspring after $t - 1$ periods. Thus, if the type space **B** is discrete, we have

$$Q_t(a, b) = \sum_{k \in \mathbf{B}} Q(k, b) Q_{t-1}(a, k), \tag{2.1}$$

where $a \in \mathbf{B}$.

If the type space is continuous, then (2.1) should be rewritten as

$$Q_t(A, b) = \int_{\mathbf{B}} Q_{t-1}(A, k) Q(dk, b), \tag{2.2}$$

with an interpretation very much the same as that of (2.1). In the case of continuous state space, it is convenient to define a density function $q_t(a, b)$ corresponding to $Q_t(A, b)$. Specifically, let $q_1(., .) \equiv q(., .)$ be such that

$$Q_1(A, b) \equiv \int_A q_1(a, b) da,$$

and $q_t(a, b)$ be defined iteratively as follows:

$$q_t(a, b) \equiv \int_{\mathbf{B}} q_{t-1}(a, k) q(k, b) dk. \tag{2.3}$$

In the case with discrete state space, we assume that there are n possible types.[3] We can write $Q(i, j)$ as $Q_{i,j}$, and the $Q(., .)$ function can be represented by the following projection matrix:

$$\mathbf{Q} = \begin{pmatrix} Q_{1,1} & Q_{1,2} & \cdots & Q_{1,n} \\ Q_{2,1} & Q_{2,2} & \cdots & Q_{2,n} \\ \vdots & \vdots & \ddots & \vdots \\ Q_{n,1} & Q_{n,2} & \cdots & Q_{n,n} \end{pmatrix}.$$

The reason **Q** is called a *projection matrix* is that it can be used to project the future distribution of population types, given the current population composition. Because the expected number of offspring is never negative, $Q_{i,j} \geq 0$ must hold, and hence **Q** is a nonnegative matrix. Iterating equation (2.1), we see that the $\mathbf{Q}_t$ matrix is actually raising **Q** to the tth power:

$$\begin{aligned} \mathbf{Q}_t &= \mathbf{Q} \cdot \mathbf{Q}_{t-1} \\ &= \mathbf{Q}^2 \cdot \mathbf{Q}_{t-2} \\ &\vdots \\ &= \mathbf{Q}^t. \end{aligned}$$

For the remainder of this book, unless otherwise specified, I shall distinguish the notation in cases with discrete and continuous spaces. If a variable x is a function of t, I write it as x_t when the space of t is discrete and as $x(t)$ when it is continuous.

2.5 STEADY STATES OF BRANCHING PROCESSES

2.5.1 Discrete State Space

In the previous section, I have described the evolution of the offspring of a single individual of type b. I now proceed with the discussion of all individuals in the society. The analysis begins with the case of discrete state space.

At period 0, suppose the number of people of all types is represented by a column vector $\mathbf{N}_0$:

$$\mathbf{N}_0 \equiv \begin{pmatrix} N_{0,1} \\ N_{0,2} \\ \vdots \\ N_{0,n} \end{pmatrix}.$$

Then, by the definition of $\mathbf{Q}$, the period-t population will become

$$\begin{aligned} \mathbf{N}_t &= \mathbf{Q}\mathbf{N}_{t-1} \\ &= \mathbf{Q}^2\mathbf{N}_{t-2} \\ &\vdots \\ &= \mathbf{Q}^t\mathbf{N}_0. \end{aligned} \tag{2.4}$$

Let $\lambda_1, \lambda_2, \cdots, \lambda_n$ be the eigenvalues of $\mathbf{Q}$, and $\mathbf{w}_1, \cdots, \mathbf{w}_n$ be the corresponding right (column) eigenvectors. To avoid cumbersome discussion of degenerated cases, I assume throughout this book that the eigenvalues of $\mathbf{Q}$ are distinct, so that the eigenvectors are independent. By definition, $\mathbf{Q}\mathbf{w}_i = \lambda_i\mathbf{w}_i \; \forall i = 1, \cdots, n$. The independence of the eigenvectors guarantees that we can write any given $\mathbf{N}_0$ as

$$\mathbf{N}_0 = c_1\mathbf{w}_1 + c_2\mathbf{w}_2 + \cdots + c_n\mathbf{w}_n$$

for some set of constants $c_1, \cdots, c_n$.

The above equation, together with (2.4), gives us

$$\mathbf{N}_1 = \mathbf{Q}\mathbf{N}_0 = \sum_i c_i\mathbf{Q}\mathbf{w}_i = \sum_i c_i\lambda_i\mathbf{w}_i,$$

$$\mathbf{N}_2 = \mathbf{Q}\mathbf{N}_1 = \sum_i c_i\lambda_i\mathbf{Q}\mathbf{w}_i = \sum_i c_i\lambda_i^2\mathbf{w}_i.$$

And, in general,

$$\mathbf{N}_t = \sum_i c_i\lambda_i^t\mathbf{w}_i. \tag{2.5}$$

It is evident from (2.5) that, because c_i and $\mathbf{w}_i$ are time-invariant, as t is large, the dynamics of $\mathbf{N}_t$ will be dominated by the term associated with the largest of $|\lambda_i|$'s. The specific results are characterized by a theorem proved by Harris (1963) and Mode (1971). Before introducing this theorem, we need one more definition.

DEFINITION (D2.1) *(Mode 1971, p. 11): A nonnegative matrix $\mathbf{Q}$ is said to be irreducible if and only if for every pair of (i, j) there exists a positive integer s such that the (i, j)th element of the matrix $\mathbf{Q}^s$, denoted $Q_{i,j}^s$, is positive. If s does not depend on the pair of types (i, j), then $\mathbf{Q}$ is said to be positively regular.*

Readers who are familiar with matrix algebra might have noticed that the above positive regularity condition is essentially the same as the term primitivity used by some researchers.[4]

Now we are ready to introduce the major ergodic result in the theory of branching processes. This result, due to Harris (1963), is an application of the well-known Frobenius–Perron theorem.

THEOREM 2.1 *(Mode 1971, pp. 14–19)*
If $\mathbf{Q}$ is positively regular, then $\mathbf{Q}$ has a positive dominant eigenvalue ϱ of multiplicity one; that is, if λ is any other eigenvalue of $\mathbf{Q}$, then $|\lambda| < \varrho$. Corresponding to the eigenvalue ϱ, there is a right eigenvector $\mathbf{v}' = (v_1, \cdots, v_n)$ such that $\mathbf{Q}\mathbf{v} = \varrho\mathbf{v}$, and a left eigenvector $\mathbf{u} = (u_1, \cdots, u_n)$ such that $\mathbf{u}\mathbf{Q} = \varrho\mathbf{u}$. Both $\mathbf{v}$ and $\mathbf{u}$ have strictly positive elements with the property $\mathbf{u}\mathbf{v} = 1$. Furthermore, if $\varrho > 1$, then $\forall i \in \mathbf{B}$, the random variable $N_{t,i}/\Sigma_{j=1}^n N_{t,j}$ converges to $v_i/\Sigma_{j=1}^n v_j$ and $\mathbf{Q}^t$ converges to $\varrho^t(v \cdot u)$ almost surely as $t \to \infty$.

The almost-sure convergence of $N_{t,i}/\Sigma_{j=1}^n N_{t,j}$ to $v_i/\Sigma_{j=1}^n v_j$ can be understood intuitively. Equation (2.5) can be explicitly written as

$$\mathbf{N}_t = c_1\lambda_1^t\mathbf{w}_1 + \cdots + c_n\lambda_n^t\mathbf{w}_n. \tag{2.5'}$$

If we order the size of the n eigenvalues of $\mathbf{Q}$ in decreasing order as $\lambda_1 > \lambda_2 > \cdots > \lambda_n$, then λ_1 is denoted the dominant eigenvalue $\lambda_1 = \varrho$, and $\mathbf{w}_1$ is the dominant right eigenvector $\mathbf{w}_1 = \mathbf{v}$. As $t \to \infty$, all elements of the $\mathbf{N}_t$ vector will grow at the rate of ϱ,[5] therefore the relative size of group i will be proportional to the relative size of the ith element of the v vector.

When $N_{t,i}/\Sigma_{j=1}^n N_{t,j}$ converges to a constant as $t \to \infty$, it means that the composition of types of the population converges to a time-invariant structure. This is the typical ergodic result of the general branching process.

2.5.2 Continuous State Space

As shown in section 2.4, with continuous state space, the across-period projection mechanism is characterized not by a projection matrix but by a distribution function $Q(.,.)$ with density $q(.,.)$. The t-duplicate version of the transition density, denoted q_t, is given by the formula in (2.3). For the case of continuous state space, the condition of *positive regularity* is to require that:

CONDITION (C2.1): *There exists a positive integer t_0 such that $0 < q_{t_0}(x, y)$* $< \infty \ \forall x \in \mathbf{B}, y \in \mathbf{B}$.

As one can see, C2.1 is very much the same as D2.1. Harris (1963) showed that in the case of continuous state space other than C2.1 above, we also require an additional regularity condition:

CONDITION (C2.2): *$Q(\mathbf{B}, b)$ and $E_b(Z_1(\mathbf{B})^2)$ are both bounded functions of b.*

C2.2 is to warrant the boundedness of the first and second moments of the projection function Q. As to human population, so long as there is an upper bound for human reproduction, C2.2 will always be satisfied. Given C2.1 and C2.2, Harris proved the following theorem:

THEOREM 2.2 *(Harris, 1963, pp. 77–80; Mode, 1971, p. 236)*
If C2.1 and C2.2 are satisfied, then $Q(.,.)$ has a dominant eigenvalue ϱ, with corresponding right and left eigenfunctions $v(.)$ and $u(.)$ such that

$$pv(y) = \int_{\mathbf{B}} q(y, b)v(b)db,$$

$$pu(b) = \int_{\mathbf{B}} u(y)q(y, b)dy.$$

Let $N_t(A)$ be the number of people in the set A at period t. If $\varrho > 1$, then as $t \to \infty$, (i) $q_t(a, b) \to \varrho^t v(a)u(b)$, and (ii) $\forall A_1, A_2 \subset \mathbf{B}$, the random variable $N_t(A_1)/N_t(A_2)$ converges almost surely:

$$\frac{N_t(A_1)}{N_t(A_2)} \to \frac{\int_{A_1} v(b)db}{\int_{A_2} v(b)db}. \tag{2.6}$$

As one can see, theorem 2.2 is similar to theorem 2.1; thus, its interpretation is also the same and, hence, is omitted.

2.6 VERIFYING POSITIVE REGULARITY

It should be clear that the ergodicity property of types hinges upon whether the positive regularity conditions of theorems 2.1 and 2.2 hold true. For age-specific models, there is a special way to verify such a regularity condition, which will be demonstrated below.

2.6.1 Age-Specific Branching Processes

When age is counted by discrete units, the projection matrix of the general branching process becomes the well-known $n \times n$ Leslie matrix:

$$\mathbf{Q} = \begin{pmatrix} 0 & 0 & \cdots & 0 & F_\alpha & \cdots & F_\beta & 0 & \cdots & 0 & 0 \\ p_1 & 0 & \cdots & 0 & 0 & \cdots & 0 & 0 & \cdots & 0 & 0 \\ 0 & p_2 & \cdots & 0 & 0 & \cdots & 0 & 0 & \cdots & 0 & 0 \\ \vdots & & & & & \ddots & & & & & \vdots \\ 0 & 0 & \cdots & 0 & 0 & \cdots & 0 & 0 & \cdots & p_{n-1} & 0 \end{pmatrix}.$$

In the above matrix, F_j is the probability that a person aged j will bear a baby, α and β refer to the youngest and the oldest ages of possible female reproduction, p_i refers to the probability that a person aged i can survive to age $i + 1$, and n is assumed to be the upper bound of human age. The population dynamics are as described in (2.4).

It is easy to see that such a Leslie matrix can be decomposed into the following four blocks:

$$\mathbf{Q} = \begin{pmatrix} \mathbf{A} & \mathbf{0} \\ \mathbf{D} & \mathbf{C} \end{pmatrix},$$

where $\mathbf{0}$ is an $(n - \beta) \times (n - \beta)$ zero matrix, $\mathbf{A}$ is $\beta \times \beta$, $\mathbf{D}$ is $(n - \beta) \times \beta$, and $\mathbf{C}$ is $\beta \times (n - \beta)$. Such a block decomposition implies that females older than β can never produce any offspring of type (age) $\alpha \le \beta$ in the future. This obviously violates the condition of irreducibility, so that theorem 2.1 cannot be applied directly.

We know from (2.4) that the dynamics of $\mathbf{N}_t$ will be determined by the tth power of $\mathbf{Q} : \mathbf{Q}^t$. But as we raise $\mathbf{Q}$ to the tth power, it is not difficult to verify that

$$\mathbf{Q}^t = \begin{pmatrix} \mathbf{A}^t & \mathbf{0} \\ \mathbf{D}_t & \mathbf{C}^t \end{pmatrix}, \tag{2.7}$$

where $\mathbf{D}_t \equiv \Sigma_{j=0}^{t-1} \mathbf{C}^j \mathbf{D} \mathbf{A}^{t-j-1}$. Furthermore, since $\mathbf{C}$ is a matrix with nonnegative elements only in terms below the diagonal, we have $\mathbf{C}^t \to \mathbf{0}$ as $t \to \infty$. Finally, since $\mathbf{D}_t$ involves linear combinations of powers of $\mathbf{A}$ less than t, $\mathbf{D}_t$ should behave like $\mathbf{A}^t$, but less dramatically.

The above discussion tells us that all the relevant information about $\mathbf{Q}$ is contained in $\mathbf{A}$ and that the age group beyond the upper bound of reproduction, β, does not contribute to the intrinsic growth rate of the whole population. Formally, Parlett (1970) proved the following theorem.

THEOREM 2.3 *(Parlett 1970, p. 194)*
(i) The eigenvalues of $\mathbf{A}$ *and the eigenvalues of* $\mathbf{C}$ *constitute the eigenvalues of* $\mathbf{Q}$. *(ii) No eigenvalue of* $\mathbf{A}$ *is zero, and all eigenvalues of* $\mathbf{C}$ *are zeros. (iii)*

For any eigenvalue λ of $\mathbf{A}$, let $\mathbf{v}$ and $\mathbf{u}$ be the right and left eigenvectors; that is, $\mathbf{A}\mathbf{v} = \lambda\mathbf{v}$, $\mathbf{u}\mathbf{A} = \lambda\mathbf{u}$. The right and left eigenvectors of $\mathbf{Q}$ are determined by

$$\mathbf{Q}\begin{pmatrix} \mathbf{v} \\ \tilde{\mathbf{v}} \end{pmatrix} = \begin{pmatrix} \mathbf{v} \\ \tilde{\mathbf{v}} \end{pmatrix}\lambda, \tag{2.8}$$

$$\left(\mathbf{u}, \tilde{\mathbf{u}}\right)\mathbf{Q} = \lambda\left(\mathbf{u}, \tilde{\mathbf{u}}\right),$$

where $\tilde{v}_1 = D_{1,\beta}v_\beta/\lambda$, and $\tilde{v}_j = C_{j,j-1}\tilde{v}_{j-1}/\lambda$, $j = 2, \cdots, n - \beta$; $\tilde{u}_k = 0$, $k = 1, \cdots, n - \beta$.

Theorem 2.3 tells us that, to understand the ergodic properties of an age-specific branching process, it is sufficient to concentrate upon the block matrix $\mathbf{A}_{\beta\times\beta}$. Parlett (1970) showed that $\mathbf{A}$ is nonnegative and positively regular. Intuitively, people who are still reproductive can produce children of age 1, who in turn have a positive probability to move to any age equal to or younger than β; so $\mathbf{A}$ is irreducible. For the irreducible $\mathbf{A}$ matrix to be primitive, Sykes (1969) showed that it is sufficient to have two adjacent age classes with a positive expected fertility. This is certainly true for human populations. So $\mathbf{A}$ is indeed positively regular, and theorem 2.1 can apply.

Restricting our attention to the subset $[0, \beta]$, theorem 2.1 tells us that the age structure for ages younger than β will be proportional to elements of $\mathbf{v}$ as $t \to \infty$. Then we can use theorem 2.3 to calculate $\tilde{\mathbf{v}}$ and use (2.8) to infer the time-invariance of the overall age structure in $[0, n]$.

When the age space is continuous, the discussion is very much the same and will not be repeated here.

2.6.2 General Branching Processes

For general branching processes, there is no easy way to check the positive regularity condition; we have to verify whether $\mathbf{Q}$ is positively regular case by case. Although there is no general rule, there are some useful insights we can follow.

The reducibility of $\mathbf{Q}$ means that there is a proper subset $\mathbf{C} \subset \mathbf{B}$ such that $\forall c \in \mathbf{C}$, the offspring of c can never move out of $\mathbf{C}$; that is, $\mathbf{C}$ is an *absorbing* subset. Irreducibility rules out the possibility of such an absorbing subset and requires that each element of $\mathbf{B}$ has at least some chance to move to any other part of $\mathbf{B}$. In other words, irreducibility requires that there is perfect mobility across types when the period (of "moving") in question is long enough. For example, if we classify people by their income, then, according to theorem 2.1, a sufficient condition for the existence of a steady-state income distribution is that we have perfect income mobility.

If **Q** has been proven to be irreducible, then primitivity is easy to check. Essentially, an irreducible matrix **Q** will be *imprimitive* if it is *cyclic* (Caswell 1990). To rule out cyclicity, it is sufficient to have at least one positive diagonal element. The intuition is as follows. A positive diagonal element $Q_{i,i}$ means that an agent of type i has some chance to produce offspring of the same type. This result, together with the irreducibility of **Q**, means that there is no definite number of periods for which the offspring of any type of agent will become the same type.[6] Thus, cyclicity can be ruled out.

For the case of continuous state space, we have to check whether C2.1 and C2.2 are satisfied. As I mentioned in section 2.5.2, as long as there is an upper bound for human reproduction, C2.2 would always be satisfied. C2.1 essentially requires that the projection density $q(.,.)$ is positively regular. Again, this requires that there is perfect mobility across all measure-nonzero subsets of **B** and that there is no definite number of periods for the offspring of any agent to reenter the original type class of the agent. In the next few chapters I will provide some important applications of the general branching process.

2.7 Meaning of the Dominant Eigenvalue

I showed in theorems 2.1 and 2.2 that the size of the dominant eigenvalue is very important for determining the steady-state pattern of the population. I now provide a formal interpretation of the meaning of ϱ.

We learned from our discussion in the previous sections that for a given projection matrix, the following equation is true for the steady state:

$$\mathbf{Qv} = \varrho\mathbf{v}.$$

Because the size distribution of the population in the steady state is proportional to **v** by theorem 2.1, as t is sufficiently large, we can replace **v** by $\mathbf{N}_t$ and rewrite the above expression as

$$\mathbf{QN}_t \approx \varrho\mathbf{N}_t,$$

or equivalently

$$\sum_{j=1}^{n} Q_{i,j} N_{t,j} \approx \varrho N_{t,i}.$$

Summing the above equation over i, we have

$$\sum_{i=1}^{n}\sum_{j=1}^{n} Q_{i,j} N_{t,j} \approx \varrho \sum_{i=1}^{n} N_{t,i}.$$

Dividing both sides of the above equation by $\sum_{j=1}^{n} N_{t,i}$ yields

$$\varrho \approx \frac{\sum_{i=1}^{n}\sum_{j=1}^{n} Q_{i,j} N_{t,j}}{\sum_{i=1}^{n} N_{t,i}}.$$

Note that $\Sigma_{j=1}^{n} Q_{i,j} N_{t,j}$ equals $N_{t+1,i}$, the total number of type-i people in period $t + 1$; hence,

$$\varrho \approx \frac{\sum_{i=1}^{n} N_{t+1,i}}{\sum_{i=1}^{n} N_{t,i}}.$$

Thus, ϱ is the gross population growth rate in the steady state.

Intuitively, when the gross population growth rate ϱ is greater than 1, the size of population will expand; whereas when ϱ is less than one, the population size will contract. I will discuss this further in chapter 5.

2.8 GENERAL POPULATION MODELS IN PREVIOUS LITERATURE

As mentioned, separating people by their ages is the most natural division. It is also, however, the most passive classification, for age is clearly not a variable that any individual can actively choose or change. Previous literature contains very little discussion on general type-specific branching processes. Preston (1974) analyzed the interaction of occupational mobility and occupational differential fertility. Caswell (1990) presented a systematic mathematical analysis on general type-specific population models. But their approaches merely addressed other passive characteristics, such as occupation, physical size, or maturity stages, of human and other (animal or plant) populations. There has been no discussion on the role of active human decision.

In this chapter I have argued that the dynamics of a general type-specific population model can be characterized by a multitype branching process. In the next four chapters, I will show that the projection matrix of the macro branching process is actually formed by, or related to, individual micro decisions. Such a micro–macro connection enables us to analyze how a change in exogenous parameters can affect individual decisions, which in turn change the aggregate population pattern. These comparative statics or dynamics with behavioral background will be the emphasis of my later discussion.

CHAPTER 3

Age-Specific Population Models

Steady States and Companative Statics

Mainstream demographers studying the pattern of human population are used to classifying people by their ages. In the terminology of branching processes, the type space of the stochastic process is a subset of positive real numbers that characterize human ages. This chapter deals with this case and studies the corresponding steady states and comparative statics.

3.1 STEADY-STATE AGE DISTRIBUTION

I showed in chapter 2 that the dynamics of any type-specific population structure can be described by the equation $\mathbf{N}_t = \mathbf{Q}\mathbf{N}_{t-1}$ and that $\mathbf{Q}$ is block-decomposable in the age-specific case. The fact that the northeast block of $\mathbf{Q}$ being a zero matrix not only helps us derive the eigenvalues and eigenvectors of $\mathbf{Q}$ but also helps us characterize the dynamic evolution of the *birth size*. Let B_t be the size of birth at period t, $l_a \equiv p_1 \times \cdots \times p_a$ be the probability that a person can survive to age a, and m_a be the average number of births per surviving member aged a. We see that the following accounting identity must hold:[1]

$$B_t \equiv \sum_{a=0}^{n} B_{t-a} l_a m_a = \sum_{a=0}^{n} N_{t,a} m_a, \tag{3.1}$$

which is Lotka's (1939) well-known renewal equation. Equation (3.1) is useful for deriving the steady-state age distribution.

Given the assumption of a time-invariant fertility function m_a, the total size of birth B_t, which is a linear combination of birth sizes of all fertile age groups, naturally grows at a constant rate in the steady state. Specifically, as

$t \to \infty$, we can use (2.5') to replace the $B_{t-a}l_a$ in (3.1) by $c_1\varrho^t v_a$ and rewrite (3.1) as

$$B_t \to \sum_{a=0}^{n} c_1 v_a \varrho^t m_a \equiv \varrho^t \times k,$$

where $k \equiv \sum_{a=0}^{n} c_1 v_a m_a$ is a constant. Therefore B_t will grow at the rate ϱ in the steady state.[2] Substituting $B_t = B_0 \varrho^t$ into (3.1) yields

$$1 = \sum_{a=0}^{n} \frac{l_a m_a}{\varrho^a}.$$

From the above equation, ϱ can be solved.[3]

An advantage of expressing the population dynamics in terms of the birth size is that the steady-state age structure is easy to derive from (3.1): because at period t there are $B_{t-a}l_a$ of people aged a, the proportion of aged-a people, denoted $g_{t,a}$, is

$$g_{t,a} = \frac{B_{t-a}l_a}{\sum_{b=0}^{n} B_{t-b}l_b}.$$

In the steady state, substituting in $B_t = B_0\varrho^t$, we have

$$g_{t,a} \to g_a = \frac{\dfrac{l_a}{\varrho^a}}{\sum_{b=0}^{n} \dfrac{l_a}{\varrho^a}}.$$

So the age structure in the steady state is indeed time-invariant, as theorem 2.3 described.

When the age group is classified continuously, the positive regularity condition C1 and the boundedness condition C2 in theorem 2.2 evidently hold in the subset $[0, \beta]$. All the insight of the analysis in the previous discussion remains, and we only have to change the notations accordingly. For instance, the continuous version of the renewal equation in (3.1) becomes

$$B(t) \equiv \int_0^n B(t-a)l(a)m(a)da,$$

and the corresponding intrinsic growth rate, which is denoted r in the continuous case,[4] can be solved from the following equation:

$$1 = \int_0^n e^{-ra}l(a)m(a)da.$$

The steady-state age structure becomes[5]

$$g(a) = \frac{e^{-ra}l(a)}{\int_0^n e^{-re}l(b)db}. \tag{3.2}$$

In order to make this presentation compatible with most related analyses in previous literature, in the rest of this chapter I will consider the case of continuous age space.

3.2 Calculating Variable Means

The key variable in an age-specific model is, of course, age. The mean age of a stable population, denoted $\bar{a}$, is the integral of ages weighted by the corresponding population density:

$$\bar{a} = \int_0^n ag(a)da = \frac{\int_0^n ae^{-ra}l(a)da}{\int_0^n e^{-ra}l(a)da}.$$

However, we are very often interested in variables other than age. As mentioned in chapter 1, in order to connect an economic variable, say x, with a population structure, we have to either classify people by the variable in question or, if we decide to classify people by ages, find some relationship between x and age. In economics, this latter approach will be the most appropriate for life-cycle models, because, by definition, every economic variable within a life cycle is age-specific.

Suppose $x(a)$ is an age-specific life-cycle variable. By definition the mean value of $x(a)$ is:

$$\bar{x} = \int_0^n g(a)x(a)da = \frac{\int_0^n e^{-ra}l(a)x(a)da}{\int_0^n e^{-ra}l(a)da}. \tag{3.3}$$

The proportion of the total quantity of x attributable to people aged a is

$$g_x(a) \equiv \frac{e^{-ra}l(a)x(a)}{\int_0^n e^{-rb}l(b)x(b)db}.$$

We can define the *mean age of x* as

$$\bar{a}_x = \int_0^n ag_x(a)da = \frac{\int_0^n ae^{-ra}l(a)x(a)da}{\int_0^n e^{-ra}l(a)x(a)da}.$$

For instance, if $x(a)$, $a \in [65, n]$, refers to a social security benefit profile, then $\bar{a}_x$ is the mean age of social security beneficiaries.

In view of (3.2), it is clear that the steady-state age structure is a function of r only. We can differentiate the logarithm of $\bar{x}$ with respect to r and get

$$\frac{d \log \bar{x}}{dr} = \bar{a} - \bar{a}_x, \tag{3.4}$$

or equivalently,

$$\frac{d\bar{x}}{dr} = \bar{x}(\bar{a} - \bar{a}_x). \tag{3.4'}$$

With the above background, I introduce below some well-received comparative static results.

3.3. WELFARE IMPACT OF POPULATION GROWTH: CONSUMPTION-LOAN MODEL

It is a well-known result of Samuelson's (1958) overlapping-generation consumption-loan model that the per capita welfare is an increasing function of population growth rate. The inference is quite simple: in Samuelson's model, considering neither production nor durable goods, we can imagine that people live in an infinite orchard. With a larger population growth rate, the older generation will have more children to pick apples for them, thereby having higher per capita welfare. Thus, higher population growth produces an intergenerational transfer effect.

Arthur and McNicoll (1977, 1978), however, found that such a result was sensitive to the neglected process of production. In general, human beings have a long period of childhood before they become productive. A higher population growth rate increases the proportion of young, and hence increases the number of dependents of the society, who have to be supported by the fewer, older productive people. This certainly shakes the robustness of Samuelson's original result. The formal argument is as follows.

Let us modify the two-period overlapping-generation setup to a scenario with continuous-age life cycle. Let $c(a)$, $y(a)$, $a \in [0, n]$, be the life-cycle profile of consumption and income. If the population age structure is stable, the societal balanced-budget (or no-saving) constraint is

$$
\begin{aligned}
\bar{c} &\equiv \frac{\int_0^n e^{-ra} l(a) c(a) da}{\int_0^n e^{-ra} l(a) da} \\
&= \frac{\int_0^n e^{-ra} l(a) y(a) da}{\int_0^n e^{-ra} l(a) da} \equiv \bar{y}.
\end{aligned}
$$

Differentiating the logarithm of both sides of the above equation yields

$$
\left(\bar{a} - \bar{a}_c\right) + \frac{\int_0^n e^{-ra} l(a) \frac{\partial c(a)}{\partial r} da}{\int_0^n e^{-ra} l(a) c(a) da} = \left(\bar{a} - \bar{a}_y\right) + \frac{\int_0^n e^{-ra} l(a) \frac{\partial y(a)}{\partial r} da}{\int_0^n e^{-ra} l(a) y(a) da}, \tag{3.5}
$$

where $\bar{a}_c$ and $\bar{a}_y$ are the mean ages of consumption and income.

In Samuelson's consumption-loan model, since a change in r will never change the life-cycle production profile, we have $\partial y(a)/\partial r = 0 \ \forall a \in [0, n]$. For demonstration purposes, suppose the proportional change in $c(a)$ is independent of a; then $\partial c(a)/\partial r = \beta c(a)$. Thus, equation (3.5) can be reduced to

$$\beta = \frac{\dfrac{\partial c(a)}{\partial r}}{c(a)} = \bar{a}_c - \bar{a}_y \quad \forall\, a \in [0, n].$$

This leads to the following theorem:

THEOREM 3.1 *(Lee 1980, p. 1134)*
In a consumption-loan economy with an age-specific stable population, consumption at all ages can be increased in proportion to the change in the population growth rate times the difference between the mean ages of consumption and production.

Theorem 3.1 provides us with a simple formula for evaluating the welfare impact of a change in population growth rate. Leaving aside the size of the change, its "sign" only hinges upon the relative scales of the two mean ages. Lee (1980) showed that, if there is no population growth, and if the working age range is 20–65 and the consumption age range is 0–75, then $\bar{a}_c = 37.5$ and $\bar{a}_y = 42.5$. Thus, an increase in population growth rate will not increase the steady-state per capita consumption, in contrast to Samuelson's original result. This is the case because a higher population growth means more children being supported by relatively fewer productive people.

3.4 Welfare Impact of Population Growth: Neoclassical Growth Model

The model in the above section has not taken into account individual savings, and hence there is no capital accumulation. Arthur and McNicoll (1978) studied the impact of a change in r on the steady-state per capita consumption in a neoclassical growth model. As before, the population structure is assumed to be stable: $B(t) = B_0 e^{rt}$, and the total population size is

$$N(t) = B(t)\int_0^n e^{-ra}l(a)\,da.$$

With an age-specific labor-force participation function $h(a)$, the total size of labor is

$$L(t) = B(t)\int_0^n e^{-ra}l(a)h(a)\,da.$$

Let $K(t)$ be the size of period-t capital. Total output is determined by a production function F: $F(K(t), L(t)) = Y(t)$, which is to be spent on consumption $C(t)$ and capital accumulation $\dot{K}(t)$:

$$Y(t) = C(t) + \dot{K}(t).$$

The usual assumption in neoclassical growth models is that F is homogeneous of degree one. Thus, for $k(t) \equiv K(t)/L(t)$ and $c(t) \equiv C(t)/L(t)$, we have

$$\frac{F\big(K(t),\, L(t)\big)}{L(t)} = F\!\left(\frac{K(t)}{L(t)},\, 1\right)$$

$$\equiv f\big(k(t)\big) = c(t) + \frac{\dot{K}(t)}{L(t)}. \tag{3.6}$$

In a steady state in the sense of Solow (1956), $K(t)$, $L(t)$, and $C(t)$ all grow at the same rate, which is r. Thus, dropping the time subscript t in the steady state, we have $\dot{K} = rK$, and hence (3.6) becomes $c = f(k) - rk$, or

$$c \cdot L = \big[f(k) - rk\big] \cdot L. \tag{3.6'}$$

If the economy follows Samuelson's (1965) "golden rule" path, then $f'(k) = r$.

The left-hand side of (3.6') is the societal total consumption, whereas the right-hand side is the total net output. Substituting in the formula of $L(t)$ under a stable population, we see that the societal budget constraint (3.6') can be rewritten as

$$\int_0^n e^{-ra}l(a)c(a)\,da = \big[f(k) - rk\big]\int_0^n e^{-ra}l(a)h(a)\,da.$$

Differentiating the logarithm of both sides of the above equation with respect to r, and noting that $(\partial k/\partial r) \cdot (f'(k) - r) = 0$ by the golden-rule assumption, we have

$$\frac{\displaystyle\int_0^n e^{-ra}l(a)\frac{\partial c(a)}{\partial r}\,da}{\displaystyle\int_0^n e^{-ra}l(a)c(a)\,da} = \big(\bar{a} - \bar{a}_l\big) - \frac{k}{c} + \frac{\displaystyle\int_0^n e^{-ra}l(a)\frac{\partial h(a)}{\partial r}\,da}{\displaystyle\int_0^n e^{-ra}l(a)h(a)\,da}, \tag{3.7}$$

where $\bar{a}_l$ is the mean age of the participation-weighted labor. The reader should have noticed the similarity between (3.5) and (3.7).

Suppose, for demonstration purposes, that the labor-force participation rate $h(.)$ is not affected by the change in r; then the right-hand side of (3.7) has only two terms. The first term is the difference of mean ages $\bar{a}_c - \bar{a}_l$, which is the same as in (3.5). The new term, $-k/c$, was called by Arthur and McNicoll (1978) the *capital-widening effect*. There is such a capital widening because an increase in population growth rate calls for greater investment to maintain the steady-state level of capital per head, and this would divert resources from capital deepening. Lee summarized the result as follows.

THEOREM 3.2 *(Lee 1980, p. 1146)*
Along a neoclassical golden-rule path with an age-specific stable population structure, the proportional change of per capita consumption equals the change in population growth rate times the difference between the mean ages

of consumption and earning, minus the capital widening effect, plus the proportional induced change in the labor-force size.

3.5 Welfare Impact of Population Growth: Income Inequality

Lam (1984) extended the age-specific comparative statics introduced in the above two sections to higher moments and studied the impact of a change in population growth rate on income inequality. For the variable y, Lam defined the steady-state proportion of the kth (central) moment of y attributable to age group a to be

$$g_k(a) = \frac{e^{-ra}l(a)\left[y(a) - \bar{y}\right]^k}{\int_0^n e^{-rs}l(s)\left[y(s) - \bar{y}\right]^k ds}.$$

The corresponding weighted mean age is therefore

$$\begin{aligned}
\bar{a}_k &= \int_0^n a g_k(a)da \\
&= \frac{\int_0^n a e^{-ra}l(a)\left[y(a) - \bar{y}\right]^k da}{\int_0^n e^{-ra}l(a)\left[y(a) - \bar{y}\right]^k da}.
\end{aligned} \tag{3.8}$$

The kth moment of y in the steady state is

$$M_k(y) \equiv \int_0^n e^{-ra}l(a)\left[y(a) - \bar{y}\right]^k da.$$

Differentiating the logarithm of $M_k(y)$ with respect to r and simplifying, we have

$$\frac{d \log M_k(y)}{dr} = \bar{a} - \bar{a}_k - \bar{y}(\bar{a} - \bar{a}_y)k\left[\frac{M_{k-1}(y)}{M_k(y)}\right]. \tag{3.9}$$

Lam's focus was the variance of (age-specific) incomes, denoted $V(y)$, which is M_k for the case of $k = 2$. For this case, we see that the last term on the right-hand side of (3.9) vanishes, since the first central moment $M_1(y)$ is zero. Thus, Lam arrived at the following conclusion.

THEOREM 3.3 *(Lam 1984, p. 120):*

$$\frac{d \log V(y)}{dr} = \frac{d \log M_2(y)}{dr} = \bar{a} - \bar{a}_2. \tag{3.10}$$

In the above expression, a_2 is the weighted mean age in (3.8) with $k = 2$. This is one line of extension of the work of Lee (1980).

3.6 EXTENSIONS AND COMMENTS

Another line of comparative static analysis is to consider a more complex life-cycle resource transfer problem, such as the contributions by Willis (1988), Lee and Lapkoff (1988), and Lee (1994). In these papers, transfers among individuals are extended to include expenses of child rearing and other intergenerational transfers, such as bequests and old-age support, the aggregate demand and supply of credits, and taxes and transfers to and from the government sector. Comparative static analyses along these lines also generate results that are related to the difference between mean ages of various sorts. Because such analysis is related to topics of demographic transition, details will be provided in chapter 11.

One advantage of the analysis presented in sections 3.3–3.5 is that the comparative static formulas are neat and can be easily evaluated using empirical data. For instance, Lam (1984) and Lee and Lapkoff (1988) have used the data of Brazil and the United States to evaluate the sign of expressions similar to those in (3.7) and (3.10). A major criticism of the comparative static analysis presented above has to do with the difficulty of interpreting the results. As I pointed out in the previous sections, we have to find a connection between economic variables and the individual age profile so that the economic phenomenon can be analyzed within an age-specific model. But even if we find such a connection in the context of life-cycle models, it may still be difficult to understand the meaning of terms such as *the mean age of income variance*, shown in (3.10). Furthermore, ideally, we hope to discover comparative static results that hinge upon exogenous behavioral assumptions or patterns. Mean ages are, however, calculated purely from nonbehavioral age accounting, and hence economists can say relatively little about the results. Finally, the intrinsic growth rate (r) of all branching processes is endogenously determined in the model; so differentiation with respect to r is slightly different from the general idea of comparative statics in economics.

CHAPTER 4

Income-Specific Population Models

Steady States and Comparative Dynamics

4.1 BACKGROUND

I mentioned in chapter 1 that the standard new household economics model of fertility, derived and modified by Becker (1960), DeTray (1973), Willis (1973), and later followers, emphasized the parental choices and tradeoffs between the quantity and the quality of their children. As Becker (1960) pointed out, one motivation for the new household economics approach to fertility decisions is to construct a demand-side household-decision structure to replace Malthus's out-of-date supply-side population theory. The fertility decision theory along these lines has been called by Schultz (1981, 1988) and Dasgupta (1995) the *demand-side* demography theory.

One difference between the demand-side demography theory and the classical Malthusian theory is that the former approach emphasized the static decision of a micro agent, whereas the Malthusian theory described the macro dynamic pattern of the population. Thus, from a theoretical point of view, the development of the demand-side demography lacks a macro dynamic counterpart. In this chapter I shall establish a macro dynamic population theory based on a fairly general version of Becker's and others' static setup of fertility demand.

Once we shift our focus to the household fertility decision, it is natural that the household economic variables that affect female fertility decisions, such as her wages, family income, or the opportunity cost of babysitting, will become important explanatory variables of aggregate demographic patterns. Given that the fluctuation of mortality is no longer significant in recent years and that human fertility decisions are largely affected by the above-mentioned household economic variables, then in order to explain the aggregate pattern of population movement, it is natural to classify people by these economic variables rather than by ages. This is another motivation for the derivation of a non-age-specific stable population theory.

4.2 HOUSEHOLD FERTILITY DECISION

4.2.1 Suppressing the Age Structure

As we focus upon the macro dynamic implications of Becker's micro static fertility decision model, it is convenient to ignore sex differences and suppress the age structure of a person by assuming that everyone lives two periods, young and old. This is very much the same as the one-sex Samuelsonian (1958) overlapping-generation model: individuals who remain in the parental household are called young; they become old when they form their own families. Within each family, decisions are made by the family head. Observe that in this overlapping-generation setup, the across-period transition of types actually refers to the change of types between parents and children. This is different from the age transition across periods for the same individual. The household decision will be explained in detail in this chapter, and similar structures in later chapters will be introduced only briefly.

4.2.2 Quantity–Quality Tradeoff

Given the family head's initial endowment b, at the beginning of the second period one has to determine the number of children one plans to have (denoted m). Besides the parent's planned fertility, there are some reproductive uncertainties, denoted by a random variable ε_m, which may represent contraception, fecundity, child mortality uncertainty, or parental taste parameters. Thus, the actual number of offspring of a parent is $m + \varepsilon_m$. The subscript m on fertility uncertainty means that the realized number of children is correlated with the planned size, which is reasonable in practice.

After the fertility size is realized, the family head has to divide the family income y into current consumption c and child-quality investment (or bequest savings) $s \equiv y - c$. If a family has m children, then each child receives an equal share, s/m. Using this bequest, the child can then produce his or her own income and form his or her own family. If a child receives b dollars of human capital investment or bequest when he or she is young, it is assumed that his or her old-age income is determined by $y = f(b, \eta)$, where η is a random variable characterizing the luck or ability uncertainty of the child. This is a setup similar to that in Loury (1981) and Chu (1988). The luck variable is assumed to be independently and identically distributed for all individuals.

All agents are assumed to be expected-utility maximizers. The utility of a family head is assumed to depend on family consumption during his tenure and on the quantity and quality of his children. If family bequest is the factor that determines children's quality, then bequests enter as an argument in parents' utility function. For demonstration purposes, suppose, as adopted in Chu (1990), that the head's objective function can be written as

$$U = u\left(c, m\right) + m \cdot \delta \cdot L\left(\frac{y - c}{m}\right),$$

where u represents the utility flow of family happiness, $0 < \delta < 1$ is a discount factor, $L(.)$ characterizes the family head's perceived quality satisfaction from a child with initial endowment $(y - c)/m$, and $m\delta L$ is the total quality satisfaction a parent perceives.

With the assumption that the parent's fertility decision is made before the realization of his lifetime income,[1] the parent's utility maximization problem can be written as follows.

$$\max_{m}\left\{ E_{\eta\,\varepsilon_m} \max_{s}\left[u\left(f\left(b, \eta\right) - s, m + \varepsilon_m\right) + \left(m + \varepsilon_m\right) \cdot \delta \cdot L\left(\frac{s}{m + \varepsilon_m}\right)\right]\right\}.$$

The above maximization problem gives rise to two optimal solution functions: $m^* = m(b)$, $s^* = s(f(b, \eta), m(b) + \varepsilon_{m(b)})$. Therefore the endowment of each child will be $s^*/[m^* + \varepsilon_{m^*}]$. If the endowment of the parent is appended with a subscript t and that of a child with a subscript $t + 1$, then we have the following dynamic endowment transition rule:

$$b_{t+1} = \frac{s^*\left(f\left(b_t, \eta\right), m^*\left(b_t\right) + \varepsilon_{m^*\left(b_t\right)}\right)}{m^*\left(b_t\right) + \varepsilon_{m^*\left(b_t\right)}}. \tag{4.1}$$

4.2.3 Combining Individual Decisions

Equation (4.1), together with the endowment-specific reproductive rule, that a parent with endowment b will have $m^*(b) + \varepsilon_{m^*(b)}$ children, constitutes an endowment-specific branching process. Specifically, let

$$P_{a,b}^i \equiv \text{Prob}\left(\frac{s^*\left(f\left(b, \eta\right), i\right)}{i} = a\right)$$

be the transition probability for a child of a parent having endowment b to move to a point $a \in \mathbf{B}$, given that the parent has i children. Then the discrete version projection matrix $\mathbf{Q}$ in equation (2.2) can be specified as

$$Q_{a,b} = \sum_{i=1}^{\bar{m}} i \cdot \text{Prob}\left(m^*\left(b\right) + \varepsilon_{m^*(b)} = i\right) \cdot P_{a,b}^i, \tag{4.2}$$

where $\bar{m}$ is the upper bound of human reproduction.

So far we have seen that a typical Becker–Willis micro level family fertility decision model will generate a macro level branching process. The state (type) variables for classifying individuals are those that affect the parents' fertility decision. In the framework given above, the type variable is chosen to be b, the economic endowment of a person. In general, the type variable may contain other information related to the family fertility decision.

Given that (4.2) constitutes the element of the projection matrix of a branching process, our job now is to check whether the projection matrix $\mathbf{Q}$ given in (4.2) satisfies the positive regularity condition. If it does, then we can apply theorem 2.1 to infer the ergodic properties in the steady state.

4.3 Verifying Positive Regularity

Our discussion in section 2.6 tells us that the essence of the positive regularity condition is the perfect mobility throughout the type space. So we have to check whether a parent with any endowment $b \in \mathbf{B}$ has some positive probability of having offspring with possible endowments in any relevant subset of $\mathbf{B}$ after some transitional periods. We will show that such a condition can be satisfied under very weak technical and economic assumptions. Specifically, we suppose that (i) $u(.,.)$ and $f(.,.)$ are increasing and concave in their first argument and $L(.)$ is also increasing and concave; (ii) $u(.,.)$ and $f(.,.)$ satisfy the Inada condition with respect to their first argument and $L(.)$ also satisfies the Inada condition;[2] (iii) the random variable η is continuously distributed in $[\underline{\eta}, \bar{\eta}]$ and $f_\eta(., \eta) > 0$; (iv) $f(b, \underline{\eta}) < b$.

Assumptions (i)–(iii) are quite regular in almost all related economic analyses. Assumption (iv) says that a parent who experiences the worst possible luck will deteriorate the endowment background of his children. These assumptions all appear to be reasonable. Given (i)–(iv), Chu (1990) proved the following theorem:

THEOREM 4.1 *(Chu 1990, pp. 178–179)*
Given assumptions (i)–(iv), the positive regularity condition corresponding to the endowment transition rule in (4.2) will be satisfied.

Detailed proofs can be found in Chu (1985); here we only provide a sketch. To verify the positive regularity condition under assumptions (i)–(iv), it is only necessary to check whether $\mathbf{Q}^t$ will be a positive matrix for some large enough t; the size of its arguments does not matter. Thus, so long as the reproductive uncertainty ε is such that everyone has a positive probability of having one realized child, without loss of generality, we can concentrate upon the event that every person has one child. This can greatly simplify the evolution rule of b_t. If we can show that the $\mathbf{Q}$ matrix derived under such a one-child event is positively regular, it is certainly true that $\mathbf{Q}$ is positively regular in general.

Given that $m + \varepsilon_m = 1$, the transition rule of b becomes

$$b_{t+1} = \frac{s\left(f\left(b_t,\, \eta\right),\, 1\right)}{1} \equiv g\left(b_t,\, \eta\right).$$

First, let us look at two specific paths of the realization of η. From assumption (iv) above, we see that the sequence generated by $b_{t+1} = g(b_t, \eta)$ is decreasing in t. On the other hand, the sequence $b_{t+1} = g(b_t, \bar{\eta})$ is bounded above by b^*, where b^* is (see figure 4.1):

$$b^* \equiv \inf\left\{b \in B \,\middle|\, b = g\left(b,\, \bar{\eta}\right)\right\}.$$

Thus, for any endowment b_0 within the interval $[0, b^*) \equiv B^*$, it is impossible that b_t will ever diverge from B^*. Since B^* is an absorbing set, in reality it is also unlikely that we would ever find a person with $b \notin B^*$. Thus, the range of endowment $[b^*, \infty)$ is not relevant to our analysis.

Next, we shall argue that, starting with any $b_0 \in B^*$, there is a positive probability that b_t will fall in any measure-nonzero subset of B^*. The reasoning is as follows. Suppose we measure incomes in dollars or cents, which have small enough units. The analysis can be approximated as if we assume a continuous state space. The concavity of u, f, and L guarantees that s has a unique interior solution. The theorem of the maximum (Varian, 1992) says that s^* is a continuous function of f. Because $f(b_t, .)$ is continuous in b_t, so is $g(b_t, .) = s(f(b_t, .), 1)$. Thus, for any given b_0, the possible range of endowments of the tth generation, $t = 2, 3, \cdots$, will cover the interval $[L_t(b_0), U_t(b_0)]$ (see figure 4.2), where

$$L_1\left(b_0\right) = g\left(b_0,\, \underline{\eta}\right) \qquad U_1\left(b_0\right) = g\left(b_0,\, \bar{\eta}\right),$$
$$L_t = g\left(L_{t-1},\, \underline{\eta}\right) \qquad U_t\left(b_0\right) = g\left(U_{t-1}\left(b_0\right),\, \bar{\eta}\right).$$

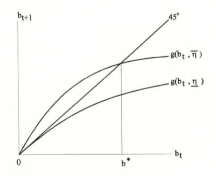

FIGURE 4.1 The upper bound of b is b^*.

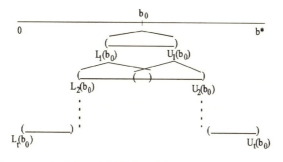

FIGURE 4.2 As $t \to \infty$, $L_t(b_0) \to 0$, $U_t(b_0) \to b^*$.

As t increases, U_t and L_t approach b^* and 0; hence, any subset of B^* can indeed be approached by future offspring of a person with endowment b_0. Thus, for all $b \in [0, b^*]$, $A \subset [0, b^*]$, the positive regularity condition of $Q(A, b)$ is indeed satisfied.

4.4 INCOME-SPECIFIC STABLE POPULATION

The analysis in the previous section allows us to apply theorem 2.1 and conclude that the population dynamics governed by the transition rule (4.2) will converge to a steady state. In the steady state the population will grow at a constant rate, which is the dominant eigenvalue of the **Q** matrix, and the societal distribution of endowment b will be time-invariant. Since the lifetime income y is a stochastic function of b: $y = f(b, \eta)$, the convergence of the distribution of b also implies the convergence of the distribution of income (y). Thus, the dynamic implication of a Becker–Willis static fertility demand theory is an income-specific stable population theory, in contrast to the popular Lotka–Leslie age-specific stable population model that demographers are familiar with.

Alternatively, since our dynamic implications are derived from a Becker–Willis static fertility demand model, our results can also be viewed as a dynamic macro counterpart of the static micro demand-side demography. As I mentioned in chapter 1, this is a theoretical extension expected by Schultz (1988) and Dasgupta (1995).

The analysis presented above is just one example of establishing a general stable population theory on the basis of individual economic decisions. When the decision scenario changes, one can establish other kinds of stable population theories analogously. We should remind the readers that the crucial step is always to verify the positive regularity condition, and the key idea is the long-run perfect mobility in the type space.

4.5 Comparative Dynamics of Income Distribution

I show in chapter 2 that the steady-state distribution of types will be proportional to the arguments of the dominant eigenvector, which in turn will be affected by the entries of the projection matrix. When exogenous variables or policies change, entries of the projection matrix will be different, thereby affecting the steady-state type distribution. In this section I shall demonstrate the comparative static analysis for the income-specific population model.

4.5.1 Theoretical Background

We can partition the projection matrix Q into two product parts:

$$Q = M \times F,$$

where the (i, j)th element of M, denoted $M_{i,j}$, is the transition probability that a child of income class j becomes a member of class i, and F is a diagonal matrix with type-specific reproduction rates as the diagonal elements. Population dynamics are characterized by $N_t = QN_{t-1}$. I showed in theorem 2.1 that if v is the dominant right eigenvector of Q, the steady-state proportion of type-i population will converge to $\pi_i \equiv v_i/\Sigma_{j=1}^n v_j$. Comparative static analyses of the general branching processes refer to the study of the change in the π vector when exogenous variables, such as elements of M or F, change.

According to theorem 2.1, the steady-state type distribution of general Markov branching processes is always characterized by the equation

$$\pi_i \varrho = \sum_{j=1}^n F_j M_{i,j} \pi_j. \tag{4.3}$$

Summing both sides of the above equation and using the property $\Sigma_i M_{i,j} = 1 = \Sigma_i \pi_i$, we have

$$\varrho = \sum_{j=1}^n F_j \pi_j. \tag{4.4}$$

There are $n + 1$ variables in (4.3), but in view of (4.4) we see that only n of them are independent. We can use (4.3) to solve for ϱ and the $n - 1$ independent proportions $\pi_1, \pi_2, \cdots, \pi_{n-1}$. Traditional comparative static analysis starts by totally differentiating the n equations of (4.3) with respect to an exogenous variable, say F_1, and then checks the sign of terms such as $\partial \pi_j/\partial F_1$.

The above-mentioned comparative static problem is indeed a difficult one. A simplified case is when $F_i = 1\ \forall i \in \{1, \cdots, n\}$, which makes the Markov branching process of N_t degenerate to a Markov process. But even in this simplified case, comparative statics are not straightforward. In a survey article, Futia (1982) argued that the only known results along these lines appeared in Daley (1968),[3] which required strong restriction upon the transition probability matrix **M**. Specifically, Daley's (1968) and Kalmykov's (1962) analysis required that the transition probability satisfy the condition of stochastic monotonicity (*SM*):

$$\sum_{i=1}^{I} M_{i,1} \geq \sum_{i=1}^{I} M_{i,2} \geq \cdots \geq \sum_{i=1}^{I} M_{i,n}, \quad 1 \leq I \leq n. \qquad (SM)$$

If the type space refers to income, and we order income in ascending order, with income type j having more income than type $k < j$, then the *SM* condition says that a child in a poor family is more likely than a child in a rich family to fall into the poorest I income classes for any I.

Suppose $\pi_{t,i}$ is the proportion of type-i individuals at period t, and suppose there is an exogenous parameter change in θ that affects the size of the $M_{i,j}$ element. To establish a comparative static result, Daley (1968) showed that one has to establish a comparative dynamic argument as follows. The first step is to show that $\partial \pi_{1,i}/\partial \theta$ has a particular sign. The second step is to show that if the *SM* condition holds, when $\partial \pi_{t,i}/\partial \theta$ is positive (or negative), $\partial \pi_{t+1,i}/\partial \theta$ will also be positive (or negative). The third step is to use mathematical induction to infer the sign of $\partial \pi_{\infty,i}/\partial \theta$, which is the steady-state result. But Futia (1982) also revealed that it is unlikely that we can get results in any general sense along these lines; we can only probe into the problems on a case-by-case basis.[4]

Other than the survey by Futia, the only effort that we know concerning the research of comparative statics of branching processes was done by Caswell (1990). Starting from the characteristic equation $\mathbf{Q}\mathbf{v} = \varrho\mathbf{v}$, Caswell (1990) solved the exact formulas of comparative statics *of π_{∞}* with respect to a change in $Q_{i,j}$. Those formulas, however, involve all the eigenvalues of **Q**, which are themselves endogenous and difficult to interpret. So far as we can see, Caswell's formulas are only useful for computer simulations or very simple age-structured models.

4.5.2 Application: Family Planning and Income Inequality

In the past two decades, considerable attention has been given to the investigation of the relationship between population growth and the distribution of income. Many researchers have found, based on empirical evidence, that population growth rate is positively related to income inequality.[5] Besides the econometric problems involved in this empirical research that Boulier (1982) criticized, there are also some conceptual difficulties. When referring to income distribution, it goes without saying that we are thinking about an economy that comprises various income groups. As long as the reproduction rates or the crude fertility rates are different across income groups, as is especially obvious in most developing countries, the property of income-specific differential fertility has to be included in the model. With differential fertility, population growth rate by definition becomes the weighted average of reproduction rates of all income groups, and this suggests that the causal relationship between income inequality and population growth as a whole is not a very meaningful topic. The key question that needs to be addressed instead is the relationship between income distribution and the reproduction behavior of some particular income groups.

Such a question is also highly policy-relevant. As pointed out by Ahluwalia (1976), the most important link between population growth and income inequality is provided by the fact that "different income groups grow at different rates, with the low-income groups typically experiencing a faster rate of natural increase" (p. 326). For many developing countries, family-planning policies are targeted at low-income families with a high fertility rate. The inequality impact of such policies is an interesting subject of investigation.

The income-specific branching process introduced in section 4.4 serves as a perfect framework to study the impact of changing the fertility rate of low-income people on income inequality. Along this line, Chu and Koo (1990) proposed two assumptions:

Assumption A4.1:

$$F_1 \geq F_2 \geq \cdots \geq F_n.$$

Assumption A4.2:

$$\frac{\sum_{i=1}^{I} M_{i,1}}{\sum_{j=1}^{J} M_{j,1}} \geq \frac{\sum_{i=1}^{I} M_{i,2}}{\sum_{j=1}^{J} M_{j,2}} \geq \cdots \geq \frac{\sum_{i=1}^{I} M_{i,n}}{\sum_{j=1}^{J} M_{j,n}}, \quad 1 \leq I \leq J \leq n. \qquad (CSM)$$

A4.1 characterizes a stylized fact in developing countries that was referred to by Ahluwalia (1976) in the above quote. A4.2 requires that the transition probability matrix obey the property of conditional stochastic monotonicity (CSM), which is a variant form of Kalmykov's stochastic monotonicity condition (SM). Notice that CSM implies SM (by letting $J = n$ in CSM) but not vice versa, and hence CSM is a stronger assumption. In our context of income-specific models, A4.2 means that, conditional on the event that a child from a poor family and a child from a rich family both fall into the poorest J classes, it is more likely that the poor child will be poorer than the rich child. This seems to be an intuitively appealing assumption. With A4.1 and A4.2, Chu and Koo (1990) proved the following theorem.[6]

Theorem 4.2 (Chu and Koo, 1990, p. 1130)
Suppose M and F are the original transition probability and fertility matrices, with π_0 the initial distribution of incomes. At period 0 there is a family-planning policy which reduces F_1 by δ. After such a reduction in F_1, let π_1,

$\pi_2, \cdots, \pi_t \cdots$ *be the series of distribution vectors that evolves. If A4.1 and A4.2 hold, then*

$$\frac{\sum_{i=1}^{I} \pi_{t,i}}{\sum_{j=1}^{J} \pi_{t,j}} \leq \frac{\sum_{i=1}^{I} \pi_{0,i}}{\sum_{j=1}^{J} \pi_{0,j}}, \quad 1 \leq I \leq J \leq n, \quad \forall t. \qquad (CSD)$$

When J = n in particular,

$$\sum_{i=1}^{I} \pi_{t,i} \leq \sum_{i=1}^{I} \pi_{0,i}, \quad 1 \leq I \leq n, \quad \forall t. \qquad (FSD)$$

Expression *FSD* is the conventional first-degree stochastic dominance relation, and expression *CSD* is a conditional stochastic dominance relation which is stronger than *FSD*. This is the reward of the stronger *CSM* assumption imposed. The *FSD* relation established is particularly helpful for inequality analysis. For the class of Benthamite social welfare functions $W_t = \Sigma_j U(y_j)\pi_{t,j}$ with monotonically increasing $U(\cdot)$, it has long been understood (see Hadar and Russell, 1969) that π_t exhibiting *FSD* to π_0 implies

$$\sum_j U(y_j)\pi_{t,j} \equiv W_t \geq W_0 \equiv \sum_j U(y_j)\pi_{0,j}.$$

Therefore, one can conclude that, if A4.1 and A4.2 are satisfied, then a reduction in F_1 can increase welfare for a very large class of social welfare functions.[7]

4.5.3 Further Results

The above-mentioned analysis has not taken into account the possible change in the **M** matrix when F_1 changes. Presumably, as poor parents have fewer children, each of their children can share more per capita human capital investment, and hence their upward mobility will be further improved. Suppose such an improvement in upward mobility makes the first column of the transition matrix change from $M_{1,j}, j = 1, \cdots, n$, to $\bar{M}_{1,j}, j = 1, \cdots, n$. Suppose further the following assumption holds.

ASSUMPTION A4.3:

$$\frac{\sum_{i=1}^{I} M_{i,1}}{\sum_{j=1}^{J} M_{j,1}} \geq \frac{\sum_{i=1}^{I} \bar{M}_{i,1}}{\sum_{j=1}^{J} \bar{M}_{j,1}}, \quad 1 \leq J \leq I \leq n.$$

The interpretation of A4.3 is similar to that of (*CSM*) and is therefore omitted. Chu and Koo (1990) proved the following theorem.

THEOREM 4.3 *(Chu and Koo, 1990, p. 1133)*
If the upward mobility of the poor family improves in such a way that A4.3 holds, and if **M** *and* **F** *satisfy A4.1 and A4.2, then as F_1 increases, the CSD and FSD relation characterized in theorem 4.2 must also hold.*

4.6 COMPARATIVE STATICS OF GROWTH RATE

In the income-specific models specified in the above sections, it is also important to evaluate the impact of a family-planning project (usually targeted at the low-income families in developing countries) on aggregate population growth. The population growth rate ϱ is the dominant eigenvalue of the income-specific projection matrix. Clearly, as F_k changes, ϱ will also change. Our purpose is to evaluate the size of $\partial\varrho/\partial F_k$. Again, if we adopt (4.3) and (4.4) and go through the ordinary comparative static analysis, it is unlikely to produce a neat result. The following is an alternative.

Let us consider a change in the reproduction rate of a particular type F_k, $k \in [1, \cdots, n]$. Suppose at period zero F_k increases from F_k^* to $F_k^* + \delta$, and suppose further that at period zero the steady state corresponding to $\delta = 0$ has been achieved. Let $\pi_t(\delta)$ denote the dynamic path of the type distribution at period t for a certain δ. By the definition of the steady state, we have $\pi_{t,i}(0) = \pi_i^* \, \forall t$ and $\varrho_t(0) = \varrho^* \, \forall t$. The dynamic version of (4.3) can be written as

$$\pi_{t,i}(\delta)\varrho_t(\delta) = \sum_{j=1}^{n} Q_{i,j}(\delta)\pi_{t-1,j}(\delta), \tag{4.5}$$

where we let the δ's that follow all variables remind us that the dynamic system (4.5) is affected by the variable δ.

Differentiating (4.5) with respect to δ and evaluating the result at $\delta = 0$ yields

$$\varrho^* \frac{d\pi_{t,i}}{dF_k} = -\pi_k^* \frac{d\varrho_t}{dF_k} + \frac{Q_{i,k}}{F_k^*}\pi_k^* + \sum_j Q_{i,j}\frac{d\pi_{t-1,j}}{dF_k}. \tag{4.6}$$

One can iteratively lag (4.6) one period and substitute the lagged result in the last term on the right-hand side of (4.6) to obtain

$$
\begin{aligned}
\varrho^* \left(\frac{d\pi_{t+1,i}}{dF_k} - \frac{d\pi_{t,i}}{dF_k} \right) = &-\pi_i^* \frac{d\varrho_{t+1}}{dF_k} + \frac{\pi_k^*}{F_k^*} \cdot \frac{Q_{i,k}^{t+2}}{(\varrho^*)^{t+1}} \\
&+ \sum_j \frac{Q_{i,j}^{t+1} \cdot \left(d\pi_{0,j}/dF_k \right)}{(\varrho^*)^t} \\
&- \sum_j \frac{Q_{i,j}^{t} \cdot \left(d\pi_{0,j}/dF_k \right)}{(\varrho^*)^{t-1}},
\end{aligned} \tag{4.7}
$$

where $Q_{i,j}^{t+1} = \Sigma_l Q_{i,l}^t Q_{l,j}$.

The almost-sure convergence property of the branching process characterized in theorem 2.1 tells us that ϱ and π will eventually converge to a new steady state, and therefore the changes in ϱ and π will also converge to constants: $d\varrho_i/dF_k \rightarrow d\varrho^*/dF_k$ and $d\pi_{i,i}/dF_k \rightarrow d\pi_i^*/dF_k$. Furthermore, theorem 2.1 tells us that as $t \rightarrow \infty$, $Q_{i,j}^t \rightarrow (\varrho^*)'u_j v_i$, which implies that the last two terms of (4.7) cancel each other out. With the above information, (4.7) can be further simplified as

$$0 = -\pi_i^* \frac{d\varrho^*}{dF_k} + \frac{\pi_k^*}{F_k^*} u_k v_i \varrho^*.$$

Because $\pi_i^* = v_i/\Sigma_j v_j \; \forall_i$ by theorem 2.1, the above equation can be rearranged to get the following theorem:

THEOREM 4.4:

$$\frac{d\varrho^*}{dF_k} \cdot \frac{F_k^*}{\varrho^*} = u_k v_k, \quad k = 1, \cdots, n,$$

where u_i and v_i are the ith element of the left and right dominant eigenvectors.

Theorem 4.4 is a simple formula that enables us to easily predict the steady-state change of population growth as a result of changes in the reproduction rate for any type group. Notice that this theorem does not depend on A4.1 or A4.2 and is true for all branching processes. Moreover, since **uv** = 1 by theorem 2.1 and **u** and **v** are vectors with positive elements, it is clear that $u_k v_k < 1$ for $k = 1, \cdots, n$. Thus, theorem 4.4 signifies that a reduction in F_k will entail a corresponding decrease in the steady-state population growth rate, but the elasticity of changes is less than one.

4.7 Empirical Estimation of the Transition Matrix

Vital rates in a Leslie matrix are easy to estimate and are available in almost all countries in the world. But for an income-specific population model, estimating the parameters in the projection matrix $\mathbf{Q} = [\mathbf{M} \times \mathbf{F}]$ is not a straightforward job. In an overlapping-generation model with suppressed age structure, an element in the transition matrix, say $M_{i,j}$, denotes the cross-generational transition probability that a child from a family of income class j becomes a member of income class i. Since a specific parent–child line has to be traced in order to calculate a meaningful transitional probability, in general we have to have family-based panel data to estimate elements of the **M** matrix. Moreover, even if family-based panel data are available, the sample period has to be very long in order to calculate the across-generation $M_{i,j}$. Besides the NLS and the PSID of the United States, there are not any panel surveys that cover such a long period of time.[8] The existing literature has some discussion on the estimation of across-period income mobility, but that is different from the across-generation mobility that we are interested in.[9]

Because most countries in the world do not have panel data that covers a long enough period, Cheng and Chu (1997) proposed to use pseudo-panel data to estimate the **M** matrix. *Pseudo-panel data* refers to the panel data set constructed by aggregating cross-sectional sample points over various cohorts. Specifically, people belonging to the same cohort are pooled and treated as one observation. The state variable of this pooled observation is the average value of all members of this cohort. Since the size of each cohort is large, by averaging the state variable values over each cohort, we can treat an observation of a cohort aged $b + s$ in period $t_0 + s$ as a 'descendant' of the cohort aged a in period t_0, given that the age-a cohort has children aged b in period t_0. Thus, at each period we have several cohort observations 'connected' with various other cohorts in other periods, and a pseudo-panel data set is therefore constructed. For instance, for the data period 1976–1995 and the cohort range aged 31–55, the pseudo-panel data set is shown in table 4.1. The boldface X's indicate the trace of one particular cohort.

Cheng and Chu (1997) divided the observations of the same cohort into n income groups and obtained n cohort-income observation pairs in each period. Let $\pi_{t,i}^a$ be the proportion of observations of income group i in period t (among all observations of cohort group aged a). In each period we observe the proportion vector $\Pi_t^a \equiv [\pi_{t,i}^a, \ldots, \pi_{t,n}^a]$ for all a. Following our previously adopted notations, let F_i be the completed fertility of income group i, **F** be the corresponding fertility matrix, s be the length of a generation, and $\mathbf{M} = [M_{i,j}]$ be the across-generation transition probability matrix. For parents having a child aged b in period t, our analysis in chapter 2 tells us that the following equation is true:

$$\Pi_{t+s-b}^a = \left[\mathbf{M} \times \mathbf{F}\right]\Pi_t^a, \quad \forall a, t. \tag{4.8}$$

Because cross-sectional household surveys are quite common in many countries over fairly long periods of time, observations of Π_t^a are usually abundant. Given the income-specific fertility matrix **F**, we can then search

TABLE 4.1. Representative Individuals in Pseudo-Panel Data

Data Period	31	32	...	49	50	...	55
1976	$\mathbf{X}_{31,76}$	$x_{32,76}$	...	$x_{49,76}$	$x_{50,76}$	...	$x_{55,76}$
1977	$x_{31,77}$	$\mathbf{X}_{32,77}$		$x_{49,77}$	$x_{50,77}$		$x_{55,77}$
1978	$x_{31,78}$	$x_{32,78}$		$x_{49,78}$	$x_{50,78}$		$x_{55,78}$
$\vdots$	$\vdots$	$\vdots$	$\ddots$	$\ddots$	$\ddots$		$\vdots$
1994	$x_{31,94}$	$x_{32,94}$		$\mathbf{X}_{49,94}$	$x_{50,94}$	...	$x_{55,94}$
1995	$x_{31,95}$	$x_{32,95}$		$x_{49,95}$	$\mathbf{X}_{50,95}$	...	$x_{55,95}$

for an estimate of **M**, denoted **M̃**, which maximizes the likelihood function corresponding to (4.8).[10]

For the case of $n = 3$ (three income classes), the estimated transition matrix is

$$\tilde{\mathbf{M}} = \begin{pmatrix} .3322 & .2370 & .2655 \\ .3767 & .5172 & .2396 \\ .2911 & .2458 & .4949 \end{pmatrix}.$$

All estimates in the above matrix are statistically significant at the .01 level. This estimated matrix can be used to calculate the steady-state income distribution of the society. Details can be found in Cheng and Chu (1997) and will not be repeated here.

CHAPTER 5

Lineage Extinction and
Inheritance Patterns

5.1 BACKGROUND

Perhaps the most basic biological instincts of all creatures are to survive and to produce offspring. In ancient times, poor hygienic environment and occasional widespread epidemics obviously gave people strong reasons to worry about the possible extinction of their own lineage. But to transform such a worry into a mathematical problem, it is helpful if the upper class of the society, which has the ability and the leisure to think about the problem on an abstract level, also feels the possibility of such an extinction. Indeed, this was the case in eighteenth-century western Europe.

The development of the theory of branching processes in fact started with the calculation of the probability of family surname extinction. Mode (1971) argued that one of the reasons for the decay of family names was that "physical comfort and intellectual capacity were necessarily accompanied by a diminution in fertility." This statement, that parents choose to have fewer children because they want increase their enjoyment of life, seems to be a more suitable characterization of the argument of Becker's (1991) contemporary household economics. Others, such as Chu and Lee (1994), argued that it was the scourges of war and famine that were responsible for the major rises of mortality in ancient history.

Whatever the cause of lineage extinction, as a large proportion of family surnames continued to die out, Francis Galton (1873), one of the founders of the theory of branching processes, presented his concern with lineage extinction on an abstract level:

Problem 4001: A large country, of whom we will only concern ourselves with adult males, N in number, and who each bear separate surnames, colonize a district. Their law of population is such that, in each generation,

p_0 percent of the adult names have no male children who reach adult life; p_1 have one such child; p_2 have two, and so on up to p_5, who have five.

Find (i) what proportion of the surnames will have become extinct after r generations; and (ii) how many instances will there be of the same surname being held by m person.

The problem of family surname extinction concerns part (i) of problem 4001; part (ii) is about the distribution of surnames (types), which was the focus of chapter 4 of this book.

Problem 4001 did not attract much attention until Agner Krarup Erlang became interested in this problem because his mother's surname, Krarup, was about to become extinct. Erlang arrived at the solution below.

First, we remove the restriction in problem 4001 that a man can have at most five sons, and let p_k be the probability of having k surviving male children. Erlang argued that the probability of surname extinction is the solution to the equation

$$\zeta = p_0 + p_1\zeta + p_2\zeta^2 + \cdots.$$

Erlang realized that the above equation will have a root in $[0,1]$ other than the root $\zeta = 1$ if and only if the average number of sons of the parent $\Sigma_{k=0}^{\infty} kp_k$ is greater than 1.

Erlang's analysis was very close to the correct solution, but a rigorous and complete answer was provided only after his death. Furthermore, the original problem 4001 concerned the extinction probability of a particular surname, where offspring of the family were assumed to have the same surname and the same reproductive vital rates. Mathematically, this corresponds to the study of a single-type branching process, where the type is the surname in question. The general case occurs when people have more than one type, and each type of individual has a different reproduction rate. For instance, people with different social status may have different reproduction rates and survival probabilities, and the status of a person may change over time. Modifying problem 4001 accordingly will change the problem to one of studying extinction, which is clearly a degenerated steady state, of a multitype branching process. Because extinction refers to the situation of nonexistence for any type of individuals, naturally the focus of extinction-related research is not on the degenerated steady-state type distribution but on the probability of becoming extinct. This is what we will study in section 5.3. Before moving on to such an analysis, I shall persuade the readers in the next section that lineage extinction is related to economic decisions.

5.2 Economic Decisions to Reduce Extinction Probability

One drawback of the discussion along the lines of problem 4001 is that the family head was assumed to react very passively to the pressure of lineage extinction. Although it may be true that in ancient times the extension of a family line mainly hinged upon the exogenously determined risk of mortality, family members do have some choices in reducing such a risk. For instance, Chu and Lee (1994) pointed out that when ancient Chinese peasants could not tolerate the pressure of famine and high taxes that threatened the survival of their families, many peasants chose to become bandits. This is a *job* transition choice in response to outside mortality pressure.[1]

Another more conventional choice by which the parent could reduce the probability of family line extinction in ancient times was through a *division of bequests* within the family. For example, in their study of the rule of bequest division in historic southern Tirol, Cole and Wolf (1974) gave the following explanation for the emergence of primogeniture:

> He would like to see every daughter well married and every son with land enough to support a family. Then too, he would like to see the holding that he has maintained against the world for a lifetime remain essentially intact to provide a material basis for perpetuation of the family line. However, the meager resources at his disposal are, more often than not, insufficient to fulfill both these goals. He must balance his desire to perpetuate his name against the future of his children. (p. 176)

Adam Smith ([1776] 1937) also provided a similar argument for the emergence of unequal sharing, with more emphasis on the economy-of-scale property of land. He stated that in ancient western Europe "when land was considered as the means, not of subsistence merely, but of power and protection, it was thought better that it should descend undivided to one. · · · The security of a landed estate · · · depended upon its greatness. To divide it was to ruin it" (pp. 361–362). Smith concluded by saying that primogeniture was "introduced to preserve a certain lineal succession" (p. 362). Although in his discussion the property to be inherited is restricted to land, the reason he gave for the choice of unequal division of bequests, namely, the preservation of the lineal succession, is indeed not unlike Cole and Wolf's argument of perpetuation of the family line.

Similar and more detailed observations of unequal human and physical investment among children can also be found in the East. Ho (1959, 1962) and Freedman (1966) pointed out that in imperial China not only family members but also whole clans often pooled their money together to subsidize just one child in a family for his human capital investment (education fund). The anticipated result is that the particular child who gets the extra help would pass the civil service examination and move up the social ladder by becoming an "official" with guaranteed sizable income and immense power. It was hoped that this civil service position would also bring honor and prestige to the family and the clan and broaden the prospects for the future lineage as well.

After studying kinship relations in historic Japan, Nakane (1967) concluded that "in order to keep the succession line firm, there is a tendency to earlier appointment of successor, and thus to primogeniture" and that "succession by primogeniture also tends to appear in the wealthy sector of the family. The degree of institutionalization of the household becomes greater, and the line of succession becomes more important" (pp. 10–11). Nakane believes that the primogeniture rule has the advantage of establishing the line of control within the family, which is deemed important for rich and large families, and the purpose of primogeniture is to *keep the succession line firm.*

There are many other anthropological discussions on the decision of bequest division against other cultural backgrounds, but the above examples provide the clearest explanation as to *why* such a phenomenon existed. Because of the high mortality rate in ancient times, family heads cared not only about their own well-being but also about the *firmness* of their lineage succession. Indeed, as Freedman (1966) and Nakane (1967) pointed out, family-line succession was viewed as a duty of the family head in traditional societies in both China and Japan. This notion of lineal succession seems to be consistent with Smith's "preserving the lineal succession" or Cole and Wolf's "perpetuation of the family line" in ancient Europe. Although Cole and Wolf, Nakane, and Smith all argued that the choice of the division of bequests might be an effective way to achieve the objective of preserving lineal succession, none of them made any clear expositions of it.

The discussion above clearly does not present the whole picture of the historical social structure of various countries, but it does provide strong evidence showing how people choose their division of bequests to reduce the probability of lineage extinction. In the next section, I will first derive the probability of lineage extinction without parental choices. This is the case analyzed by most probability theorists. In section 5.4, I will modify the formula of the lineage extinction probability in cases when parents can make their bequest division decision to *minimize* such a probability. Finally, I will analyze when the primogeniture rule will become a parent's optimal decision.

5.3 PROBABILITY OF LINEAGE EXTINCTION

5.3.1 Role of the Dominant Eigenvalue

I showed in chapter 2 that the dominant eigenvalue is the population growth rate in the steady state. Intuitively, population extinction is less likely if the steady-state growth rate is larger. In this subsection I will derive the exact formula for lineage extinction probability and demonstrate that the above intuition is by and large correct.

The evolution of N_t, characterized in chapter 2 as $N_t = QN_{t-1}$, can be started from any initial vector N_0. If we consider a vector $N_0' \equiv (0, \ldots, 0, 1, 0, \cdots, 0) \equiv \delta_i$, where 1 is the ith element of this vector, then the N_t evolved will be the distribution of period-t offspring of a type-i person at period zero. Let $\zeta_{t,i}$ be the probability that the offspring of a period-0 type-i agent will become extinct at period t:

$$\zeta_{t,i} \equiv \text{Prob}\left[N_t = 0 \middle| N_0' = \delta_i \right].$$

So the probability of eventual extinction corresponds to

$$\lim_{t \to \infty} \zeta_{t,i} = \zeta_i.$$

Because the event $[N_t = 0]$ implies the event $[N_{t+1} = 0$, we have $\zeta_{t,i} \le \zeta_{t+1,i} \le 1$. Because every increasing bounded sequence has a limit, the limit of the above expression certainly exists.

The formal relationship between the probability of lineage extinction and ϱ, the dominant eigenvalue of Q, is given in the following theorem:

THEOREM 5.1 *(Mode, 1971, p. 16)*
Suppose the population projection matrix Q is positively regular, and ϱ is its dominant eigenvalue. (i) If $\varrho \le 1$, then $\zeta_i = 1 \; \forall i = 1, 2, \cdots, n$. (ii) If $\varrho > 1$, then $\zeta_i < 1 \; \forall i = 1, 2, \cdots, n$.

So far I have only characterized the definition of lineage extinction probability and its relationship with the dominant eigenvalue. I now show how to calculate this probability.

5.3.2 Deriving the Extinction Probability

Let $r \equiv (r_1, \cdots, r_n)$ be an n-vector of nonnegative integers. Let $p_i(r)$ be the probability that a person of type i will have r_1 children of type $1, \cdots,$ and r_n children of type n. For all n-dimensional vectors of real numbers $s = (s_1, \cdots, s_n)$ such that $\|s\| \le 1$, we define a *generating function* as follows:

$$h_i(s) = \sum_r p_i(r) s_1^{r_1} s_2^{r_2} \cdots s_n^{r_n}. \tag{5.1}$$

We note that if person i has r_1 surviving children of type $1, \cdots,$ and r_n surviving children of type n in the first period, the lineage following person i will become extinct after t periods if and only if *all* the lineages of these $(r_1, \cdots, r_n)$ children become extinct after $t - 1$ periods. This event will happen with probability

$$\zeta_{t-1,1}^{r_1} \times \cdots \times \zeta_{t-1,n}^{r_n}.$$

But the event that person i has $\bar{r}$ surviving children of the various types and the event that person i has $\tilde{r}(\tilde{r} \ne \bar{r})$ surviving children are mutually exclusive, so person i's overall probabilities of extinction after t periods need to be added together:

$$\zeta_{t,i} = \sum_{\mathbf{r}} p_i(\mathbf{r})\zeta_{t-1,1}^{r_1} \times \cdots \times \zeta_{t-1,n}^{r_n} \equiv h_i(\zeta_{t-1,1}, \cdots, \zeta_{t-1,n}). \quad (5.2)$$

Let ζ_t denote the vector $(\zeta_{t,1}, \cdots, \zeta_{t,n})$ and $\mathbf{h}$ denote $(h_1, \cdots, h_n)$. We see that (5.2) can be rewritten as $\zeta_{t,i} = h_i(\zeta_{t-1})$, or in vector form

$$\zeta_t = \mathbf{h}(\zeta_{t-1}). \quad (5.2')$$

It is easy to see that the probability of extinction after one period is simply

$$\zeta_{1,i} = p_i(\mathbf{0}), \quad i = 1, \cdots, n.$$

Given ζ_1, equation (5.2') gives us a way to calculate ζ_t through iteration. In fact, Mode (1971) tells us that through (5.2') we can eventually get the correct value of extinction probability. Specifically, we have

THEOREM 5.2 *(Mode, 1971, p. 16)*
Regardless the value of ϱ, the probability of lineage extinction is always the smallest nonnegative solution to the vector equation

$$\zeta = \mathbf{h}(\zeta). \quad (5.2'')$$

Since $\zeta_{t,i}$ is increasing in t for any i, in view of figure 5.1, we see from theorem 5.2 that the $h_i(.)$ function must first intersect the 45° line from above.[2] So starting with $\zeta_{1,i} = p_i(\mathbf{0}), i = 1, \cdots, n$, we will eventually get the true extinction probability ζ.

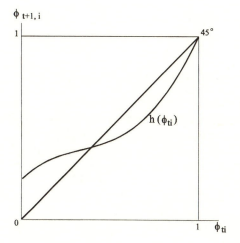

FIGURE 5.1 The shape of $h(\cdot)$.

5.4 LINEAGE PRESERVATION DECISIONS

The discussion in section 5.3 is of the case without endogenous parental decisions. When parents are aware of, and also care about, the probability of lineage extinction, they will want to do something to avoid this eventuality. As I mentioned in section 5.2 above, one popular way in ancient times was to choose a rule of bequest division so that the overall probability of lineage extinction could be minimized. Below I will establish an economic model of bequest division compatible with the historical observations made in section 5.2. We want to investigate under what circumstances a parent will choose to divide bequests unevenly and what kinds of implications we can derive from this behavioral model.

5.4.1 An Overlapping-Generation Model

In order to concentrate on the parental decision on bequest division, as in chapter 4, we suppress the age structure and consider a variant version of Samuelson's (1958) overlapping-generation model. Each individual in the society lives for either one or two periods. People who die in the first period of life (childhood) will not be able to produce any children. People who survive to the second period (adulthood) will be able to reproduce m^* children; among those children, some may die before they reach adulthood from causes such as malnutrition, disease, or poor hygiene. More generally, one can say that people make m^* reproduction attempts, and instances of miscarriage or sterility can be interpreted as failures to raise children to adulthood. To avoid deliberations on the impact of different mating systems and on the sex preferences of bequests, I shall not differentiate sexes in this chapter. For analyses of phenomena at a time when women were not allowed to play important roles in most societies, this assumption seems to be a reasonable one. Thus, in this chapter there is no difference between "primogeniture" and "one child receives most or all the bequests." The situation here is the same as in Pryor (1973).

5.4.2 Family Incomes and Bequests

Assume that the factors affecting child mortality can be summarized by a single variable: family income (y), with a high- (low-) income family having better (worse) nutrition and better (worse) hygiene and, hence, a low (high) probability of child mortality. For $0 \leq m \leq m^*$, let $p(m|y)$ denote the probability that m out of the m^* children survive to adulthood in a family with income y. Clearly, $\sum_{m=0}^{m^*} p(m|y) = 1$. Because child mortality rates are related to family incomes, it is therefore analytically convenient to classify people by their incomes rather than by their ages.

As in chapter 4, we assume that the income of a family depends on the family head's productivity, which in turn depends on both his endowed bequests (b) and luck. A person's luck is characterized by a random variable η_b, which may represent his fortune in operating his business. Here the subscript on η implies that its distribution may be affected by b. The relationships among income, bequests, and luck is summarized by a production function

$$\tilde{y} = f(b, \eta_b). \tag{5.3}$$

Within each family, let e be the total expenses of consumption and child rearing. Then clearly e will be a function of y and m: $e = e(y, m)$. The total bequests left will therefore be

$$y - e(y, m) \equiv B(y, m).$$

The determination of the $B(., .)$ function is assumed to be exogenous and is beyond the scope of our analysis in this chapter.

5.4.3 Parental Preferences and Bequest Division

Given the above simplified setup, the only decision that is left to the family head is the division of his bequests among his m surviving children. How the family head is going to divide his bequests will certainly depend on the objective function he carries. Following the evidence presented in section 5.2, we assume that the parent tries to avoid, to the greatest extent possible, lineage extinction.

Consider a family head A with total bequests $B(y, m)$ to be divided. Suppose $m \neq 0$, and let the bequest received by the ith child be b_i. Then according to (5.3), the ith child will have $\tilde{y}_i \equiv f(b_i, \eta_{b_i})$ as his income to start with. The number of surviving offspring the ith child will have will be determined by the probability distribution $p(m|\tilde{y}_i)$. The problem A faces is the division of $B(y, m)$ into b_i's, $i = 1, \cdots, m$, in such a way that the probability of extinction of his lineage can be minimized. Now we want to derive the corresponding version of the iterative equations in (5.2) with endogenous bequest division decision.

Let $E_{u|v}$ be the expectation operator of u conditional on v, $\mathbf{b} \equiv (b_1, \cdots, b_m)$, and Ω be the feasible set of allowable bequest division:

$$\Omega(y, m) \equiv \left\{ \mathbf{b} \middle| \sum_{i=1}^{m} b_i = B(y, m) \right\}.$$

Chu (1991) proved the following theorem:

THEOREM 5.3 *(Chu, 1991, p. 84)*
Suppose the stochastic event that one child has no surviving offspring at time $t + 1$ is independent of the event that any other child has no surviving offspring.[3] The solution to the problem of minimizing lineage extinction probability is characterized by the following iterative functional equation:

$$\zeta_{t+1,y} = \sum_{m=0}^{m^*} p\left(m|y\right) \cdot \min_{b \in \Omega(y,m)} \left\{ \prod_{i=1}^{m} E_{\tilde{y}_i|b_i}\left(\zeta_{t,\tilde{y}_i}\right) \right\}, \quad t \ge 1. \tag{5.4}$$

Equation (5.4) is in fact a variation of (5.2); its meaning will become clear as we proceed. Suppose the current time is zero. The term $\zeta_{t,\tilde{y}_i}$ is the probability that a child with income $\tilde{y}_i$ in period 1 has no surviving offspring t periods later, which will be in period $t + 1$. Let $G(\tilde{y}_i|b_i)$ be the conditional probability mass of $\tilde{y}_i$ given b_i. Then

$$E_{\tilde{y}_i|b_i}\left(\zeta_{t,\tilde{y}_i}\right) = \sum_{\tilde{y}_i} \zeta_{t,\tilde{y}_i} G\left(\tilde{y}_i|b_i\right)$$

will be the ith child's conditional expected probability of having no surviving offspring t periods later, given that i receives b_i. Then the product of m terms in the curly brackets of (5.4) will be the probability that *all* the m succession lines vanish at $t + 1$. Note that this product term is similar to the power product term in (5.2).

Since the parent can choose his desired bequest division rule within the domain Ω, with the assumed preferences of minimizing extinction probability, he will choose a division rule that minimizes the terms in the curly brackets in (5.4). Because the events of bringing up different numbers of children to adulthood are mutually exclusive, the probability of each should be summed together, with the respective probability values as weights. The meaning of (5.4) is now clear. Furthermore, since the extinction probability after one period is

$$\zeta_{1,y} = p\left(0|y\right) = 1 - \sum_{m=1}^{m^*} p\left(m|y\right),$$

we have an initial value for starting the iteration, and ζ_t $\forall t > 1$ can be easily obtained.

5.5 Some Analytical Examples

For demonstration purposes, let us consider some simple examples from which one can see how comparative static analysis can be executed. Suppose that (i) there are only three income groups in the society: H, M, and L (indicating, respectively, high, medium, and low) and that (ii) each parent rears either zero or two surviving children—that is, for $y \in \{y_H, y_M, y_L\}$, $p(m|y) > 0$ only when $m = 0$ or $m = 2$. Let $p_{H0} \equiv p(0|y_H)$ be the probability that a high-income person fails to secure an heir; then clearly $p(2|y_H) = 1 - p_{H0}$. The terms p_{M0} and p_{L0} are similarly defined. Let the total bequests left by family heads of various income groups be b_L, b_M, and b_H, respectively. Assume that (i) b_L cannot be further divided and can be left to only one child; (ii) $b_M = 2b_L$, that is, it can be either left to one child or divided into two equal shares, with each child receiving b_L; and (iii) $b_H = 2b_M$, interpretated similarly to (ii).[4]

If the head of a middle-income family decides to divide the bequests into two equal parts, each child will receive b_L, and the division of bequests will be denoted as (b_L, b_L). If the same family head decides to let one child receive all the bequests, this division will be denoted $(b_M, 0)$. Let Ω_M be the feasible division set of a middle-income family; then $\Omega_M = \{(b_L, b_L), (b_M, 0)\}$. With similar notations, we have $\Omega_H = \{(b_M, b_M), (b_H, 0)\}$. Finally, $\Omega_L = \{(b_L, 0)\}$ by assumption.

Suppose the bequest–income functional relation $y = f(b, \eta_b)$ is characterized by the following transformation matrix:

	y_L	y_M	y_H
0	T_{0L}	T_{0M}	0
b_L	T_{LL}	T_{LM}	0
b_M	0	T_{MM}	T_{MH}
b_H	0	T_{HM}	T_{HH}

In the above table, for instance, T_{MH} is the probability that a child with b_M endowment turns out to have y_H income. It goes without saying that $\Sigma_j T_{ij} = 1 \ \forall i$. There are some assumed zero-probability items because we want to simplify the presentation of the calculation later.

To calculate the probability of lineage extinction, we have to write down the steady-state equation (5.2″) for our example. First, let us consider the case under the rule of equal bequest division. It turns out that the corresponding equations of (5.2″) are as follows.

$$p\big(2\big|y_L\big)\Big[T_{0L}T_{LL}\zeta_L^2 + \big(T_{0L}T_{LM} + T_{LL}T_{0M}\big)\zeta_L\zeta_M + T_{0M}T_{LM}\zeta_M^2\Big] + p\big(0\big|y_L\big)$$
$$= \zeta_L, \tag{5.5}$$

$$p\big(2\big|y_M\big)\Big[T_{LL}^2\zeta_L^2 + 2T_{LL}T_{LM}\zeta_L\zeta_M + T_{LM}^2\zeta_M^2\Big] + p\big(0\big|y_M\big)$$
$$= \zeta_M, \tag{5.6}$$

$$p\big(2\big|y_H\big)\Big[T_{MM}^2\zeta_M^2 + 2T_{MH}T_{MM}\zeta_M\zeta_H + T_{MH}^2\zeta_H^2\Big] + p\big(0\big|y_H\big)$$
$$= \zeta_H. \tag{5.7}$$

Solving $(\zeta_L^*, \zeta_M^*, \zeta_H^*)$ jointly from the above three equations, we get the respective values of the extinction probability of the three income groups.

If the middle-income parents decide to divide their bequests unevenly, then (5.6) will become

$$p\big(2\big|y_M\big)\Big[T_{0L}T_{MM}\zeta_L\zeta_M + T_{0L}T_{MH}\zeta_L\zeta_H + T_{0M}T_{MM}\zeta_M^2$$
$$+ T_{0M}T_{MH}\zeta_M\zeta_H\Big] + p\big(0\big|y_M\big) = \zeta_M. \tag{5.8}$$

If the high-income parents decide to choose an unequal division, equation (5.7) will have to be rewritten as

$$p\left(2|y_H\right)\left[T_{0L}T_{HM}\zeta_L\zeta_M + T_{0L}T_{HH}\zeta_L\zeta_H + T_{0M}T_{HM}\zeta_M^2\right.$$
$$\left. + T_{0M}T_{HH}\zeta_M\zeta_H\right] + p\left(0|y_H\right) = \zeta_H. \tag{5.9}$$

One can clearly see that if the bequest division rule is changed from equal sharing to unequal sharing, the extinction probability should be solved from (5.5), (5.8), and (5.9). We denote the extinction probability vector solved out in this case $(\tilde{\xi}_L, \tilde{\xi}_M, \tilde{\xi}_H)$. If the $(\tilde{\xi}_L, \tilde{\xi}_M, \tilde{\xi}_H)$ values solved out in the latter case are smaller than $(\zeta_L^*, \zeta_M^*, \zeta_H^*)$ in the former case, high- and middle-income parents will *choose* to divide their bequest unevenly, provided that their objectives are to minimize the probability of lineage extinction. Of course, this is an extreme case; it is also possible that the optimal solution involves equal bequest sharing for some income classes and unequal bequest division for some other classes.

5.6 EMPIRICAL OBSERVATIONS IN HISTORY

5.6.1 Population Growth and Lineage Extinction

As Habakkuk (1955) pointed out, many French demographers believed that the provision for mandatory equal division of bequests in the Napoleonic Code tended to retard population growth in that period. He argued that "the peasant who worked to keep his property intact had a powerful incentive to limit the number of children between whom his property would be divided" (p. 5). Here I can provide an alternative explanation to the negative correlation between mandatory equal division of bequests and the low population growth rate that Habakkuk mentioned.

I believe that with lineal prosperity as the family's objective, as assumed by many anthropologists who were mentioned in section 5.2, if an unequal division policy appears to be optimal, this optimal policy is more efficient in achieving such an objective. If, however, all kinds of unequal division are prohibited by law, the degree of lineal prosperity that the family head can manage to achieve will also be restricted. Thus, other things being equal, it does not seem astonishing to observe a negative relationship between population growth and the degree of equal division that turned up in the period in which the Napoleonic Code was enacted.

5.6.2 Population Growth and Social Mobility

Another interesting historical study of the interaction between primogeniture and population growth is Ho's (1962) analysis of imperial China. Ho discovered that China experienced almost continuous population growth from the late fourteenth century through 1850, despite the ceaseless wars in this period. According to Ho, the civil service examination, which was instituted in 1371 and lasted until 1904, had opened up the opportunity for children of low- and middle-income families to move upward socially. Most poor or middle-income parents could afford to send only one of their children to try the civil service examination. The designated child received a larger share of educational investment from his parents. Thus, the civil service examination contributed to the unequal distribution of parental investment in children. The fact that it was a popular method of investment division during the period revealed in turn that unequal division was indeed a more efficient way of attaining the objectives all parents had in mind. If parents' objectives in imperial China were to make family lines prosperous, as Freedman (1966) described, then Ho's finding concerning the continuous population growth during the period in which civil service examinations were in force should not come as a surprise.

5.6.3 Why Was There Widespread Primogeniture In Ancient Times?

Having characterized the problem of minimizing the probability of lineage extinction, one natural question is, Uunder what circumstance will an unequal division of bequests be the solution to this problem? If we have no reason to believe that parents are concerned more about the extinction of a *particular* line of their offspring, why would there be prevalent institutions of unequal bequest division in ancient times, as described in section 5.2? This question is difficult to answer analytically, but I can provide some conjectures.

I believe that the structure of the capital market is an important factor influencing the parents' decision. If the capital market is nearly perfect, parents' incentive to choose an unequal sharing rule will be weakened for two reasons. First, with a perfect capital market, funds can be easily borrowed, and hence the role of bequests (private fund) is less important. Second, a perfect capital market also implies high intergenerational mobility of income groups, and hence the long-term benefit of enabling one child to move to a higher income group will not look attractive because any hard-won family fortune does not matter much in the long run.

When the capital market is imperfect, and hence income mobility of the society is rigid, a family head may be more amenable to an unequal division of his bequests because he knows that once the best-endowed child becomes rich, it is more likely that the offspring of this child are going to *stay* rich for some time to come. Furthermore, with rigid income mobility, family heads of the poor- or middle-income group may resort to the tried-and-true wisdom of unequal bequest division to break the intrinsic rigidity so that some of their offspring, who would most probably stay poor if bequests were divided evenly, may now stand a better chance of joining the rich. As such, although primogeniture does cause *atemporal* income inequality, it can break the *intertemporal* rigid upward mobility and may eventually help to equalize the steady-state income distribution. The reasoning given above is clearly different from that of Pryor (1973) and Blinder (1976), who in essence argued that primogeniture would *cause* more income inequality. Instead, I argue that primogeniture may be *caused by* the intrinsic rigid structure of income mobility.

It is not my purpose here to provide an analytical answer to the question of *when* parents will divide their bequests unevenly. But equation (5.5) clearly shows that parents can reduce the chance of surname extinction by appropriately allocating the size of bequests to children, even if all children are *ex ante* equal. This gives a theoretical foundation to the historical observations given in section 5.2. A numerical example and some extensive analysis were given by Chu (1991). He showed that when the intrinsic social mobility is rigid, parents will indeed choose to divide their bequests unevenly, which increases the intergenerational upward mobility of the low-income class and eventually *improves* the income inequality in the steady state. This is consistent with the argument presented above.

CHAPTER 6

Sex Preferences and Two-Sex Models

6.1 BACKGROUND

The demographic models I reviewed in previous chapters are all one-sex models, in which the sex referred to is usually the female. This setting can be justified if we assume either that the life-cycle vital rates (as functions of state variables) for both sexes are the same or that the population dynamics are determined by one sex alone, independent of the possibly relative abundance of the other sex. However, at least for human population, neither assumption is valid. The ratio of newborn girls and newborn boys is close to one, but is less than one for almost all countries in the world. The age-specific mortality rates of women are also lower than those of men worldwide. This is called *sexual dimorphism* in the demography literature.[1] Such a dimorphism makes the study of two-sex models indispensable.

If we look at the male and female vital rates, we find that the differences are small. Despite this small difference, population dynamics derived solely from male vital rates and those derived solely from female vital rates will show ever-increasing differences with the passage of time. Furthermore, because the intrinsic growth rates derived from male and female lines, respectively, are distinct, we cannot avoid the undesirable conclusion that, if we do not incorporate males and females in a unified model, eventually the sex ratio will become either zero or infinity, which is never the case in reality. This is the inconsistency we have to overcome while dealing with population models with two sexes.

Another technical difficulty with two-sex modeling has to do with the irreducibility of the state-transition matrix. I mentioned in chapters 2 and 3 that in an age-specific one-sex model, because people older than a particular age, say β, are not fertile anymore, the age group older than β is an absorbing set; hence, our focus of population dynamics can be restricted to the age set $[0, \beta]$. This is why we can transform the $n \times n$ Leslie matrix to a Lotka renewal equation. In a two-sex model, however, there does not exist a common upper bound for the reproduction of both sexes, for a male older than β can marry a female younger than β and become fertile again. Thus, as Pollak (1990) pointed out, in a two-sex model we cannot simplify our analysis by dropping some age groups; hence the convenient Lotka equation does not apply.

The problem of sexual dimorphism is more serious in the present than in the past, particularly in areas with prevalent sex preferences. Sex-based abortions made possible by modern medical technology have enlarged the gap between the sizes of male and female newborns. This would certainly affect the population sex ratio in the long run. Furthermore, given assartative mating, parents' uneven resource allocation to boys and girls would certainly affect the matching in the marriage market, which in turn would change the equilibrium distribution of wealth in the economy. This chapter will devote to the discussion of the two-sex models, with more emphasis on the role of parental sex preferences.

6.2 Two-Sex Models

In his series of publications, Robert Pollak (1986, 1987, 1990) made a significant contribution to solving the two-sex problem. Pollak's discussion contains two parts: the case with permanent marriage (or permanent *union* more generally), and the case with one-period "southern California" marriage. In this subsection I introduce the simpler one-period marriage analysis.

6.2.1 The BMMR Model

Pollak (1990) proposed a Birth Matrix-Mating Rule (BMMR) model to deal with the problem of sexual dimorphism in the one-sex setup. Specifically, a BMMR model contains the following elements:

(i)   An age-specific birth matrix $\{m_{i,j}\}$, where $m_{i,j}$ is the expected number of female offspring born in a period to a couple with female and male aged i and j, respectively.

(ii) A union or marriage function that maps the societal age-specific female–male vectors, denoted N^- and N^+, respectively, into an age-specific number of unions $u_{i,j}$. Thus, $u_{i,j}(N^-, N^+)$ gives the total number of next-period unions with female aged i and male aged j, given that there are N^- females and N^+ males in the society in this period. We require that $u_{i,j}(x,y)$ be nonnegative for any x and y, and that $u_{i,j}(x, y) \le x$ and $u_{i,j}(x, y) \le y$.[2]

(iii) A sex-specific survival schedule (p_i^-, p_i^+), where p_i^- (p_i^+) is the female (male) survival probability from age i to age $i + 1$, similar to the schedule in any one-sex age-specific model.

It is believed that this BMMR model contains the most heuristic approach to analyzing the two-sex problems of human population, and I shall provide a preliminary introduction below.

Given the BMMR setup, it is straightforward to derive the dynamic state-transition rule of this sex/age-specific model. It is important to note that the state space in Pollak's model is age–sex rather than age alone.

The total number of newborn females in period $t + 1$, denoted $N_{t+1,1}^-$, is

$$N_{t+1,1}^- = \sum_i \sum_j m_{i,j} u_{i,j}\left(\mathbf{N}_t^-, \mathbf{N}_t^+\right) \equiv \omega_0^-\left(\mathbf{N}_t^-, \mathbf{N}_t^+\right). \tag{6.1}$$

If the ratio of male-to-female newborns is σ, then

$$N_{t+1,1}^+ = \sigma \sum_i \sum_j m_{i,j} u_{i,j}\left(\mathbf{N}_t^-, \mathbf{N}_t^+\right) \equiv \omega_0^+\left(\mathbf{N}_t^-, \mathbf{N}_t^+\right). \tag{6.2}$$

As to other age groups, the state-transition rule is even simpler. Let $N_{t,a}^-$ and $N_{t,a}^+$, respectively, be the number of females and males aged a at period t. Then

$$N_{t+1,a+1}^- = p_a^- N_{t,a}^- \equiv \omega_a^-\left(\mathbf{N}_t^-, \mathbf{N}_t^+\right) \quad a \ge 1, \tag{6.3}$$

$$N_{t+1,a+1}^+ = p_a^+ N_{t,a}^+ \equiv \omega_a^+\left(\mathbf{N}_t^-, \mathbf{N}_t^+\right) \quad a \ge 1. \tag{6.4}$$

Equations (6.1)–(6.4) together constitute the dynamics of all age classes. The state space can be written as $(\mathbf{N}_t^-, \mathbf{N}_t^+)$, and the dynamics can be expressed as

$$\left[\mathbf{N}_{t+1}^-, \mathbf{N}_{t+1}^+\right] = \left[\omega^-\left(\mathbf{N}_t^-, \mathbf{N}_t^+\right), \ \omega^+\left(\mathbf{N}_t^-, \mathbf{N}_t^+\right)\right] \equiv \omega\left(\mathbf{N}_t^-, \mathbf{N}_t^+\right),$$

where $\omega^- \equiv (\omega_0^-, \cdots, \omega_{n-1}^-)$ and $\omega^+ \equiv (\omega_0^+, \cdots, \omega_{n-1}^+)$. It is clear from (6.3) and (6.4) that for $a \ge 1$, ω_a^- and ω_a^+ are linear functions of $(\mathbf{N}_t^-, \mathbf{N}_t^+)$. But because $u_{i,j}$ is in general a nonlinear function of $\mathbf{N}_t^-$ and $\mathbf{N}_t^+$, ω_0^- and ω_0^+ are nonlinear. So what we have in (6.1)–(6.4) is essentially a nonlinear branching process with expanded (age–sex) state variables.

6.2.2 The Steady State

Notice that if a steady state of the two-sex model exists, it must be such that $\mathbf{N}_t^-$ and $\mathbf{N}_t^+$ grow at the *same* rate, otherwise the sex ratio will eventually be either zero or infinity. Thus, Pollak (1990) proposed the following definition of steady state for the two-sex model: a steady state is a triplet $(\hat{\mathbf{N}}^-, \hat{\mathbf{N}}^+, \hat{\varrho})$ such that

$$\left(\hat{\varrho}\hat{\mathbf{N}}^-, \hat{\varrho}\hat{\mathbf{N}}^+\right) = \omega\left(\hat{\mathbf{N}}^-, \hat{\mathbf{N}}^+\right). \tag{6.5}$$

In view of (6.3) and (6.4), we see that $\forall a \geq 1$, if $(N_{t,a}^-, N_{t,a}^+)$ is doubled, $(N_{t+1,a+1}^-, N_{t+1,a+1}^+)$ will also double. Thus, because $u_{i,j}$ is the only source of nonlinearity, in order to sustain a steady state as defined in (6.5), unavoidably we must assume $u_{i,j}$ to be homogeneous of degree one in $(\mathbf{N}^-, \mathbf{N}^+)$.[3] This assumption means that doubling the number of males and females will double the pairs of unions formed and precludes the possible influence of population density on the formation of unions.

The last technical assumption needed to establish the steady state of a two-sex model is that the reproduction rate of the society is not terribly low; otherwise, the population will certainly become extinct. This assumption can be explicitly specified using the idea of a ϱ-*normalized* population. To construct a ϱ-*normalized* population, we divide $\mathbf{N}_t$ by ϱ^t:

$$\left(\mathbf{N}_t^-(\varrho), \mathbf{N}_t^-(\varrho)\right) = \left(\frac{\mathbf{N}_t^-}{\varrho^t}, \frac{\mathbf{N}_t^+}{\varrho^t}\right).$$

Thus, a steady state can be characterized by a $\hat{\varrho}$ such that

$$\left(\hat{\varrho}\mathbf{N}^-(\hat{\varrho}), \hat{\varrho}\mathbf{N}^+(\hat{\varrho})\right) = \omega\left(\mathbf{N}^-(\hat{\varrho}), \mathbf{N}^+(\hat{\varrho})\right).$$

We say that a population structure is ϱ-*productive* if there exists a value of ϱ for which $\omega_0^-(\mathbf{N}^-(\varrho), \mathbf{N}^+(\varrho)) > \varrho$. That is, there are some ϱ's such that the number of females born by the normalized population is at least ϱ. This is essentially a technical condition, and Pollak (1986) showed that it is likely to be satisfied for human populations.

We notice that the intrinsic growth rate ϱ is the key parameter of the model, for once ϱ is determined, the relative size of each age–sex composition can be calculated from the sex-specific mortality schedule. Thus, Pollak concentrated upon the determination of the equilibrium $\hat{\varrho}$, Pollak (1986) proved the following theorem:

THEOREM 6.1 *(Pollak, 1986, pp. 251–253)*
Suppose (i) $u_{i,j}(x,y)$ is well defined for all pairs of (x, y); (ii) $u_{i,j}(x, y)$ is continuous in (x, y); (iii) $u_{i,j}(x, y)$ is homogeneous of degree one in (x, y); and (iv) the population is ϱ-productive. Then there exists a steady state satisfying (6.5).

6.2.3 BMMR with Persistent Union (BMMRPU)

The above discussion refers to the case with one-period unions, which is somewhat restrictive. Because the family decision period for a complete fertility is quite long, a multiperiod setup with persistent marriage is evidently necessary. Pollak (1987) extended his analysis to this case and derived a similar result, which is shown below.

Because we are going to separate each family union into several dimensions, to simplify the notations I shall list them as elements in parentheses instead of in the subscript. Let us denote $u_t(i, j, n^+, n^-)$, $m^-(i, j, n^+, n^-)$, and $m^+(i, j, n^+, n^-)$, respectively, the number, the probability of bearing a girl, and the probability of bearing a boy associated with unions of females aged i and males aged j, having n^+ boys and n^- girls at period t. The fertility rates m^- and m^+ are assumed to be time-invariant, and hence do not have a time subscript. The total number of newborn babies of each sex is then

$$N^s_{t+1,1} = \sum_i \sum_j \sum_{n^+} \sum_{n^-} u_t\left(i, j, n^+, n^-\right) m^s\left(i, j, n^+, n^-\right), \quad s = +, -. \qquad (6.6)$$

Summing $u_t(i, j, n^+, n^-)$ over n^+ and n^- yields the total number of female i–male j unions at period t. Thus, the available number of aged i females for possible period-$(t + 1)$ union is

$$N^{a-}_{t,i} = N^-_{t,i} - \sum_j \sum_{n^+} \sum_{n^-} u_t\left(i, j, n^+, n^-\right),$$

where the superscript a refers to availability. Similarly, the number of aged j available males for possible period-$(t + 1)$ union is

$$N^{a+}_{t,i} = N^+_{t,i} - \sum_i \sum_{n^+} \sum_{n^-} u_t\left(i, j, n^+, n^-\right).$$

The number of new unions at period $t + 1$ is a linear homogeneous function of $N^{a-}_{t,i}$ and $N^{a+}_{t,j}$:[4]

$$u_{t+1}\left(i + 1, j + 1, 0, 0\right) = \mu\left(N^{a-}_{t,i}, N^{a+}_{t,j}\right). \qquad (6.7)$$

Besides this new union, there is a probability $\delta(i, j, n^+, n^-)$ of determining whether an old union will persist in the next period:

$$u_{t+1}\left(i + 1, j + 1, \tilde{n}^+_{t+1}, \tilde{n}^-_{t+1}\right) = \delta\left(i, j, n^+_t, n^-_t\right) u_t\left(i, j, n^+_t, n^-_t\right), \qquad (6.8)$$

where $\tilde{n}^+_{t+1}$ and $\tilde{n}^-_{t+1}$ are the random numbers of boys and girls at period $t + 1$, depending on how many sex-specific children are born in that period. Equations (6.7) and (6.8) provide a full characterization of the unions at period $t + 1$.

Let $\mathbf{N}^-_t$ and $\mathbf{N}^+_t$ be vectors of females and males of all ages and $\mathbf{U}_t$ be the vector of all types of unions. The state variables now become $(\mathbf{N}^-_t, \mathbf{N}^+_t, \mathbf{U}_t)$, and equations (6.3)–(6.4) and (6.6)–(6.8) can be treated as a transformation from $(\mathbf{N}^-_t, \mathbf{N}^+_t, \mathbf{U}_t)$ to $(\mathbf{N}^-_{t+1}, \mathbf{N}^+_{t+1}, \mathbf{U}_{t+1})$. A steady state of this BMMRPU model can be similarly defined, Pollak (1987) proved that such a steady state exists as long as the union function μ is homogeneous of degree one.[5]

6.2.4 Applications to Other Type Spaces

Pollak's formulation of the two-sex problem is neat and can be applied to other type-specific population models as well. All we have to do is to specify an expanded type–sex space, a type–type union function, and a union-specific reproduction function. Then we can apply Pollak's theorem almost directly and establish the corresponding type–sex steady state. An application will be briefly mentioned in the last section of this chapter.

6.3 FERTILITY DECISIONS AND SEX PREFERENCES

6.3.1 Two Types of Sex Preferences

Economists have mentioned two types of sex preferences in the literature. In the first type, parents have a desired sex composition planned for their children; and when the existing sex ratio of children is inconsistent with their desired composition, they either have more children (Ben-Porath and Welch, 1976,1980; DeTray, 1984) or shorten the birth interval (Rosenzweig, 1986) so as to facilitate the realization of their desired ratio. The second type of sex preference is related not to the birth decision but to the resource allocation among children (Behrman et al., 1986; Chu, 1991). Parents with son preferences would give more resources to sons than to daughters. Although there are cases of daughter preferences or one-of-each-sex preferences, the prevailing type in most societies is son preference. The question is: How would these prevailing micro household preferences affect the macro population characteristics in the equilibrium?

The first type of sex-preference behavior has been rigorously studied by Leung (1991), and the discussion of the second type of sex preference will be left to the last section of this chapter. The background of Leung's study was based on the premise that no techniques such as amniocentesis-based abortion or sex-based selective implantation are allowed to be used. If these techniques that have high probability of success are available and legal, then sex selection will involve little risk, and there is no need at all for parents to bear more or to shorten the birth interval. Because amniocentesis and selective implantation for sex selection were not widespread even in the 1990s and are still illegal in many places around the world,[6] Leung's analysis is still relevant.

Leung assumed that a typical couple faces the following T-period decision problem:

$$\max_{h_1, \cdots, h_{T+1}} E_0 \left\{ \sum_{t=0}^{T} \delta^t \left[U\left(n_t^+, n_t^-, c_t\right) - W\left(h_{t+1}\right) \right] + V\left(n_{t+1}^+, n_{t+1}^-\right) \right\}$$

$$\text{s.t. } p_t n_t^+ + q_t n_t^- + c_t = y_t, \quad t = 0, 1, \cdots, T,$$

where h_{t+1} is the probability of birth in period $t + 1$, which is a variable chosen by the parents at period t; $W(h_{t+1})$ is the cost associated with choosing h_{t+1}; n_t^+ and n_t^- are the number of boys and girls the parents have at period t; p_t and q_t are the costs associated with rearing a boy and a girl, respectively; δ is the discount rate; y_t and c_t are the household income and consumption, respectively, at period t; E_0 is the expectation operator; $U(.,.) - W(.)$ characterizes the utility flow at period t; and $V(.,.)$ is the value function at period $t + 1$. The derivation of V will be specified below.

6.3.2 The Optimal Stopping Rule of Birth

In the above maximization problem, the state variables are n_t^+ and n_t^-, and the parents have to determine the "optimal stopping rule" of childbearing. Of course, if the parents intend to have one more child in period $t + 1$ by raising h_{t+1}, whether they will have one more boy or girl is a random event. It is assumed that women would become infertile in period $T + 1$ so that, other than incidence of mortality, the stock of children will become unchanged after period $T + 1$.

Let σ be the probability of giving birth to a boy. Standard analysis of dynamic programming tells us that the solution to the above problem can be characterized by the following Bellman equation:[7]

$$V_t\left(n_t^+, n_t^-\right) = \max_{h_{t+1}}\left\{U\left(n_t^+, n_t^-, y_t - p_t n_t^+ - q_t n_t^-\right) - W\left(h_{t+1}\right)\right.$$
$$+ \delta\left[\left(1 - h_{t+1}\right)V_{t+1}\left(n_t^+, n_t^-\right) + h_{t+1}\left[\sigma V_{t+1}\left(n_t^+ + 1, n_t^-\right)\right.\right.$$
$$\left.\left.\left. + \left(1 - \sigma\right)V_{t+1}\left(n_t^+, n_t^- + 1\right)\right]\right]\right\}. \tag{6.9}$$

Notice that the functional form of V_t is derived instead of assumed.

6.3.3 A Testable Hypothesis

After period $T + 1$, the time of becoming infertile, $h_t = 0$, and the size of (n_t^+, n_t^-) will not change $\forall\ t \geq T + 1$. By definition, $V_{T+1}(n_{T+1}^+, n_{T+1}^-)$ is the discounted sum of all future utility flow:[8]

$$V_{T+1}\left(n_{T+1}^+, n_{T+1}^-\right) = E_{T+1}\left\{\sum_{t=T+1}^{n}\delta^t U\left(n_{T+1}^+, n_{T+1}^-, y_t - p_t n_{T+1}^+ - q_t n_{T+1}^-\right)\right\}.$$

Substituting V_{T+1} into (6.9) and iterating, we can derive V_t for every t. Suppose $p_t = \bar{p}$ and $q_t = \bar{q}$ for all t, and parental utility function has the following specification:

$$U = u\left(\alpha_t + \beta n_t^+ + \gamma n_t^-\right), \quad \beta > \gamma \geq 0, \tag{6.10}$$

where β and γ are time-invariant parameters. Since $T + 1$ is the time of becoming infertile, given (6.10), we see that V_{T+1} will be a function of $(a_{T+1} + \beta n^+_{T+1} + \gamma n^-_{T+1})$. Substituting this back to (6.10) and iterating, we see that V_t is also a function of $(\beta n^+_t + \gamma n^-_t)$ $\forall t$. Given this result, Leung proved the following theorem:[9]

Theorem 6.2 *(Leung, 1991, p. 1082)*
Let the optimal h_{t-1} chosen at period $t + 1$ be h^*_{t+1}. If (6.10) holds and $p_t = \bar{p}$ and $q_t = \bar{q}$ for all t, then

$$\left. \frac{\partial h^*_{t+1}}{\partial n^+_t} \right|_{n^+_t + n^-_t = const.} < 0.$$

For any two families with the same number of children, the above theorem provides us with a testable prediction: the family with more boys tends to have a smaller probability of having one more birth. Or in a cross-sectional context, theorem 6.2 predicts that in a society with stronger son preferences, the fertility rate of all periods (certainly including the steady state) should be higher. This is the first implication of son preferences, which has induced extensive research. Repetto (1972), Ben-Porath and Welch (1976, 1980), and Leung (1994) all used micro data about family decisions to test whether the existing male/female composition of children has any (significantly) negative impact on parents' decision to have more children. The empirical evidence by and large does support such a negative impact.

The premise of theorem 6.2 is equation (6.10), which means that there is a fixed tradeoff between sons and daughters. If son preferences originate from productivity differences between men and women, then (6.10) essentially assumes that such a productivity difference is roughly constant.

6.4 MICRO SEX PREFERENCES AND MACRO SEX RATIOS

The sex preferences presented above are characterized by the parents' attempt to change the boy/girl ratio within their family. Our question is whether these (widespread) micro attempts would affect the macro characteristics of the population. Specifically, if parents with son preferences have an "at least one boy" fertility decision rule, how would the steady-state sex ratio be affected? The question was raised by Ben-Porath and Welch (1976), and there has been much biological research trying to answer this question in the past ten years.

6.4.1 Comparative Statics of the Sex Ratio

The sex ratio of males to females older than 2 years will certainly be affected by the age-specific mortality schedule. So the number of age-specific newborn babies (N_1^-, N_1^+) should be more appropriate for us to use to study the impact of parental sex preferences.

If the relative schedules of $m^-(.)$ and $m^+(.)$ are independent of parental sex preferences, then the resulting aggregate sex ratio will not be affected by the prevalence of sex preferences. The reasoning is simple: if the probability of bearing a boy or a girl is $\sigma: (1 - \sigma)$, then the intention of parents with son preference to bear more children will only make them face more $\sigma: (1 - \sigma)$ chances; the realized societal sex ratio *outcome* of newborn babies, by the law of large numbers, however, must always be $\sigma: (1 - \sigma)$.

But recent biological studies have come up with strong evidence that points in a different direction. According to James (1990, 1992, 1995a, 1995b) and Williams and Gloster (1992), bearing a male or female baby is not a totally random event. They pointed out that factors such as follicular phase length, parental hormone level, race, parental coital rates, and caloric intakes all have influence on the newborn sex ratio of humans and other mammals.[10] Among these factors that influence the sex ratio, some (such as the hormone level or the parental coital rates) are not society-based but indeed individual-specific. For instance, if a mother has a lower-than-normal hormone level, according to the series of research by James, she is more likely to bear girl babies. In general, there are certain parents with low hormone level or other characteristics who have larger probability than others to bear female babies, and they are called *girl producers* by Ben-Porath and Welch (1976). Similarly, parents who have larger probability than others to bear male babies are called *boy producers*.[11] I will show that this finding has helped in establishing the relationship between parental sex preferences at the micro level and population sex ratio at the macro level, a relationship strongly related to the main focus of this volume.

If parents have strong son preferences, then the boy producers are likely to be satisfied to keep the family size relatively low, whereas the girl producers will have to bear many girls before they finally have enough boys. As such, we would predict that for regions without sex preferences or with even-handed sex preferences, the aggregate sex (male/female) ratio of newborn babies should be nearly *uncorrelated* with the fertility rate; whereas for regions with strong son preferences, the male/female ratio of newborn babies should show a pattern *negatively correlated* with the fertility rate. Conversely, the existence of a significantly negative correlation coefficient in some countries provides objective evidence of their son preferences. This is a relationship against which one can test the data.

The above negative-correlation prediction is in fact robust even for regions known for prevalent (albeit illegal) sex-based abortion. In these regions, parents do not have to have a lot of births to achieve the number of sons they desire. They can keep on aborting until a boy is on its way, so that the resulting male/female ratio of newborns may be high but the fertility rate will remain low. Thus, even with prevalent sex-based abortions, there is still a negative *correlation* between the fertility rate and the male/female ratio of newborn babies in areas with strong son preferences.

In summary, we have

THEOREM 6.3
Suppose the probability of having a male or female baby is individual-specific. Then, other things being equal, for areas without sex preferences or with one-of-each-sex preferences, the aggregate sex (male/female) ratio of newborn babies should be uncorrelated with the fertility rate; whereas for areas with strong son preferences, the male/female ratio of newborn babies should have a pattern negatively correlated with the fertility rate.

6.4.2 An Empirical Test

Let the fertility rate and the sex ratio (boys/girls) of newborn babies of country i at period t be, respectively, $m_{i,t}$ and $r_{i,t}$. The above analysis clearly predicts that, other things being equal, $r_{i,t}$ and $m_{i,t}$ should be more negatively correlated in areas with stronger son preferences. Chu and Yu (1996) tested this hypothesis using the United Nations data, which will be discussed below. For countries lacking reliable micro data of fertility, such a macro estimation and testing may be an interesting alternative.

Based on extensive review of the literature, Williamson (1976) provided a summary of rank orderings of parental sex preferences for different societies. Because there are some "areas" (instead of countries) in Williamson's study for which fertility rate data are not available, Chu and Yu (1996) chose 15 countries from Williamson's summary for their statistical analysis.

A premise of the negative-correlation prediction in the previous subsection is that fertility is an active control variable of parents. If parents have very high fertility rates and continue to give birth, then they will not stop bearing children even after they have several boys. So in countries with a high fertility rate, son preferences will not be revealed in birth decisions and will not have anything to do with the fertility rate. Thus, sample points that, for religion or other reasons, have persistently high or increasing fertility rates and appear not to practice birth control should be ruled out. Furthermore, because in the postwar baby-boom periods there are high fertility rates that are not related to sex preferences, those observations should also be ruled out.

Sometimes men and women in the same region were found by Williamson to have different intensities of son preferences, but usually the difference is not large. In their empirical analysis, Chu and Yu used women's (mother's) son-preference index.[12] As shown in table 6.1, among the sample countries, Tunisia and Egypt are ranked +4 by Williamson, meaning that

TABLE 6.1. Data Period and Son-Preference Index of 16 Countries

Group	Country	Data Period	Son Preference Index
1	Egypt	71–74, 77–89, 91	+4
	Tunisia	74, 78–80, 85–89	+4
	Korea	78–89, 91, 93	+3
	Taiwan	71–94	+3
2	Denmark	71–92	+1
	Finland	71–90	+1
	Norway	71–92	+1
	Sweden	71–93	+1
	United States	71–88, 91,	+1
	Israel	82–85, 87–93	0
	Chile	71, 73, 77–91, 93	−1
	Cuba	71, 76–88, 91	−1
	Mexico	74, 76, 78, 80,	−1
		83, 88, 93	
	Puerto Rico	71–85, 87–92	−1
	Uruguay	71–79, 83–88	−1
	Venezuela	71–79, 81–89	−1

Sources: $m_{i,t}$ and $r_{i,t}$ are from the United Nations *Demographic Yearbooks* and Taiwan *Population Statistics Yearbooks*. Son-preference indexes for all countries are provided by Williamson (1976).

there are "very strong son preferences" in these two countries. Women in Taiwan and South Korea also share "strong son preferences," receiving an index of +3. All other countries have son-preference indexes equal to or less than 1 or negative (daughter preferences).

The data needed for the empirical analysis are yearly time series of fertility rates and newborn male/female sex ratios for 16 countries. So essentially we have a panel data set of $r_{i,t}$ and $m_{i,t}$. Because observations of any single country may be too narrow in scope, Chu and Yu (1996) decided to separate the observations into two diverse groups and test whether there is any distinction between these two groups. The first group includes Korea, Taiwan, Tunisia, and Egypt, which, according to table 6.1, have strong ($\geq$ +3) son preferences. The other group includes Latin America and the Caribbean countries, the United States, Israel, and Nordic countries. These 12 countries have weak sex preferences. The analysis in the previous section tells us that there should be a (significantly) negative correlation between $r_{i,t}$ and $m_{i,t}$ for countries in group 1 and almost no correlation for countries in group 2.

In order to obtain an estimation of the correlation coefficient between $r_{i,t}$ and $m_{i,t}$, we have to control the countrywise difference in fertility rates. There is also a trend toward a general decline in fertility pattern for almost all our sample countries. To take into account the above cross-section and time-trend effects, Chu and Yu (1996) considered the following two-factor fixed-effect model:[13]

$$m_{i,t} = \alpha_0 + \alpha_i + \gamma_t + \zeta r_{i,t} + \varepsilon_{i,t}, \qquad (6.11)$$

where $\varepsilon_{i,t}$ is the error term associated with the (i, t)th observation. There are also two constraints, $\Sigma_i \alpha_i = \Sigma_t \gamma_t = 0$, which are imposed to normalize the total country effect and time effect to zero.

Given that the country effect and the time effect are controlled, the sign of the coefficient of $r_{i,t}$ tells us whether there is any correlation between $r_{i,t}$ and $m_{i,t}$.[14] Chu and Yu's estimation result shows that while $\tilde{\zeta}$ is not significantly different from zero for group 2 countries, it is significantly negative for group 1 countries. They also carry out an F test: the null hypothesis is that the ζ coefficients for the two groups of countries are equal, and the alternative hypothesis is that the ζ coefficients for group 1 countries should be significantly smaller. The result shows that the null hypothesis is rejected in a one-tailed test at the .01 level.

6.5 Unequal Resource Division

Besides having *ex ante* preferences for a particular sex ratio of children before they are born, *ex post* parents may allocate resources differently among children that are already born. Boys and girls may receive different resources from their parents and then mate with someone from another family. The wealth of the new family may be affected by the size of both the dowry from the female side and the gift from the male side. Because sex preferences are revealed by the difference of resource allocation sizes, it seems more appropriate to classify people by income rather than by age. The analysis in this section is similar to the one in chapters 4 and 5, and I will provide only a brief discussion here. The difference is that, since the evolution of family incomes involves a union of two sexes, the state space of the branching process we study in this section is income/sex.

Let us suppress the age structure and consider an overlapping-generation model in which everyone lives two periods. The first period is childhood and the second is adulthood. Male and female adults with resources i and j from different families can form a new union with new *family* income $f(i, j, \tilde{w}) = \tilde{w} + r \cdot (i + j)$, where $\tilde{w}$ is the random wage income, characterizing parents' overall ability, and $r \cdot (i + j)$ is the property income. Each unmarried adult has his or her own income, which is assumed to be consumed by this adult before death. Married couples will save a proportion of their income and leave it as bequests to children. The bequests will be divided among female and male children and become their resources i and j, respectively, in their adulthood.

There are two general types of mating environments to be discussed. The first is random mating, where for any male with endowment i, the realization of j is independent of i. The second type is assortative mating, where the realization of the mate's resource j is (imperfectly) correlated with that of i.[15] There are also two broad types of bequest division rules to be studied.

The first is to divide all bequests equally among all boys and girls. And the second, which characterizes some kinds of son preferences, is to leave a larger (smaller) share to boys (girls) and divide the bequests evenly among children of the same sex.

Suppose the mating environment is random. Then parents' decision to leave a larger bequest to boys will shift the *ex ante* endowment distribution of boys to the right and that of girls to the left. Intuitively, compared with the case of no son preferences, a scenario with son preferences in a society that has random mating will result in a steady-state distribution of endowments with an equal mean but a larger variance and a larger endowment inequality. This can be seen as we compare figures 6.1 and 6.2. Without son preferences, the endowment distribution among all children is the same, and a random mating is a random selection of two points from the same compact pool. But with son preferences, the endowment pools of boys and girls are separated, and a random selection of two points will evidently have a more variable result.

Now consider assortative mating. Suppose the positive correlation between i and j is strong; then rich (poor) boys will be more likely to mate with rich (poor) girls, so that intergenerational mobility is weak. In this case,

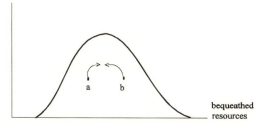

FIGURE 6.1 Without sex preferences, a random mating is a probabilistic matching of two points (a, b) from the same bequest distribution.

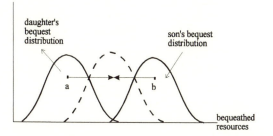

FIGURE 6.2 With son preferences, a random mating is a probabilistic matching of two points (a, b) from two dispersed bequest distributions.

the analysis in chapter 5 tells us that an unequal division of bequests in the poor group may be an effective way to improve the upward mobility of the poor class, and the steady-state inequality may be reduced by such sex preferences. Here we have only provided the above sketch; a detailed analysis would be similar to that in Chu (1991).

PART II

Cycles and Transitions

CHAPTER 7

Cyclical Patterns of Human Population

Summary of Previous Research

7.1 BACKGROUND

According to Chesnais (1992), the fluctuation of human populations can be summarized into three broad categories: the pretransitional, transitional, and posttransitional cycles. In the pretransitional period before the Industrial Revolution, population fluctuations appear to reflect natural constraints of the environment. In more recent centuries, there were changes of the vital rates from high fertility–high mortality to low fertility–low mortality, which are referred to as *demographic transitions*. In this transitional period, because the decline of mortality usually leads that of fertility, fluctuations in the population age structure are a natural consequence of such a transition. After this transitional period, in many developed countries the mortality rate is stabilized, and female fertility becomes a typical family decision. Since family fertility decisions are related to other market institutions, the posttransitional population cycles have close interactions with these institutional elements.

Although the population cycles can be separated into the three abovementioned types, these cyclical movements share one common feature: the Malthusian environmental check always plays a direct or indirect role. In the next few chapters, I will discuss how the environmental checks interact with human decisions and institutions and how these interactions affect the cyclical movement of the population.

Thomas Malthus argued that all populations are subject to environmental constraints and that these constraints operate through a variety of checks to population growth. If there are no such checks, we have a stationary branching process as described in chapters 2–6. In that case, the population will converge to a steady state under weak assumptions, and there are fluctuations only in the process of convergence. When there are environmental checks, the strength of the checks determines the speed with which the system tends toward equilibrium; this speed, relative to response lags that are intrinsic to the process, heavily influences the dynamic behavior of the economic–demographic system. When checks are weak, shocked populations tend to converge slowly without overshooting and to move in cycles one generation long (Lee, 1974). If checks are stronger, overshooting may occur, and longer cycles of periodicity spanning two generations or more are possible, as population size and growth rates oscillate about their equilibrium values. If checks are sufficiently sensitive, then the amplitude of these oscillations will grow rather than damp, and limit cycles and chaotic cycles can in principle occur (Tuljapurkar, 1987; Wachter and Lee, 1989). This chapter presents a summary of the major mathematical results on population cycles, which will serve as the basis for our later discussion. The first section is about cycles in stationary branching processes, and subsequent sections are about cycles in time-variant branching processes. Readers who are not interested in the mathematical foundation of demographic cycles can skip this chapter and move on to chapter 8.

7.2 STATIONARY BRANCHING PROCESSES

I showed in chapter 2 that the dynamics of a general branching process can be characterized by

$$\mathbf{N}_t = \mathbf{Q}\mathbf{N}_{t-1}, \tag{2.4}$$

where $\mathbf{Q}$ is a time-invariant projection matrix. Let $\lambda_1, \lambda_2, \cdots, \lambda_n$ be the eigenvalues of $\mathbf{Q}$ and $\mathbf{w}_1, \cdots \mathbf{w}_n$ be the corresponding right (column) eigenvectors. We also showed that the population vector in period t can be written as

$$\mathbf{N}_t = \sum_i c_i \lambda_i^t \mathbf{w}_i \tag{2.5}$$

for some set of constants $(c_1, \cdots, c_n)$. In chapter 2 I use ϱ to denote the dominant eigenvalue λ_1; here I shall use λ_1 instead to distinguish it from the other eigenvalues.

Dividing both sides of (2.5) by λ_1^t yields

$$\frac{\mathbf{N}_t}{\lambda_1^t} = c_1\mathbf{w}_1 + c_2\left(\frac{\lambda_2}{\lambda_1}\right)^t \mathbf{w}_2 + c_3\left(\frac{\lambda_3}{\lambda_1}\right)^t \mathbf{w}_3 + \cdots. \tag{7.1}$$

If we list the λ's in descending order with $|\lambda_1| > |\lambda_2| > \cdots > |\lambda_n|$, then we see from (7.1) that

$$\left[\left(\frac{\mathbf{N}_t}{\lambda_1^t}\right) - c_1\mathbf{w}_1\right] \to c_2\delta^{-t}\mathbf{w}_2,$$

where $\delta \equiv \lambda_1/|\lambda_2|$ is called the *damping ratio* of convergence. Thus,

$$\lim_{t \to \infty} \left\| \frac{\mathbf{N}_t}{\lambda_1^t} - c_1 \mathbf{w}_1 \right\| \le k\delta^{-t}$$

for some constant k. The above equation says that the convergence of $\mathbf{N}_t$ to a stable population structure is asymptotically geometric, at a rate as fast as δ.

In the process of convergence, the path may well be cyclical. In particular, λ_j may be a complex number and may be written as $\lambda_j = \sigma_j + i\omega_j$. In terms of polar coordinates, we have

$$\lambda_j = |\lambda_j| (\cos\theta_j + i \sin\theta_j),$$

where $\theta_j = \tan^{-1}(\omega_j/\sigma_j)$. The period of oscillation is therefore $P_j \equiv 2\pi/\theta_j$. Although all complex eigenvalues of $\mathbf{Q}$ may contribute to the cyclical pattern of the converging path, the most important and longest lasting of these is of course associated with λ_2. Coale (1972) showed that for the age-specific human population model, P_2 is approximately equal to the mean age of childbearing in the steady state, roughly 25–30 years.

This single-generation cycle of human population found by Coale was also compatible with some historical evidence. Using a long series of data on baptisms, burials, and marriages, Goubert (1965) and Lee (1977) verified a 30-year wave in baptisms in several parishes. Although there were some small density-dependent feedbacks, the generation cycle was virtually unaffected.

7.3 TIME-VARIANT BRANCHING PROCESSES

7.3.1 General Discussion

The general formulation of a time-variant branching process is characterized by the following equation:

$$\mathbf{N}_{t+1} = \mathbf{Q}_t \mathbf{N}_t = \mathbf{Q}_t \mathbf{Q}_{t-1} \cdots \mathbf{Q}_0 \mathbf{N}_0. \tag{7.2}$$

When the projection matrix $\mathbf{Q}$ is time-variant, it is not surprising that the population structure will have fluctuations. Therefore, the focus of previous research is *not* about the cyclicity of $\mathbf{N}_t$, but rather the question of when the intrinsically fluctuating series $\mathbf{N}_t$ will have an ergodic (time-invariant) property.

There are two subcases to be considered, depending on whether $\mathbf{Q}_t$ is stochastic. When $\mathbf{Q}_t$ is nonstochastic, the ergodicity of N_t hinges upon the question of when the N_t sequence will *forget* its initial state (Tuljapurkar, 1990). Specifically, let the Hilbert metric distance between $\mathbf{x}$ and $\mathbf{y}$ be[1]

$$d(\mathbf{x}, \mathbf{y}) = \max_{i,j} \left\{ \ln \left(\frac{x_i y_j}{x_j y_i} \right) \right\},$$

and let a *contraction coefficient* of $\mathbf{Q}$ be defined as

$$\tau(\mathbf{Q}) = \sup_{x,y} \frac{d(\mathbf{Qx},\mathbf{Qy})}{d(\mathbf{x},\mathbf{y})}.$$

Let $H_{t,s}$ denote the series product of $\mathbf{Q}$'s:

$$H_{t,s} = \mathbf{Q}_t\mathbf{Q}_{t-1}\cdots\mathbf{Q}_s.$$

Caswell (1990) summarized the conclusion of Cohen (1979) and provided the following theorem.

THEOREM 7.1
If

$$\lim_{t\to\infty}\tau(H_{t,s}) = 0 \quad \forall s,$$

then the population structure $\mathbf{N}_t$ will be weakly ergodic in the sense that any two initial populations exposed to the same sequence of environments $\mathbf{Q}_t$, $t \in \{0, 1, \cdots\}$, will converge to the same population type distribution.

The second case is when the $\mathbf{Q}_t$ matrix is stochastic. The general formulation is to assume that $\mathbf{Q}_t$ follows a Markov process, that is, the realization probability of $\mathbf{Q}_t$ only depends on $\mathbf{Q}_{t-1}$. Cohen (1976) showed that, because $\mathbf{Q}_t$ depends on $\mathbf{Q}_{t-1}$ and $\mathbf{N}_t$ depends on $\mathbf{Q}_{t-1}$ and $\mathbf{N}_{t-1}$, we see that $\mathbf{Q}_t$ and $\mathbf{N}_t$ *jointly* form a Markov process. The ergodicity of $(\mathbf{Q}_t, \mathbf{N}_t)$ means that two populations with different initial $\mathbf{N}_0$ and different realization of $\mathbf{Q}_t$'s will eventually have the same type distribution.

7.3.2 Density-Dependent Models

In the above discussion, the analysis is less about cycles and more about the steady state of the type distribution, which is irrelevant to the focus of this chapter. The most relevant time-varying branching process that can generate various forms of cycles is the density-dependent model characterized by

$$\mathbf{N}_{t+1} = \mathbf{Q}_{\mathbf{N}_t}\mathbf{N}_t. \tag{7.3}$$

Evidently, (7.3) says that the projection matrix $\mathbf{Q}$ depends on the previous-period population composition $\mathbf{N}_t$.

There are many different ways to model density dependency in the literature. Usher (1972) and others assumed that elements of $\mathbf{Q}$ are all inversely related to the total population size. Cushing (1989) proposed a weaker assumption, supposing that density, not necessarily represented by the total population size, affects all the vital rates equally, so that $\mathbf{Q}_{\mathbf{N}_t} = h(\mathbf{N}_t)\mathbf{Q}$. Lee (1974) assumed that fertility rates are functions of the size of cohorts or the size of total labor force. Hasting (1978) considered the case when the net reproduction rate, instead of the individual vital rate, is a function of population size. In Samuelson's (1976) model, reproduction is assumed to depend on the *ratio* of the birth sizes of the previous two generations. In a regular predator–prey mode (Volterra, 1931), the reproduction of each species also depends on the relative abundance of the two species in question.

For any kind of specification of the density-dependent model, its local stability can be analyzed as follows. The derivation is due to Beddington (1974). Let us first detrend the population vector so that the steady-state growth rate is 1 and the steady-state vector is N*. Let $\Delta_t \equiv N_t - N^*$; then (7.3) can be rewritten as

$$\Delta_{t+1} + N^* = Q_{\Delta_t + N^*} \cdot \left[\Delta_t + N^*\right].$$

Expanding the **Q** matrix in a Taylor series around N* yields

$$N^* + \Delta_{t+1} \approx \left(Q_{N^*} + \sum_i \Delta_{t,i} \frac{\partial Q}{\partial N_{t,i}}\Big|_{N^*}\right)\left[\Delta_t + N^*\right]$$

$$= Q_{N^*}N^* + Q_{N^*}\Delta_t + \left(\sum_i \Delta_{t,i} \frac{\partial Q}{\partial N_{t,i}}\Big|_{N^*}\right)\left[\Delta_t\right]$$

$$+ \left(\sum_i \Delta_{t,i} \frac{\partial Q}{\partial N_{t,i}}\Big|_{N^*}\right)N^*. \tag{7.4}$$

Since $Q_{N^*}N^* = N^*$ by definition, the first terms on both sides of (7.4) can be canceled out. When Δ_t is sufficiently small, we can eliminate the third term on the right-hand side, which is of order Δ_t^2, and get

$$\Delta_{t+1} \approx Q_{N^*}\Delta_t + \left(\sum_i \Delta_{t,i} \frac{\partial Q}{\partial N_{t,i}}\Big|_{N^*}\right)N^*. \tag{7.5}$$

Thus, the local stability of the population hinges upon the first-order terms on the right-hand side of (7.5).

We derive (7.5) not to study the local stability of N_t but to analyze its possible sources of instability. If there is no density dependency, then the second term on the right-hand side of (7.5) drops out, and the dynamics of N_t will be stable, as described in chapter 2. The second term of (7.5) actually characterizes the sensitivity (elasticity) of vital rates with respect to density pressure. When this elasticity is small, the dynamic system of N_t will remain stable. When the elasticity is larger, the density feedback effect is strong, which in turn generates a momentum of cyclical (and perhaps unstable) movement of N_t. When this elasticity is even larger, the N_t series may have a more volatile cyclical movement, even limit cycles or chaos. Such a feedback effect is called *homeostasis*.

7.4 AGE-SPECIFIC DENSITY DEPENDENCY

To study the age-specific density-dependency model, Lee (1974) started with Lotka's renewal equation (3.1), which is restated below:

$$B_t \equiv \sum_{a=0}^{n} B_{t-a} l_a m_a = \sum_{a=0}^{n} N_{t,a} m_a, \qquad (3.1)$$

where l_a and m_a are, respectively, age-specific surviving probability and fertility rate. Let $\phi_a \equiv l_a m_a$ be the age-specific net maternity function, and $R \equiv \Sigma_a \phi_a$ be the net reproduction rate. Then (3.1) above can be rewritten as

$$B_t = \sum_{a=0}^{n} \phi_a B_{t-a}. \qquad (7.6)$$

7.4.1 General Settings

Density dependency is characterized by the assumption that the age-specific fertility rate at period t is a function of the vector of previous birth numbers

$$m_{a,t} = m_a\left(B_{t-1}, B_{t-2}, \cdots B_{t-n}\right),$$

where n is the upper bound of human survival. We use a boldface $\mathbf{B}_t$ to denote the vector $(B_{t-1}, B_{t-2}, \cdots, B_{t-n})$. Then we have $m_{a,t} = m_a(\mathbf{B}_t)$ and $\phi_{a,t} = l_a m_a(\mathbf{B}_t) = \phi_a(\mathbf{B}_t)$. Thus, (7.6) now becomes

$$B_t = \sum_a \phi_a\left(B_t\right) B_{t-a}.$$

Without loss of generality, we can detrend the birth series by its growth rate and consider a steady-state $\mathbf{B}_t$ series with zero growth. Let $\mathbf{B}^*$ be the steady-state birth vector with all its entries equal to B^*; then in the steady state we have

$$1 = \sum_a \phi_a\left(\mathbf{B}^*\right). \qquad (7.7)$$

In the steady state, since the net maternity function is time-invariant, we denote $\phi_{a,t} = \phi_a(\mathbf{B}^*) \equiv \phi_a$. Let

$$\eta_a \equiv \frac{\partial R_t}{\partial B_{t-a}} B^*$$

be the elasticity of the net reproduction rate with respect to the number of births a years earlier, evaluated at the steady-state birth (i.e., $B_{t-a} = \mathbf{B}^*$ $\forall_{t-a}$). Expanding the right-hand side of (7.6) in a Taylor series around $\mathbf{B}^*$ and using (7.7), Lee (1974) showed that (7.6) can be approximated by

$$B_t \approx B^* + \sum_a \left(\phi_a + \eta_a\right)\left(B_{t-a} - B^*\right). \qquad (7.8)$$

Let $b_t \equiv (B_t - B^*)/B^*$ be the proportional deviation of B_t; then the above equation can be rewritten as follows:

$$b_t \approx \sum_a (\phi_a + \eta_a) b_{t-a}. \qquad (7.8')$$

7.4.2 Cohort and Period Models

In equation (7.8), η_a characterizes the sensitivity of fertility with respect to deviations of B_{t-a} relative to the steady-state size. Lee (1974) proposed two alternative hypotheses that can further simplify (7.8') to a testable form. The first simplification is the *cohort* hypothesis, which assumes that age-specific fertility is affected by the number of births at that age: $m_{a,t} = m_a(B_{t-a})$. In this case, $\partial Rt/\partial B_{t-a}$ is equal to $\partial \phi_{a,t}/\partial B_{t-a}$. Let α_a denote the elasticity of ϕ_a with respect to B_{t-a}, then (7.8') becomes

$$b_t \approx \sum_a (1 - \alpha_a) \phi_a b_{t-a}.$$

If all age-specific elasticities equal the same value α, then the above equation can be further simplified as

$$b_t \approx (1 - \alpha) \sum_a \phi_a b_{t-a}.$$

Another formulation of the cohort model was proposed by Frauenthal and Swick (1983), who assumed that $m_{a,t} = m_a \cdot M(B_{t-a})$. With this special assumption, equation (7.8) can be written analogously as

$$b_t \approx (1 - \gamma) \sum_a \phi_a b_{t-a},$$

where γ is the elasticity of $M(.)$ with respect to B_t evaluated at $B_t = B^*$.

An alternative hypothesis is to assume that fertility is affected not by the cohort size but by the total labor force, more in the spirit of Easterlin (1961). In this case, $m_{a,t} = m_a(L_t) \equiv m_a(\Sigma_j r_j l_j B_{t-j})$, where $L_t \equiv \Sigma_j r_j l_j B_{t-j}$ is the total labor force and r_j is the age-specific labor-force participation rate. The model so specified is called the *period* model. Let the elasticity of R_t with respect to L_t be $-\beta$ and the elasticity of L_t with respect to B_{t-a} be k_a. Then, for the period model, (7.8) becomes

$$b_t \approx \sum_a (\phi_a - \beta k_a) b_{t-a}.$$

7.5 Hopf Bifurcation and Cycles

This section summarizes major theorems of Hopf bifurcation. More details are available in Golubitsky and Schaeffer (1985) and Tuljapurkar (1987). The theorems presented are important for studying existence and stability of population cycles.

7.5.1 General Results

Consider the following nonlinear dynamic system:

$$\frac{du}{dt} + F(u, \gamma) = 0, \tag{7.9}$$

where $F: R^n \times R \to R^n$, and γ is a bifurcation parameter. Assuming that $u = 0$ is a fixed point of (7.9) at $\gamma = \gamma^*$, then $F(0, \gamma^*) = 0$. By the implicit function theorem, we know that in the neighborhood of γ^* the solution to (7.9) can be expressed as $u(\gamma)$. For a dynamic system such as (7.9), we say that $\gamma = \gamma^*$ is a *bifurcation* point if a small change of γ around γ^* causes a significant change in the solution path $u(\gamma)$. There are several kinds of bifurcation, and the one related to our later discussion is Hopf bifurcation.

Applying the first-order Taylor approximation to (7.9) around $u = 0$ yields

$$\frac{du}{dt} = -A(\gamma)u, \tag{7.10}$$

where $A(\gamma)$ is the $n \times n$ Jacobian matrix of F evaluated at $u = 0$. Suppose the characteristic roots of $A(\gamma)$ can be written as $\sigma(\gamma) \pm i\omega(\gamma)$.

We make the following two assumptions.

ASSUMPTION A7.1: *$A(\gamma^*)$ has only one pair of purely imaginary eigenvalues, that is, $\sigma(\gamma) = 0$.*

ASSUMPTION A7.2: $\sigma'(\gamma^*) \neq 0$.

A7.1 and A7.2 say that $\gamma = \gamma^*$ is a Hopf bifurcation point. Now we introduce Hopf's first theorem:

THEOREM 7.2
If A7.1 and A7.2 hold, then there exists a periodic solution to (7.9).

Given assumptions A7.1 and A7.2, theorem 7.2 says that at $\gamma = \gamma^*$, there is a unique pair of purely imaginary roots for the characteristic equation $|A(\gamma)| = 0$. In this case the solution $u = 0$, which forms either a limit cycle or a closed-orbit solution, is called *neutrally stable*. Specifically, for any given initial value u_0, a solution or *trajectory* to (7.9) is denoted $u(t) = \Phi_t(u_0)$. An *attractor* is a set to which trajectories starting at initial points in a neighborhood of the set will eventually converge. A point is said to be in a *closed orbit* if there exists a $t \neq 0$ such that $\Phi_t(u) = u$. If a closed orbit is an attractor, then it will be called a *limit cycle* (for a two-dimensional case, see figures 7.1 and 7.2).[2]

Without loss of generality, we assume that for $\gamma < \gamma^*$, the steady state $u = 0$ is stable (i.e., orbits spiral into the origin), and for $\gamma > \gamma^*$, the steady state $u = 0$ is unstable (i.e., orbits spiral away from the origin).

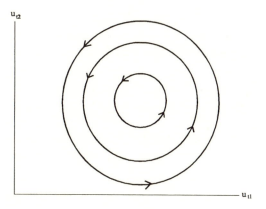

FIGURE 7.1 Closed orbit.

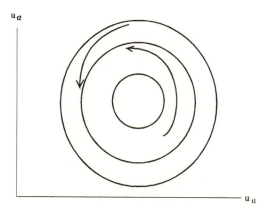

FIGURE 7.2 Limit cycle.

When we take into account the higher order terms of the Taylor expansion, the situation becomes more complicated, but more information concerning the stability of the limit cycles will appear. We can write the nonlinear version of equation (7.9) as

$$\frac{du}{dt} = -A(\gamma)u + O(u^2), \tag{7.11}$$

where $O(u^2)$ is the higher order term. In equation (7.11), periodic solutions may exist not just at the point $\gamma = \gamma^*$. The concrete result is Hopf's second theorem. Before we introduce this theorem, we need another definition.

Suppose at some γ there exists a periodic solution $u^*(t)$ to the system (7.11). Around $u^*(t)$ we can consider a "nearby" solution $u^*(t) + v(t)$. Tuljapurkar (1987) showed that, for the case of population renewal equations, the stability of $u^*(t)$ in fact depends on the sign of the exponent of a linearized expression of $v(t)$. That is, the stability of (7.11) hinges on the sign of φ, where φ is such that $v(t) = \omega(t)\exp(\varphi t)$ for some $\omega(t)$. Here φ is called the Floquet exponent.[3] Now we introduce the following stability theorems.

THEOREM 7.3
If the stability condition corresponding to (7.11) is satisfied, then the system will (i) converge to the assumed fixed point $u = 0$ when $\gamma < \gamma^*$; (ii) converge to a limit cycle when $\gamma > \gamma^*$. In the latter case, the amplitude of the limit cycle will increase in γ.

For the case of population renewal equations, the stability condition in Theorem 7.3 refers to the requirement that the Floquet exponent is negative. I will skip the general expression of the Floquet exponent for now and come back to it when I discuss the special model of population dynamics. I shall now introduce the theorem of *exchange of stability*.

THEOREM 7.4
If the Floquet exponent is negative, then the periodic solution on one side of γ^* and the fixed-point solution on the other side of γ^* are both stable (this case is called supercritical). If the Floquet exponent is positive, then the periodic and fixed-point solutions on both sides of γ^* are unstable (this case is called subcritical; see figure 7.3).

A *subcritical* case means that a periodic solution with a positive amplitude is never stable.

7.5.2 Testing and Estimation

For all the density-dependent models, the sensitivity of density dependency always hinges upon the elasticities of the birth function with respect to previous births, and the size of previous births characterizes the pressure of population density. These elasticities can all be estimated from empirical data. The usual approach is to put the age-specific fertility rate on the left-hand side of the regression equation and the numbers of previous-period

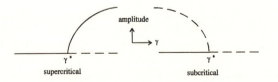

FIGURE 7.3 Super- and subcritical cases. Dashed lines indicate unstable solutions.

births (or the weighted average of previous births) on the right-hand side. The estimated elasticity, denoted $\bar{\gamma}$, can be obtained from the regression result. Tuljapurkar (1987) applied the general Hopf bifurcation theory to age-specific density-dependent renewal equations and showed that there is a "critical" elasticity beyond which there will be limit cycles or chaotic movements. Then the estimated elasticities can be compared with the theoretical critical elasticities to see whether our real-world birth data sequence will generate persistent cycles.

Lee's (1974) estimation showed that the U.S. data cannot generate a strong enough elasticity that is consistent with limit cycles. Guckenheimer, Oster, and Ipakchi (1977) even concluded that "most populations operate in the parameter region corresponding to a stable equilibrium." Frauenthal and Swick (1983) and Swick (1981), however, argued that they could derive from the U.S. population data an elasticity strong enough to generate a limit cycle. But their analysis was later shown by Wachter and Lee (1989) to be incorrect.

Notice that all the above empirical analysis only concerns the *existence* of a limit cycle or closed-orbit solution. To study whether such a solution is *stable* is another, more complicated, matter.

7.6 PREDATOR–PREY MODELS

As was shown in section 7.2, a density-dependent model can be written as follows: $N_{t+1} = \mathbf{Q}_{\mathbf{N}_t} N_t$. Another way to interpret this expression is that N_{t+1} is a *nonlinear* function of N_t. Such a nonlinearity property of the density-dependent model is in fact a key factor in creating erratic cycles. One particular example of the density-dependent model to which biologists have paid much attention is the predator–prey model, introduced by Lotka (1925) and Volterra (1931).

The simplest formulation of the predator–prey model, following the notations in the literature, is characterized by the following (continuous time) differential equations:

$$\dot{N}_{t,1} = aN_{t,1} - bN_{t,1}N_{t,2}$$
$$\dot{N}_{t,2} = -cN_{t,2} + dN_{t,1}N_{t,2}, \quad a, b, c, d > 0, \tag{7.12}$$

where $N_{t,1}$ is the total prey population and $N_{t,2}$ is the predator population. The prey are considered the only food resource available to the predator. Thus, if $N_{t,1} = 0$, the predator population decreases exponentially at the rate c. The prey population does not need the predator to survive, and with the nonexistence of predators, the prey population grows exponentially at the rate a.

In the steady state of (7.12) with $\dot{N}_{t,1} = \dot{N}_{t,2} = 0$, there are two solutions: $(N_1^*, N_2^*) = (c/d, a/b)$; and the trivial solution $(N_1^*, N_2^*) = (0, 0)$. The Jacobian matrix of (7.12) around the nontrivial solution is

$$J = \begin{pmatrix} a - bN_2^* & -bN_1^* \\ dN_2^* & -c + dN_1^* \end{pmatrix} = \begin{pmatrix} 0 & -bc/d \\ ad/b & 0 \end{pmatrix}.$$

Since $|J| = ac > 0$ and the trace of J is zero, we know that the eigenvalues of J are purely imaginary. The equilibrium is therefore neutrally stable, meaning that no stability conclusion about (N_1^*, N_1^*) can be drawn. That is, besides the equilibrium $(c/d, a/b)$, the solution trajectories of (7.12) are closed orbits, but none of them is a limit cycle. This was formally proved by Hirsch and Smale (1974).

Such a closed-orbit solution derived from the reasonable model in (7.12) was called by Samuelson (1972) a "universal cycle." Samuelson also proposed several other alternatives to (7.12). The first is a predator–prey model with density dependency:

$$\frac{\dot{N}_{t,1}}{N_{t,1}} = a - xN_{t,1} - bN_{t,2}$$

$$\frac{\dot{N}_{t,2}}{N_{t,2}} = -c + dN_{t,1} - yN_{t,2}, \quad a, b, c, d > 0. \qquad (7.13)$$

Samuelson added the $-xN_{t,1}$ term to characterize the diminishing-return effect of the prey population, and the $-yN_{t,2}$ term is to characterize the crowding effect among the predator group. These two effects may both be related to density pressure. By checking the Jacobian matrix of the local approximation of (7.13), it is easy to see that the two eigenvalues become negative and the solution becomes locally stable. This demonstrates the power of the density-dependency effect.

Samuelson also tried another setup:

$$\frac{\dot{N}_{t,1}}{N_{t,1}} = a + xN_{t,1} - bN_{t,2}$$

$$\frac{\dot{N}_{t,2}}{N_{t,2}} = -c + dN_{t,1} + yN_{t,2}, \quad a, b, c, d > 0, \qquad (7.14)$$

which characterizes some kind of increasing return in reproduction. It can be shown that system (7.14) becomes unstable. The point here is that the predator–prey scenario is not a concept independent of economic institutions; it can be combined with a density-dependent model or an increasing-return model to generate qualitatively different results. Chu and Lee (1994) gave an example of combining the predator–prey setup with the density-dependent model; this scenario will be discussed in detail in chapter 9.

7.7 REMARKS

Lee (1987) distinguished the variations in human populations into two categories: those related to resource availability, such as variations in carrying capacity or in incomes, which are *density-dependent*; and those unrelated to resource availability, reflecting wars, epidemics, cultural, political and social changes, and medical advances, which are *density-independent*. But when we take into account the role of human economic decisions, the distinction between density dependency and density independency is not an unambiguous one.

In human history, very often famines or food deficiencies, which are density-dependent themselves, might cause conflicts and wars between two tribes, events which we classify as density-independent. Density pressure or food deficiency may also induce peasants to become bandits, who (as predators) rob and deprive peasants of food (preys). Thus, human economic decisions often transform a density-dependent pressure on human reproduction into a density-independent one. It is therefore important to investigate the role of human decision on population cyclicity, instead of restricting ourselves to the abstract classification of density-dependence or independence. We are interested in *how* human decisions interact with density pressure; only with this question answered are we able to provide a more accurate prediction of the pattern of population cycles.[4]

Lee (1987) also pointed out that density-dependency is a prevalent phenomenon for all animals and that it is more or less "biological." It is expected that rational human decisions may be able to weaken the biological response of fertility and mortality to density while strengthening the nonbiological response of fertility through institutional and rational regulation. But this conjecture can only be accurately analyzed within a model which *explicitly* concerns human decisions. I will present such an analysis in the chapters that follow. Chapter 8 provides a general characterization of behavioral interactions in individual *attitudes*, of which the combination forms the *custom* of the society. In chapter 9, I study a case in ancient that human history. In that period, there were several decisions that humans could make to change the vital rates. I will show that the institutions they generate in response to density pressure, although *rational* individually, may not be able to relieve the overall density pressure. In chapter 10, I study the most popular type of modern birth cycles, the Easterlin cycles. I analyze how the labor market, a human institutional design, interacts with the fertility behavior of individual family heads.

CHAPTER 8

Attitude-Specific Population Models

Dynamic Custom Evolution

8.1 BACKGROUND

In the predator–prey model introduced in chapter 7, two types of individuals interact with each other. The key features are that the reproduction rate of each type depends on the size of both types and that each individual's welfare depends on his or her interaction with other individuals. Besides the predator–prey interaction described above, there are several other well-known two-type interactions in economic literature. Hardin's (1968) classic paper on "tragedy of the commons" is a typical example.

The scenario of decision interaction Hardin considered is as follows: there is a pasture open to all, and each herdsman considers whether to add an animal to his herd. The benefit of adding an animal goes to each individual, but the social (overgrazing) cost is born by all herdsmen. Thus, it is a dominant strategy for each herdsman to add more cattle, which, however, leads to a Pareto-inferior overgrazing result. If we consider the interaction between any two herdsmen as a 2×2 game, then the game Hardin had in mind is similar to the "prisoners' dilemma." When the concern with herd size is replaced by the concern with population size, the problem becomes one of population/environment interaction. This kind of decision interaction will be discussed in chapter 14.

In this chapter we will study another kind of two-type population interaction, the *critical-mass* model proposed by Schelling (1978). In the critical-mass setup, people can choose different behavior types in different periods, and their choice depends on the overall behavioral pattern in the previous period. The key idea is described in the following example.

Suppose we use the [0,1] interval to characterize the behavioral pattern of the population. When the behavioral pattern is close to 0, then the rational decisions of most people will sustain 0 as a stable equilibrium. When the overall pattern exceeds a certain critical mass, *the tide turns*; as people gradually change their micro decisions, the macro behavioral pattern eventually changes to 1, which is another stable equilibrium. Schelling (1978) proposed many empirical examples that have the above-mentioned critical-mass property. For instance, in universities we often observe that one's decision whether or not to attend a seminar depends on the attitude of other colleagues. If most other people go, then I go; if most other people do not go, then I decide to do likewise. In the former case, the seminar can continue; in the latter case, the seminar will have to be canceled. Both are equilibria with stable population composition.

Besides Schelling's classic example, economists found that many other phenomena in society have the same properties. Jones (1976) showed that if most people use a certain commodity as a medium of exchange, then that commodity will be more readily acceptable to general exchangers, which in turn will attract more people to use it. Eventually it will become the only commodity money. Lui (1986) and Chu (1990) argued that if most officials take bribes, in general it is more difficult to collect evidence from the colleagues of an official suspected of corruption. As a result, the probability of conviction and the deterrence perception will be low, leading to further corruption. Benjamini and Maital (1985) and Schlicht (1985) noted that if most of one's neighbors evade taxes, the perception that the expected peer-group condemnation will be low if one does the same facilitates the decision of tax evasion. Chu (1993) showed that if most drivers drive rudely (or politely), then it is also optimal for others to do the same, so that overall traffic patterns will become different. In daily life, one double-parks if many others do; one surges to the ticket window if most other people do; and one crosses the lawn if plenty of others do. So in short, what the critical-mass model involves is some macro population activity that is self-sustaining once the magnitude of that activity crosses a certain threshold.

The above examples refer to different aspects of macro population behavior, but they share a common property: micro individual decisions combine to form the macro behavior pattern of the population. Put differently, suppose we classify people by their *attitude* in an environment; then the social custom is simply the aggregate characterization of such an attitude. This aggregate attitude will become the *custom* in the next period, which in turn will affect individual decisions in that period. In order to analyze the evolution of a population's custom, it is certainly convenient to classify people by their attitudes instead of by their ages. In the next few sections I will set up a two-attitude population model, demonstrate how the macro social custom is affected by the micro decision, and show when the population dynamics will be of cyclical patterns.

There are various ways to model the decision interdependency among rational individuals; here we propose a framework consistent with the spirit of Schelling (1978). To make the following scenario more practical, it may be helpful to think of the macro index of custom as the proportion of rude drivers in a country or a city and of people's attitudes as reflected by the way they drive. It goes without saying that the model here also applies to many other interpretations in Schelling (1978).

8.2 THE CRITICAL-MASS MODEL

8.2.1 Individual Decision Making

We shall consider a population with a very large size N_t at period t. Each member of the population randomly meets (one by one, say, at a crossroads) n others in each period. Because no one is in a position to know in advance whom he is going to come across, any *ex ante* cooperative negotiation is out of the question. The interactions between any two individuals will be characterized by the following symmetric 2×2 game. There are two choices in everyone's pure strategy space: 1 and 2. Let us interpret strategy 1 as driving rudely and strategy 2 as driving courteously.

The magnitude of payoffs is assumed to be as follows. $\omega \equiv r \cdot \pi$ is the expected penalty of adopting strategy 1, where π is the size of penalty on all detected rude drivers and r is the probability of detection. Now let us consider the situation without enforcement and penalty ($\omega = 0$) and explain the relative magnitude of a, b, c, and d. The ideal situation is for both sides to drive courteously ($\max\{a, b, c, d\} = d$). If one expects the other driver to drive rudely, he would be inclined to requite like for like ($a > c$). Conversely, if one drives rudely but the driver he comes across happens to be courteous, he would be mortified for what he has done ($d > b$).

	1	2	
1	$a - \omega, a - \omega$	$b - \omega, c$	$d > b, \ d > a > c$
2	$c, b - \omega$	d, d	

In the above payoff expression, row chooser's payoffs are listed first.

Let θ_r (θ_c) be the probability that the row (column) player takes strategy 1. There are three obvious Nash equilibria in this symmetric 2×2 game: $(\theta_r, \theta_c) = (1, 1)$, $(\theta_r, \theta_c) = (0, 0)$, and $(\theta_r, \theta_c) = (x, x)$, where

$$0 < x \equiv \frac{d - (b - \omega)}{a - \omega - c + d - (b - \omega)}$$

$$= \frac{d - b - \gamma\pi}{a - c + d - b}. \tag{8.1}$$

8.2.2 Decision Interdependency

Because one does not know in advance what strategies the others are going to adopt, he or she can only draw on experience and make an educated guess. This, as we will see, gives rise to the mutual interactions among drivers. Suppose there are p_t proportion of the population taking strategy 1 (and hence $1-p_t\%$ taking strategy 2) at period t. One may come across $n \ll N_t$ people on the street randomly, where N_t denotes the population size of the city. Thus, the number of people taking strategy 1 (denoted k) in this n-person sample will follow a binomial distribution:

$$k \sim \binom{n}{k} p_t^k \left(1 - p_t\right)^{n-k}.$$

Let $\overline{Z}_n$ be the sample mean of this n-sample; then we have

$$p_r\left(\overline{Z}_n > x \big| p_t\right) = p_r\left(n\overline{Z}_n > nx \big| p_t\right)$$

$$= 1 - \sum_{y=0}^{x^*} \binom{n}{y} p_t^y \left(1 - p_t\right)^{n-y}$$

$$\equiv h\left(p_t; x^*\right), \tag{8.2}$$

where x^* is the largest integer no greater than nx. Clearly, when $p_t = 0$, the event $\overline{Z}_n > x$ never happens, and hence $h(0; x^*) = 0$. Similarly, $h(1; x^*) = 1$.

Let us suppose, as did Schelling (1978), that people are myopic in the sense that they use the sample mean they observe at period t to predict the proportion of strategy-1 choosers in period $t + 1$.[1] Given p_t, it is shown in (8.1) that a particular individual i will have probability $h(p_t; x^*)$ to observe a sample mean (denoted $\overline{Z}_n^i$) larger than x. Let

$$\xi^i = \begin{cases} 1, & \text{if } \overline{Z}_n^i > x; \\ 0, & \text{if } \overline{Z}_n^i \leq x. \end{cases}$$

8.2.3 Macro State-Transition Rules

Suppose we pick a city of population size N_t and calculate the corresponding sample mean $\bar{\xi}_{N_t} \equiv \sum_{i=1}^{N_t} \xi^i / N_t$; then clearly $\bar{\xi}_{N_t}$ will have a sampling distribution with mean $h(p_t; x^*)$. By Khinchine's law of large numbers (see Theil, 1971), as $N_t \to \infty$, $\bar{\xi}_{N_t}$ converges to $h(p_t; x^*)$ in probability. Thus, in a city with a very large number of drivers, there will be $h(p_t; x^*)$ proportion of them who have $\xi^i = 1$ (or who observe $\overline{Z}_n^i > x$). Under Schelling's myopic-prediction assumption, person i with $\xi^i = 1$ would expect to meet more than x proportion of strategy-1 takers in period $t + 1$, and therefore, according to the specification of the 2×2 traffic interaction game, i's best response is to adopt strategy 1 in period $t + 1$. As such, we have

THEOREM 8.1

Suppose the total size of population in period t, denoted N_t, is a very large number. Given that p_t is the proportion of strategy-1 adopters in period t, the number of people who will choose strategy 1 in period $t + 1$ is $h(p_t; x^*)$, which is independent of N_t.

Notice that here the dynamics of population composition is independent of population size. The key reason for such independence is the law of large numbers. Although each individual may observe different ξ^i's, the *societal* mean, which is the common reference variable for individual decision in the next period, is always independent of the absolute size of various types.

8.2.4 Extensions

The above analysis applies to all individuals in general and has not taken into account the reproduction and possible decision difference between people with different attitudes. Let $N_{t,i}$, $i = 1,2$, be the total number of strategy-i takers in period t, and let ϱ_i be their corresponding gross reproduction rate. Clearly we have $N_t = N_{t,1} + N_{t,2}$.

People with different attitudes may be accustomed to their current behavior. For instance, rude drivers in New York may be accustomed to their style of driving. We assume that each type of people may have their own payoff matrix, so that they may have different critical values in (8.1). Let x_i, $i = 1,2$, be the critical value of type i; then the dynamics of the population can be written as

$$N_{t+1,1} = \varrho_1 N_{t,1} h\left(p_t, x_1^*\right) + \varrho_2 N_{t,2} h\left(p_t, x_2^*\right)$$
$$N_{t+1,2} = \varrho_1 N_{t,1}\left[1 - h\left(p_t, x_1^*\right)\right] + \varrho_2 N_{t,2}\left[1 - h\left(p_t, x_2^*\right)\right]. \qquad (8.3)$$

Notice that in the above expression it is x_i^*, not x_i, that enters the h function. Suppose both types of people are fairly similar in the sense that the possible difference between x_1 and x_2 can still sustain the equality $x_1^* = x_2^*$. Then we can divide both sides of (8.3) by the total number of period-$(t + 1)$ population, $N_{t+1} = \varrho_1 N_{t,1} + \varrho_2 N_{t,2}$, and get the following dynamic evolution equation of population composition: $p_{t+1} = h(p_t; x^*)$, where $x^* = x_1^* = x_2^*$.[2]

8.3 DYNAMIC CUSTOM EVOLUTION

8.3.1 Endogenous Nonconvexity of p_t

The function $h(p_t; x^*)$ in (8.2) may have several possible shapes. First, if $0 < nx < 1$, then $x^* = 0$, and $h(p_t; x^*) = 1 - (1 - p_t)^n$. This implies that $dh/dp_t = n(1 - p_t)^{n-1} > 0$ and $d^2h/dp_t^2 = -n(n - 1)(1 - p_t)^{n-2} < 0$. The second possibility occurs when $n - 1 < nx < n$ and the h function becomes $h(p_t;$

x^*) = p_t^n. Both these cases are depicted in figure 8.1. As we shall see in the next section, the value of x^* will be determined by government policy, and the above-mentioned two cases will stand only if that policy is extreme. In what follows, we shall set aside these two extremes and concentrate on the third possibility: $1 \leq nx \leq n - 1$, where we can rewrite $h(p_t; x^*)$ as

$$h(p_t; x^*) = 1 - (1 - p_t)^n - \sum_{y=1}^{x^*} \binom{n}{y} p_t^y (1 - p_t)^{n-y}. \tag{8.2'}$$

The picture of h for the case $1 \leq nx \leq n - 1$ is also drawn in figure 8.1.

Differentiating the $h(p_t, x^*)$ in (8.2') with respect to p_t yields

$$\frac{dh}{dp_t} = n(1 - p_t)^{n-1} - n \left[\sum_{y=1}^{x^*} \binom{n-1}{y-1} p_t^{y-1} (1 - p_t)^{n-y} \right.$$

$$\left. - \sum_{y=1}^{x^*} \binom{n-1}{y} p_t^y (1 - p_t)^{n-y-1} \right] \tag{8.4}$$

Since

$$\binom{n-1}{y-1} p_t^{y-1} (1 - p_t)^{n-y} \bigg|_{y=k} = \binom{n-1}{y} p_t^y (1 - p_t)^{n-y-1} \bigg|_{y=k-1},$$

by expanding the terms in the square bracket of (8.4) we see that most of them cancel with each other, and dh/dp_t can be further simplified as

$$\frac{dh}{dp_t} = n \binom{n-1}{x^*} p_t^{x^*} (1 - p_t)^{n-x^*-1} > 0.$$

Differentiating the above expression with respect to p_t once more yields

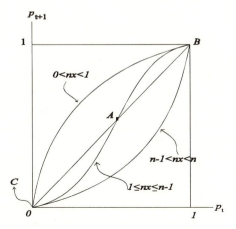

FIGURE 8.1 The shape of h (p_t; x).

$$\frac{d^2h}{dp_t^2} = n\binom{n-1}{x*}p_t^{x*-1}\left(1 - p_t\right)^{n-x*-1}\left[x* - p_t(n-1)\right],\qquad(8.5)$$

which will be positive (negative) if p_t is smaller (larger) than $x*/(n - 1)$. Equations (8.4) and (8.5) allow us to arrive at the following theorem.

THEOREM 8.2
When $1 \leq nx \leq n - 1$, the h curve is uniformly increasing in p_t and has a unique inflection point at $x*/(n - 1)$.

8.3.2 Multiple Equilibria in Population Composition

I mentioned in the previous section that $h(0, x*) = 0$ and $h(1, x*) = 1$. In view of figure 8.1, we see that when $1 \leq nx \leq n - 1$, there are clearly three steady states for p_t: 0, 1, and the one that corresponds to point A. $p_t = 0$ is clearly a Pareto optimum, and it is also locally stable. The situation is different from the one corresponding to the prisoners' dilemma game, where individual rational decisions *always* lead to a Pareto-inferior outcome.

Although there have been several models that explain the interdependency of individuals' choices, as reviewed in section 8.1, our analysis is nevertheless unique. By assuming that people make decisions on the basis of their previous binomial sampling, we were able to derive the exact formula and the *exact inflection point* of the state-transition rule. Thus, instead of proposing vaguely that there may be *multiple* equilibria, as in Arthur (1989), David (1988), or Gordon (1989), we can conclude that as long as $1 \leq nx \leq n - 1$ holds, there are *exactly three* equilibria, as shown in figure 8.1. This property, together with the interior inflection point derived, is very helpful in developing our understanding of the shape of the custom transition path and our later discussion of government policies.

Figure 8.1 shows that the dynamic evolution of population composition satisfies the four properties of a complex system characterized in Arthur (1989): namely, possible multiple equilibria, possible inefficiency, lock-in, and path dependence. These properties can be explained from figure 8.1: in the case of $1 \leq nx \leq n - 1$, the three equilibria are A, B, and C, and only B and C are stable. As long as B and C involve different social costs, one of them is inevitably inefficient. The population composition is path-dependent because different initial points (starting from (A, B) or (C, A)) lead to different steady states. A government policy can change the value of x, and hence the shape of h, but a stable equilibrium will not be responsive to any marginal change in x. This means that a stable equilibrium is "locked in," and the government has to make some significant change in order to extricate itself from a stable but inefficient situation.

To make the model more realistic for policy analysis, let us assume that there are q_1 proportion of (well-mannered) people who never drive rudely, and q_2 proportion of (rash) people who always drive rudely. With these modifications, the population custom transition rule becomes:

$$p_{t+1} = q_2 + \left(1 - q_1 - q_2\right)h\left(p_t; x\right) \equiv g\left(p_t; x\right), \qquad (8.6)$$

which is shown in figure 8.2, with the number of steady states being possibly one, two, or three.

8.4 TRYING TO CHANGE THE CUSTOM

Now we consider government enforcement policies that try to change the custom by penalizing rude drivers. Let us assume that law enforcement revenues collected by the government are paid back to the public in a lump sum, so that they are private but not social costs. Thus, if we normalize the population size to one, the expected social return of traffic interaction in period t, given the payoff values in the 2×2 game, will be

$$ap_t^2 + \left(b + c\right)p_t\left(1 - p_t\right) + d\left(1 - p_t\right)^2 \equiv B_t.$$

Enforcement cost C_t is assumed to be a linear function of detection probability: $C_t = \alpha \cdot r_t$, and hence the net social welfare would be

$$
\begin{aligned}
W_t &\equiv B_t - C_t \\
&= ap_t^2 + \left(b + c\right)p_t\left(1 - p_t\right) + d\left(1 - p_t\right)^2 - \alpha r_t \\
&\equiv W\left(p_t, r_t\right), \qquad (8.7)
\end{aligned}
$$

where the relationship between r_t and p_t is as described in (8.6). With δ the social discount rate, the present value of total social welfare is $\Sigma_{t=0}^{\infty} \delta^t W_t$.

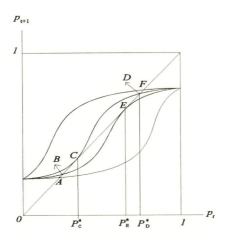

FIGURE 8.2 Points between P_E^* and P_C^* cannot be sustained by stationary policies.

8.4.1 Stationary Policies

In most law enforcement cases, the penalty size cannot be frequently altered, but the detection probability can be changed by adjusting police forces or inspecting probabilities. So in our later analysis, we shall study the impact caused by changing r. It is easy to see from (8.1) that tightened enforcement (increasing r) would decrease x. If such a decrease is significant enough to cause the threshold integer x^* to go downward, then individuals would be more likely to adopt strategy 2 (to drive courteously), the curve $g(p_i;x)$ would shift down, and the corresponding steady state would also change. Let $W(p^*(r),r)$ denote the total social welfare associated with r and its corresponding steady-state traffic order $p^*(r)$. Clearly, whether a change in r is worth implementing depends upon the sign of dW/dr.

Suppose we are now at point A of figure 8.2, which is sustained by very strict traffic law enforcement at a very high enforcement cost. Suppose the government is trying to relax enforcement in order to cut cost. When r falls, x will decrease, as we can see from (8.1). If the critical integer x^* also decreases, the curve $g(p_i;x)$ shifts up, and the steady-state value p^* increases to B. As the $g(.,.)$ curve shifts upward, a greater percentage of people are adopting strategy 1, and the traffic order is gradually worsening. However, the nonconvexity of g implies that as r falls there may be a jump in $p^*(r)$, and hence a jump in social costs. This can be seen in figure 8.2, where a slight reduction of r at the point C would make the steady-state p value change from p_C^* to p_D^*. Similarly, there will also be a jump if one tries to increase r at the point E. In fact, *no p value between p_E^* and p_C^* could ever be sustained as a steady state*. Thus, for stationary policies, the government is faced with only two choices: a good custom with a low percentage of traffic violators, sustained by strict enforcement ($\overline{AC}$ area), or a high percentage of traffic violators as a result of lax enforcement ($\overline{EF}$ area). More generally, we have the following theorem.

THEOREM 8.3
Suppose $1 \leq nx \leq n - 1$, and suppose there are $q_1 > 0$ proportion of (well-mannered) people who never adopt strategy 1 and q_2 proportion of (rash) people who always adopt strategy 1. There exists a subset $K \in [0,1]$ such that all customs $p \in K$ cannot be sustained by stationary policies.

8.4.2 Oscillatory Policies

Now consider the following oscillatory policy, which shuttles between tough (say r^1) and lax (say r^0) enforcement. Suppose at period zero $p_0 = p^*(0)$ may be very large because there is essentially no enforcement. Suppose the government decides that starting from period one, r will be increased to r^1, a very strict enforcement. Then p_t will follow the path $p_{t+1} = g(p_t; x^1)$, the traffic order will gradually improve, and the social benefit in each period will be $W_t = W(p_t, r^1)$.

The population composition p_t eventually converges to $p^*(1)$ (see figure 8.3). After staying at $p^*(1)$ for a while, suppose at period T_1 the government decides to relax enforcement to r_0 from period $T_1 + 1$ onward. The p_t will then follow the path $g(p_t; x^0)$, and the social benefit in each period will be $W_t = W(p_t, r^0)$. The government can repeat the above-mentioned cycles once p_t converges to $p^*(0)$. This cyclical enforcement policy will generate a sequence of W_t's, and the discounted total social benefit will be denoted TW^0_{cycle}, where the superscript "0" specifies the cycle's starting point $p^*(0)$.

Similarly, if at period zero $p_0 = p^*(1)$, which is very small, we assume that the government starts the cyclical policy by first reducing r to r^0, then, as p_t converges to $p^*(0)$, increasing r to r^1, and so on. Discounted total social benefits so obtained will be denoted as TW^1_{cycle}. For other starting points, the oscillatory policies can be described similarly.

Intuitively, oscillatory policies such as the ones presented in the paragraph above can never be efficient if the law enforcement agency is typically assumed to maximize a concave objective function over a convex feasible set.[3] As the convexity refers to a set of variables indexed by time, cycles cannot be optimal, because the average of two points of a cycle will exploit the convexity of the function and therefore increase the objective value achieved. However, as we explained in section 8.3, the mutual interaction of individual decisions has created a natural nonconvexity in the macro index of population composition. This in turn makes an oscillatory policy possibly better, because now the average of two points in a cycle may end up at a point which *cannot be sustained* by any stationary policy but can only be attained by an oscillatory one. Chu (1993) presents a set of

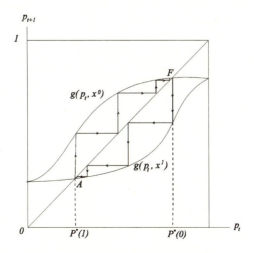

FIGURE 8.3 Cyclical policies—shuttling between γ^0 and γ^1.

examples that demonstrate when an oscillatory enforcement policy will be more socially efficient.

8.5 INDIVIDUAL INTERACTIONS AND CUSTOM CYCLES

As Cooter and Ulen (1988) and Wilson (1983) pointed out, crime statistics for the United States over the last fifty years show that the number of a wide variety of crimes declined from a peak in the mid-1930s to a trough in the early 1960s; rose rapidly from the early 1960s until the mid-or late 1970s; and finally began to fall slowly in the 1980s. There are two often-mentioned explanations for these crime cycles: the first relates the peak of the crime rate to the possibly unfair distribution of income in a period of rapid economic growth; the second hypothesis suggests that crime cycles are related to the cyclical age structure caused by fertility cycles. But a closer examination shows that these two explanations do not seem to be sufficient to account for the crime waves we observe.[4] What was rarely stressed in previous discussion of this topic was the interaction between crime waves and individual decisions.

As we mentioned in section 8.1, when the social order is weak, there usually exists public pressure for the tightening of law enforcement in order to improve order. Thus, because the crime rate is very high, there is a natural tendency for it to go down. Furthermore, since the dynamic time path of crime rates is nonconvex, a tightened law enforcement may cause a *gradual, persistent* fall of crime rates, as shown by the zigzag curve from *F* to *A* in figure 8.3. Similarly, when the crime rate is low, people may also propose to relax law enforcement in order to reduce the seemingly unnecessary enforcement costs, and this proposal could also cause a persistent increase in crime rates, as curve *A* to *F* illustrates. The movement between *A* and *F* cannot stop, for no point in the middle range can be sustained as a steady state. As such, aside from the exogenous demographic or economic shocks, the above-mentioned public pressures, together with the nonconvexity of dynamic path, form an *endogenous* force of prolonging crime cycles. This mutual interaction between social order and enforcement policy seems to be an important factor in interpreting crime cycles and perhaps other behavioral patterns of population composition as well.

CHAPTER 9

Occupation-Specific Population Models

Population and Dynastic Cycles

9.1 BACKGROUND

As Lee (1987) pointed out, vital rates of the human population are often determined by forces such as culture, institutions, technology, and individual rationality, forces that have little to do with density pressure or prior growth. Perhaps most people also expect "rational" human practice to weaken the biological responses of both fertility and mortality to density pressure, while strengthening the nonbiological response through institutional regulations. But can human institutional designs and rational responses really reduce the impact of natural checks? As we study the pattern of population dynamics in ancient China, we can provide some viewpoints different from the general opinion. The long-term relationship between human institutional designs and natural checks is discussed in chapter 14.

9.1.1 Population Dynamics in Ancient China: Some Stylized Facts

The books by Ho (1959) and Chao and Hsieh (1988; hereinafter C&H) contain the most thorough research on the history of Chinese population.[1] The data summarized in C&H have presented us with a time-population diagram, shown in figure 9.1. From this figure, as well as other related literature, the following "stylized facts" of population dynamics in Chinese history can be summarized:

1. Population declines often coincided with dynasty changes (C&H; Ho, 1959).

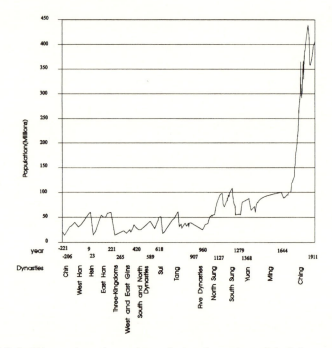

FIGURE 9.1 Chinese dynasties and population dynamics, original data are from Chao and Hsieh (1988); interpolations are done by the author.

2. Population declines were often drastic in a rather short period of time.[2]
3. Natural checks such as famine and epidemics did not independently reduce the population surplus (Ho, 1959); rather, population declines were often the direct and indirect results of internecine wars.
4. There are obvious peaks and troughs in the population data, but no regular cyclical patterns (C&H).

The fact that no serious population decline appears to have been independently due to famines and epidemics seems to suggest a weak pattern of density-dependency for ancient Chinese populations, a pattern consistent with the observation of Lee mentioned in the beginning of this chapter. However, as noted by many historians (see, e.g., Ho, 1959, and C&H 1988), the frequent clashes between soldiers and rebellious peasants in Chinese history were often *initiated* by famine or density pressure. As such, the originally weak natural checks on population were often magnified by war, and such magnified "institutional checks" caused very drastic population changes. It seems therefore that density pressure was indirectly responsible for the large and rapid historical population declines. Finally, this synchronized pattern of significant population decline and dynasty transition is not common in other countries in human history. These patterns clearly deserve further investigation.

9.1.2 Density Pressure and Peasant Revolt

The key factor that links the above-mentioned stylized facts of Chinese population data is what historians call the "peasant revolt." Here a brief background introduction to Chinese history seems to be in order. The 4,100-year history of China can be roughly divided into 23 dynasties (plus or minus two, depending on how dynasties are counted). They vary in length, with the longest being 644 years and the shortest four years. Wright (1965) and Usher (1989) both argued that major dynasties in China ended because of "peasant revolutions," although some of these uprisings were also accompanied by foreign invasions toward the end of a dynasty. When the population size was so large and/or taxes were so high that peasants' per capita income plummeted, even the traditionally obedient peasants were driven to rebellion by switching (or choosing) their "occupation" and becoming bandits, which was essentially an uprising or a revolution. This explains the interaction between density pressure and revolutionary wars. Rampant banditry seriously disrupted the farming environment and resulted in drastic population declines.

9.1.3 An Occupation-Specific Population Structure

The crucial element in the above scenario of peasant revolution is that people can switch or choose their *occupations* (remain peasants or join the revolt), and therefore we shall consider an *occupation-specific* population model. In the rest of this chapter, we separate people in ancient China into three groups: peasants, bandits, and rulers. Peasants grow and harvest crops and pay taxes, rulers collect taxes and hunt for bandits, and bandits rob and steal food and clash with peasants and rulers. We assume that people are making rational decisions when switching occupations; they choose to be bandits because the new occupation generates higher expected utility. By switching or choosing their occupations, people try to avoid the original pressure of high population density.

But the density pressure may be weakened or strengthened by people's occupation decisions, depending on whether the paradox of aggregation applies. If many peasants decide to become bandits, the war between bandits and soldiers may become devastating, which could lead to a population decline sharper than it would have been if these peasants did not make that occupation choice. When the relative power of bandits vis-à-vis soldiers exceeds some critical value, the peasant revolution succeeds, resulting in dynasty changes. These occasional internal changes in population compositions form the so-called dynastic cycles, which could be very erratic.

9.2 Occupation Switching and Population Dynamics

In order to focus attention on the occupational choice of the ancient Chinese, here as in chapters 4 and 5 I suppress the age structure of the population and consider a one-sex two-period model along the lines of Samuelson (1958). Each person in the society lives either one or two periods. The first period is called childhood; a person's childbearing occurs in the second period of life, which is adulthood. We assume that each surviving adult bears m children, where m refers to the "natural" level of fertility, and that only some of these children can survive to their second life period.[3] It is widely believed that natural fertility prevailed generally in preindustrial populations.

9.2.1 The Population Composition

As I mentioned briefly in the previous subsection, we shall consider a model with three population groups: rulers, peasants, and bandits. It goes without saying that this occupational classification only refers to adults. Rulers are the group of people who have the authority to tax peasants and go after the bandits. Rather than going into the complex theory of how a political authority comes into being, we shall concentrate on the forces behind the political regime—soldiers. Suppose there are N_{t-1} surviving children in the society at the end of period $t-1$, who will become adults at period t. The government drafts d proportion of them to be soldiers, and the remaining $(1-d)$ proportion will start to ponder their peasant/bandit occupation decision at period t. By assumption the service of soldiers is mandatory once they are drafted; hence, for them there is no occupation choice.

A civilian can choose to be a peasant and toil in the field or join the bandits and rob and steal. To protect their crops, the peasants fight the bandits. We assume there is a fighting "technology" that determines the final share of food and the survival probability of the two fighting parties. Let N_t^F be the number of adult peasants (farmers) at time t before clashing with the bandits, and N_t^B be the number of bandits at time t; then $(1-d)N_{t-1} \equiv (N_t^F + N_t^B)$ is the total number of adult civilians, and

$$b_t \equiv N_t^B / \left[(1-d)N_{t-1}\right]$$

is the ratio of bandits to civilians. We denote γ_t^i as the survival probability of group i ($i = F, B$) in the peasant/bandit clashes and s_t as the share of food peasants saved after bandits' strikes. (Thus $1 - s_t$ will be the share bandits got off with.) In general, we expect both s_t and γ_t^i to be functions of b_t. Finally, each peasant is required to pay v amount of food as head tax to the government to feed the soldiers and support the bureaucracy.

9.2.2 Individual Peasant/Bandit Occupation Decision

The choice between occupations is based on comparison of the expected utility of bandits and peasants. Suppose surviving adults all have the same utility function $u = u(x)$, where x is the per-adult food received. We also assume that the utility associated with a person's death state is zero. Let x_t^F be the food received by the surviving peasant at period t, and suppose there is no saving. Then his expected utility, denoted Eu_t^F, will be

$$Eu_t^F = \gamma_t^F \cdot u\left(x_t^F\right) + \left(1 - \gamma_t^F\right) \cdot 0$$
$$= \gamma_t^F \cdot u\left(x_t^F\right).$$

Similarly, a bandit's expected utility is

$$Eu_t^B = \gamma_t^B \cdot u\left(x_t^B\right).$$

Let f be the aggregate production function that transfers the labor input I_t, which is an increasing function of N_{t-1}, to crop output y_t:

$$y_t = f\left(I_t\left(N_{t-1}\right), D_{t-1}, \varepsilon_t\right).$$

Here D_{t-1} characterizes the damage to agriculture at the end of period $t - 1$. In particular, we expect that cultivated land would be destroyed and farmers' capital goods damaged during skirmishes and wars. ε_t is an exogenous random variable representing the output shocks in agriculture due to droughts, floods, or other natural calamities. We also assume that y_t/I_t is decreasing in I_t, in compliance with the law of diminishing return.

To simplify our presentation, we assume the following:

(i)   Because of the unpredictable nature of bandits' activities, soldiers can only hunt for bandits after the bandits strike. This *ex post* hunting increases the mortality probability of bandits, and therefore deters people from being bandits *ex ante*.

(ii) Surviving peasants divide evenly the food they saved from the bandits.

(iii) The amount of food taken by bandits and the tax collected by government do not affect the fighting efficiency of the two parties.

Given the above assumptions, Chu and Lee (1994) showed that the ratio of Eu_t^B to Eu_t^F will be a function of b_t, N_{t-1} and D_{t-1}:

$$\frac{Eu_t^B}{Eu_t^F} = \Psi\left(b_t, N_{t-1}, D_{t-1}\right). \tag{9.1}$$

Notice that for any given b_t, an increase in D_{t-1} will cause a reduction in y_t and hence an increase in Ψ. Thus, a deteriorating farming environment as a result of wars would make the occupation of farmer less attractive. This explains the effect of turmoil on occupation selection (C&H 1988; Ho, 1959). Furthermore, since y_t/N_{t-1} is decreasing in N_{t-1} by diminishing returns, we see from (9.1) that a larger population size (higher density) would also make people consider favorably the option of becoming an outlaw.

We assume that a person with attitude characteristic k will choose to be a bandit if

$$\Psi\big(b_t,\, N_{t-1},\, D_{t-1}\big) > k.$$

Thus, a person with larger k is interpreted as "more law-abiding" or "more disciplined" and is less likely to become a bandit.

9.2.3 Density Pressure, Bandit Ratio, and Population Growth

At period t, suppose the natural fertility of a surviving parent of group i ($i = F, B, S$) is m_t^i and the survival rate of children is γ_t^i. Because only surviving adults can bear children, at period t the net reproduction rate for an adult of group i is $\gamma_t^i \cdot m_t^i$. In our later analysis, we assume that natural fertility is negatively influenced by the population size ($m_t^i = m^i(N_{t-1})$), characterizing the Malthusian density pressure, and that the survival rate is negatively influenced by the bandit ratio ($\gamma_t^i = \gamma(b_t)$), characterizing the casualty impact of the turmoil. Because bandits usually were all males who operated in general areas but rarely settled down, their reproduction rate is assumed to be insignificant relative to the other two groups.

Suppose people in the same society have different values of k, and the distribution function for a child brought up by a parent of group i is $G^i(.)$, implying that children brought up in different environments may have different attitudes toward occupations. According to the decision-making process given above, the number of peasants and bandits at period $t + 1$ should be

$$N_{t+1}^B = \sum_i \big(1 - d\big)G^i\big(\Psi(b_{t+1},\, N_t,\, D_t)\big)N_t^i\gamma^i\big(b_t\big)m^i\big(N_{t-1}\big), \qquad (9.2)$$

$$N_{t+1}^F = \sum_i \big(1 - d\big)\big[1 - G^i\big(\Psi(b_{t+1},\, N_t,\, D_t)\big)\big]N_t^i\gamma^i\big(b_t\big)m^i\big(N_{t-1}\big). \qquad (9.3)$$

Adding the above two equations together, we have the following formula of gross population growth of N_t:

$$\Delta N_t \equiv \frac{N_t}{N_{t-1}} - 1 = \sum_i \alpha_t^i\gamma^i\big(b_t\big)m^i\big(N_{t-1}\big) - 1$$

$$\equiv \varrho\big(b_t,\, N_{t-1}\big), \qquad (9.4)$$

where $\alpha_t^F = (1 - d)(1 - b_t)$, $\alpha_t^B = (1 - d)b_t$, and $\alpha_t^S = d$. Equations (9.2)–(9.4) characterize the standard formulation of a two-occupation branching process, where the state variables are N_t^F and N_t^B, or, equivalently, b_t and N_t.

Normally we expect the population growth rate to slow down as the ratio of bandits b_t increases. We also expect the density pressure (N_{t-1}) to have a negative impact on population growth, an orthodox Malthusian view in the literature.

9.2.4 The Steady State

Without clear evidence as to how intergenerational occupation choices are correlated in ancient China, we assume that the decision of occupation selection is independent of the parent, so that $G^i(.) \approx G(.)$ $\forall i = F, S, B$ in (9.2)–(9.3).[4] With this assumption, we replace G^i by G $\forall i$ in (9.2), divide both sides of the equation by $(1 - d)N_t$, and use (9.4) to simplify it; we get the following simple equilibrium condition of b_{t+1}:

$$b_{t+1} \approx \left[G\left(\Psi\left(b_{t+1}, N_t, D_t \right) \right) \right]. \tag{9.5}$$

The interpretation of the above equation is as follows: the right-hand side of (9.5) gives the proportion of people who will choose to be bandits when the *expected* proportion of bandits is b_{t+1}, and the left-hand side of (9.5) is the *actual* proportion of bandits in the society. In equilibrium, people's expectations are fulfilled, and hence (9.5) holds. That is, no one wishes to change his profession when (9.5) holds.

From (9.5) we can solve for the equilibrium b_{t+1} as

$$b_{t+1} = \chi\left(N_t, D_t\right) \approx \chi\left(N_t, R_t\right), \tag{9.6}$$

where R_t is the revolt variable I use to indicate the extent of war damage to agriculture in my later analysis.[5] As mentioned in section 9.1, many historians hypothesized that the ratio of bandits b_{t+1} should increase when the population size (N_t) was large or when the damage (D_t) to agricultural capital was significant.

As the sequence (b_t, N_t) evolves, the generated relative soldier/bandit force ratio $z(b_t)$ may sometimes be smaller than a critical value $\bar{z}$. When this happens, it means that the bandits have defeated the soldiers (the fighting arm of the rulers), and the old dynasty is thus overthrown. The bandits will then become soldiers of the new ruler, and most of the soldiers of the previous regime will be demobilized, some going back to farming, some hiding out and becoming bandits. In economic theory, we do not know exactly how the old regime disintegrates. Accordingly, in my later empirical analysis, I will not stress phenomena associated with these power-transitional periods; rather I let the error term capture the variations in the initial value of b_t of a new dynasty.

My primary purpose is to estimate the population growth equation (9.4) and see if the occupation-switching hypothesis fits well with the ancient Chinese data. In the estimation process, I also want to emphasize the importance of the population composition equation (9.6).

9.3 EMPIRICAL ANALYSIS

9.3.1 Econometric Setting

The yearly data that Chu and Lee (1994) present are the population time series $\{N_t\}$ from C&H, the normalized winter temperature data $\{z_t\}$ from Chu (1973), and a warring dummy variable $\{W_t\}$. Detailed explanation of the data set is provided in later subsections. In (9.4), we expect that N_{t-1} has a negative impact on ΔN_t, characterizing the Malthusian density pressure, and, more important, that the ratio of bandits b_t also has a negative impact on ΔN_t, characterizing the impact of revolt warfare on population decline. Because we do not have historical records of bandit ratio over time, we have to find a proxy variable for b_t, denoted $\hat{b}_t$. From the discussion in the previous section, we know that the ratio of bandits is itself endogenously determined, and from equation (9.6) we get some idea how to derive $\hat{b}_t$.

Previous historians did keep written records of peasant revolts, which more or less correspond to the periods with high realizations of b_t. Thus we can observe a sequence of index variables $\{R_t\}$ in Chinese history:

$$R_t = \begin{cases} 1, \text{if a peasant revolt occurred at } t; \\ 0, \text{otherwise.} \end{cases}$$

There has been much discussion about the history of Chinese peasants' revolts; in my later empirical analysis, I adopt the data summarized in Chang (1983), which is listed in table 9.1.

Summarizing the preceding discussion, we propose the following three models for estimation, where e_t represents the error term.

MODEL A: $\Delta N_t = g\left(N_{t-1}, z_t, W_t, e_t\right).$

Model A is the same as that in Lee and Galloway (1985), who use the population size in the previous period to characterize the density pressure and the temperature data to capture the random shocks to agriculture. The effect of population composition (bandit ratio) is not reflected in this model. Notice that in our notation ΔN_t is the population growth *rate* instead of the change in population size (see [9.4]), and regressing ΔN_t on N_{t-1} is a standard estimation of the density-pressure effect.

MODEL B: $\Delta N_t = g\left(N_{t-1}, R_t, z_t, W_t, e_t\right).$

Model B uses the revolt index $\{R_t\}$ proxy variable to characterize negative impact of a large bandit ratio on population growth. Here R_t is treated as an *exogenous* variable; therefore, Ho's (1959) conjecture that population pressure might be the source of the peasant uprising is ignored.

TABLE 9.1. Farmers' Revolutions and Political Wars

Farmers' Revolutions ($R_t = 1$)	Wars Between Political Power Centers ($W_t = 1$)
B.C. 209–202	
A.D. 17–27	
184–193	A.D. 190–589 Wars between several power centers toward the end of E. Han, Three Kingdoms, Wei, Gin, and North and South dynasties.
301–315	
399–411	
432–439	
485–486	
505	
510	
523–530	
611–624	
874–901	A.D. 755–975 Wars Between military cliques toward the end of Tang dynasty (starting with the Ann-Shih rebel); wars between Five Dynasties and Ten Kingdoms.
920	
942–943	
993–995	
1120–1122	
1130–1135	A.D. 1125–1130 Large-scale invasion wars by Gin, which ended the North Sung dynasty
1204–1231	A.D. 1210–1279 Invasion wars by Yuan, which ended Sha, Gin, and the South Sung dynasties
1351–1368	
1445–1450	
1465–1471	
1510–1512	
1627–1646	
1721–1723	
1774	
1781–1784	
1786–1788	
1795–1804	
1813	
1851–1873	

Source: Constructed by the author, based on description in Chang (1983) and C&H (1988).

MODEL C: $\quad \Delta N_t = g\!\left(N_{t-1},\, \hat{b}_t,\, z_t,\, W_t,\, e_t\right),$

where the bandit ratio proxy $\hat{b}_t$ is the probit probability derived in the following manner.

By (9.6), historians at period t would observe $b_t = \chi(N_{t-1}, R_{t-1})$ proportion of bandits. They would record

$$R_t = \begin{cases} 1, \text{if } \chi\left(N_{t-1}, R_{t-1}\right) \geq C \\ 0, \text{otherwise}, \end{cases}$$

where C is the critical bandit ratio above which historians would record it as a revolt. In this model, the revolution variable is endogenized. We can test Ho's hypothesis by investigating the statistical significance of N_{t-1} in the probit equation.

9.3.2 Variable Specification

The peasant-revolt dummy variable data $\{R_t\}$ are summarized from Chang (1983) (see table 9.1). The population data $\{N_t\}$ for the period 221 B.C. to 1911 A.D. are taken from pages 536–543 of C&H, together with their interpolations for periods without data. The total number of data points is 2,133. Such data interpolations are necessary for our later probit estimation.

We also construct a dummy variable W_t (see table 9.1), which equals 1 when t is in the A.D year range (190–589), (755–975), (1125–1130), (1210–1279) and 0 otherwise. This was done to accommodate the fact that during these four time spans, China was either divided into many political centers or invaded by its powerful neighbors. In these periods, there was no central dynastic authority but rather countless conflicts and wars, and such conflicts were mostly among established political powers, different from the wars between imperial soldiers and the uprising peasants. Finally, the winter temperature data, characterizing the general weather conditions, are adopted from Chu (1975).

We first linear-detrend the log population data in three-ladder periods according to the division by C&H.[6] We keep the points at the intersection of two consecutive ladders connected by applying the Spline-regression technique (Maddala, 1977). The log trend in each ladder represents its equilibrium-carrying capacity of population, and the detrended log residuals series is therefore the (positive or negative) excessive population pressure. This residual series corresponds to the N_t variable in (9.4), and the difference of the log residual will be the ΔN_t defined in (9.4). The above procedure is standard in the empirical literature on density dependency.

9.3.3 Estimation Results

The estimation result is listed in table 9.2. In model A, where we follow the approach of Lee and Galloway (1985) and ignore the factor of peasant revolts, it can be seen that the density-dependency factor, the warring-period dummy, and the temperature variable are all significant. From the

TABLE 9.2. Regression Results on Estimation Models

Variable	Model A	Model B	Model C	Model C with AR-1	Model C Probit
Const.	.0027	.0042	.0044	.0040	−2.1859
	(4.41)	(7.15)	(7.47)	(2.84)	(−28.90)
N_{t-1}	−.0050	−.0040	−.0040	−.0122	.3387
	(−3.96)	(−3.32)	(−3.33)	(−4.19)	(1.77)
W_t	−.0060	−.0047	−.0048	−.0077	
	(−6.75)	(−5.63)	(−5.73)	(−4.03)	
z_t	.0010	.0007	.0007	−.0010	
	(1.92)	(1.73)	(1.39)	(−0.80)	
R_t		−.0178			
		(−16.06)			
R_{t-1}					(3.4144)
					(26.25)
$\hat{b}_t$			−.0193	−.0067	
			(−15.16)	(−3.37)	
$I_t(k)$					
$\bar{R}^2$	.0211	.1265	.1162	.5345	.7647
D.W.	.5560	.6365	.6422	2.4588	
				$\hat{\varrho} = .71$	

Note: $\bar{R}^2$ is the adjusted R square; numbers in the parentheses are t statistics.

statistics in table 9.2, it is clear that this model cannot capture the basic pattern of population dynamics in ancient China.

In model B, we add the variable R_t. Even before the F test, the additional explanatory power provided by this variable is obvious in table 9.2. However, since the coefficient of R_t conveys only the "average" responsiveness, our fitted curve does not match well the extreme population declines, such as the ones that occurred at the end of the East and West Han dynasties. We will discuss this phenomenon later.

Model C seems to be a satisfactory combination of equations (9.4) and (9.6). It contains a structural equation of revolution, and it explicitly characterizes the interactions between density pressure, bandit ratio, and population growth. Our estimation shows that all variables except temperature have significant coefficients with expected signs. The combination of the fact that $\partial \hat{b}_t / \partial N_{t-1} > 0$ in the probit equation and $\partial \Delta N_t / \partial \hat{b}_t < 0$ in the population growth equation suggests that the density pressure was *interacting* with the institutional factor (revolt wars) and that the former might be *magnified* by peasant revolts in Chinese history. This phenomenon is not covered by Lee's general observation, mentioned in section 9.1, and is lost in the Lee–Galloway model A. A positive coefficient of R_{t-1} in the probit equation supports the "self-enforcing" hypothesis of the revolution proposed by Ho (1959). Furthermore, a positive coefficient of N_{t-1} in the probit equation also supports the hypothesis of Ho (1959) and C&H (1988) that density pressure causes or prolongs peasant revolts. Finally, one notices that the $\bar{R}^2$ is increased by approximately five times from model A to model C as we include peasant revolts in our consideration.

As mentioned previously, the coefficient of $\hat{b}_t$ in the ΔN_t regression represents only the overtime "average" impact of the bandit ratio on population growth, which explains the failure of model C to capture the extreme declines in population in the East and West Han dynasties. A by-product of this phenomenon is that the D.W. statistic for this model is very small, indicating serially correlated prediction errors. Specifically, by underestimating the population decline, say, at the end of the East Han dynasty, we automatically are going to overestimate the population size in the following period, and with $\partial \Delta N_t / \partial N_{t-1} < 0$, this will cause a consecutive underestimation of the population change.

It is intuitively clear that one reason for such a serial correlation comes from our $\{R_t\}$ data: we have a dummy characterization for revolt, but we do not know the "scale" of the uprising, on which the magnitude of population decline depends. Thus, by not distinguishing small uprisings, such as the one in 942 A.D., from the large ones, such as the widespread revolt toward the end of East Han, the regression coefficient inevitably underestimates the impact of the latter and overestimates that of the former. There is nothing we can do with the data, so we apply the Cochrane–Orcutt AR-1 adjustment to modify the serially correlated residuals. We also list the result in table 9.2. As can be seen from these statistics, an ad hoc AR-1 adjustment can significantly improve our estimation (see figure 9.2).

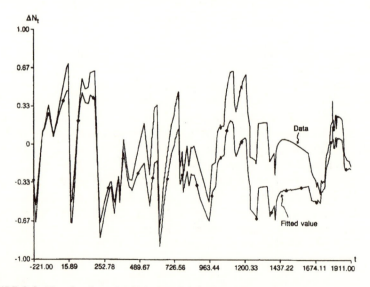

FIGURE 9.2 Fitted value of ΔN_t in Model C with AR-1 adjustment.

9.4 Dynamics of Population Composition Under Anarchy

9.4.1 Cycles Without Density Pressure

As C&H pointed out, although many dynasties went through the same phases, there were no regular patterns for China's dynastic cycles. This observation in terms of population composition means that the dynamics of b_t may be very irregular. There are two reasons for the fluctuation of b_t in our model in section 9.2: one is the exogenous influence of agricultural uncertainty and the other is the endogenous self-enforcing mechanism in the population composition structure. The following paragraph by Ho (1959) is a typical description of such a self-enforcing impact: "as the combined effect of war, devastation, famine, and epidemics began to be felt, even larger numbers of poor peasants voluntarily swarmed into the Taiping war (a peasant revolution in the Ching Dynasty)" (p. 238). Ho's observation suggested that b_t may be affected by b_{t-1}, which is more or less characterized in model C above. But there the special linear AR-1 form might have restricted our econometric estimation.

To explore the nonlinear dynamics of population composition, we are going to study an interesting special case of population composition under *anarchy*. In this anarchical situation, there are no taxes or military draft ($d = v = 0$), and we assume that surviving adults all have the Bergson-class utility function: $u(x) = x^\theta$, $\theta > 0$.

One possibility for why b_t may be affected by b_{t-1} is that people's expectations of b_t do not always conform to reality. In what follows, we shall consider a very simple adaptive-expectations model for demonstration purposes. Suppose people use the realized b_{t-1} to predict b_t in period t. It can be easily shown that equation (9.1) then becomes

$$\frac{Eu_t^B}{Eu_t^F} = \left[\frac{1 - s(b_t)}{s(b_t)}\right]^\theta \cdot \left[\frac{\gamma^B(b_t)}{\gamma^F(b_t)}\right]^{1-\theta} \cdot \left[\frac{1 - b_t}{b_t}\right]^\theta \equiv \Psi(b_t), \qquad (9.7)$$

and equation (9.5) is reduced to

$$b_{t+1} = G\big(\Psi(b_t)\big)$$

$$= G\left(\left[\frac{1 - s(b_t)}{s(b_t)}\right]^\theta \cdot \left[\frac{\gamma^B(b_t)}{\gamma^F(b_t)}\right]^{1-\theta} \cdot \left[\frac{1 - b_t}{b_t}\right]^\theta\right) \equiv \chi(bt). \qquad (9.8)$$

Notice that with our special setup, the dynamics of the population composition is totally independent of the population size or the density elasticity. This is similar to the situation in chapter 8, but the reasoning is different. In the critical-mass model of chapter 8, it is the law of large numbers that helps us establish the simple dynamic relationship of population composition. In this chapter, the simple relationship between b_t and b_{t+1} stems from the specific production technology and utility function assumed.

In equation (9.8), since $G'(.)$ is always positive, we can envisage the law of motion between b_t and b_{t+1} by inspecting (9.7). We notice that in (9.7), both $[1 - s(b_t)]/s(b_t)$ and $\gamma^B(b_t)/\gamma^F(b_t)$ are increasing in b_t, whereas $(1 - b_t)/b_t$ is decreasing in b_t. Intuitively, when the proportion of bandits b_t is very large, bandits' mortality rate may be low, and their loot may also be on the high side. But as b_t is large, then spoils are shared by a larger number of bandits. Thus, as b_t increases, there are two conflicting forces that drive the ratio of expected utilities between bandits and peasants, and this renders the possibility of alternating signs of $\Psi'(b_t)$ for b_t in the range of $[0, 1]$. For demonstration purposes, we assume the following simple survival function:

$$\gamma^F(b) = l + (1 - l)(1 - b)^c, \quad 0 < l < 1, c > 0$$
$$\gamma^B(b) = l + (1 - l)b^c, \qquad 0 < l < 1, c > 0.$$

The parameters in γ^F and γ^B are assumed equal, meaning that peasants and bandits have the same fighting skill.

The $s(.)$ function in (9.7) characterizes the peasants' "battle achievement" or "war results" in their fight against the bandits. We assume that $s(0) = 1, s(1) = 0$, and $s'(.) < 0$. It is also fair to believe that $s(.)$ is symmetric, meaning that the two fighting parties are equally efficient, and that when the size of one fighting party is about the same as (significantly larger than) the other side, the share of war result should be about equal to (significantly greater than) one half. Therefore, there must be a turning point at which the "superiority of numbers" becomes the dominant factor.[7] Thus, we expect to see a convex (concave) region for the $s(.)$ function when b is smaller (larger) than $1/2$. In our numerical analysis, we adopt the specification:

$$s(b) = \frac{1}{2} + 4\left(\frac{1}{2} - b\right)^3.$$

9.4.2 Erratic Composition Dynamics

Now I am going to demonstrate the possible erratic fluctuation of population composition and to show that such fluctuations may evolve endogenously, even without biological checks or the density pressure. In our peasant–bandit–ruler discussion, it has been affirmed that a high bandit–peasant ratio indicates a high probability that the rulers would be defeated and replaced by bandits. The above-mentioned irregular pattern of the bandit–peasant ratio can therefore be interpreted as to foretell (or facilitate) the appearance of irregular patterns of dynastic cycles. We assume

ASSUMPTION A9.1: $s(b)$ is symmetric about $b = 1/2$, $s(1) = 0 = 1 - s(0)$, $\lim_{b\to 1} s(b)/(1 - b) < \infty$, $\lim_{b\to 0} [1 - s(b)]/b < \infty$, $s''(b) > (<)0$ as $b < (>)1/2$, and $|s'(1/2)| < 1$.

Assumption A9.2: $0 < \gamma^B, \gamma^F \leq 1$, and $\gamma^{F'} < 0 < \gamma^{B'}$.

In A9.1, the assumption $\lim_{b \to 0}[1 - s(b)]/b < \infty$ says that when bandits are few in number, their per capita share is not infinitely large. The meaning of $\lim_{b \to 1} s(b)/(1 - b) < \infty$ is the same. All other parts of A9.1 and A9.2 are self-explanatory. With the above assumptions, Chu and Lee (1994, 1997) proved the following theorems.

THEOREM 9.1
Under A9.1 and A9.2, if θ is sufficiently close to 1, $\Psi(b_t)$ in (9.7) has at least two critical points for $b_t \in (0, 1)$.

THEOREM 9.2
Under A9.1 and A9.2, if θ is sufficiently close to 1, there exists a $G(.)$ function with $G'(.) > 0$ such that (9.8) generates chaotic dynamics (in the sense of Li–Yorke period-3 cycle) for b_t.[8]

Theorem 9.1 says that under some minor assumptions, $\Psi(b)$ will fluctuate for b in some subset of $[0, 1]$. As we can see, the fluctuation of $\Psi(b)$ is necessary to generate more interesting dynamics of b_t. Indeed, when we differentiate (9.8) with respect to b_t, we have

$$\chi'(b_t) = \frac{db_{t+1}}{db_t} = G'\big(\Psi(b_t)\big) \cdot \Psi'(b_t). \tag{9.9}$$

Since $G'(.) > 0$, a monotone increasing or decreasing $\Psi(q)$ will also make $\chi(b)$ a monotone function, which leads us to conclude that b_t will always converge to or diverge away from a steady state. This is not an interesting case to study. From equation (9.9), we see that the critical points of $\Psi(b_t)$ will also be those of $\chi(b_t)$ in (9.8). Because the critical points of Ψ are determined independently of the distribution function $G(.)$, rich dynamics of b_t are possible as the specification of $G(.)$ varies.

One should note that the dynamic pattern of b_t in equation (9.8) may be sensitive to variations of many variables. For demonstration purposes, in theorem 9.2 we study only the impact of changing the cumulative distribution function of people's attitude characteristics. The setup in (9.8) resembles the critical-mass model in chapter 8. Thus, we showed that with fairly reasonable assumptions about the war-result function and the survival function (A9.1 and A9.2), it is always possible to observe the most exotic dynamic pattern of b_t—chaos.

The key step in constructing a period-3 cycle in theorem 9.2 is to let the slope of the $G(.)$ function be sufficiently steep in the region where Ψ fluctuates. Making $G(.)$ steep in this region implies that a large proportion of people are moving together or interactively, so that the aggregate index of composition becomes very sensitive to small changes. Such an interaction of decision making in the background also seems to match the behavior of ancient Chinese people described by Ho (1959) and C&H (1988).

9.5 REMARKS ON INDIVIDUAL CHOICES AND INSTITUTIONAL CHANGES

Unlike animals, human beings are expected to think of sophisticated ways to ease population pressure. There are abundant examples other than the peasant-revolt scenario studied above: first, Chao (1986) pointed out that China's traditional economy was very resilient in its institutions and that its redistributive mechanisms managed to absorb the population pressure. In chapter 5, I further specified such a redistributive mechanism within the clan and argued that ancient families often reallocate their incomes or resources to reduce the probability of lineage extinction. Here the interesting feature of human population is its resulting income distribution. Second, as Ranis and Fei (1961) pointed out, the excess of laborers in the rural areas of developing countries often try to migrate to urban areas and find work under a different economic regime; thus, the two regimes interact with each other to achieve a rural–urban "dual" equilibrium. This kind of economic equilibrium is clearly more complicated and perhaps more effective in mitigating the population pressure (under the rural regime) than the equilibria that can be achieved by animal migrations. In this context, the human population is grouped under different economic regimes. Third, we know from the labor economics literature that people who were born in the baby-boom period can lessen the negative impact of population pressure by lengthening the period of their human capital investment or by changing their labor-force participation decisions. In this case, we are interested in the impact of density pressure on labor markets and on people's education decisions.

The above examples show that human beings can indeed resort to various institutional devices to relieve the density pressure. Unlike animals, people have a tremendous reserve of ingenuity that is not reflected in the traditional variables of population analysis such as age, sex, and location. Very often it is the composition dimension of population that is most interesting. Age and sex are the variables common to all populations and are not subject to change by any individual member of the population; whereas occupation, religion, and education are variables meaningful perhaps only to human populations and *are* subject to change (at some costs). In time of pressure, if rational people believe that a change in their social situation can ease the pressure to a certain degree, we would surely see a change in the population composition structure. This change may result in the lessening or worsening of the density pressure, depending on whether the paradox of aggregation applies. Thus, the observed "strength of feedback" in terms of population size covers two effects: one connects density pressure with population size directly and the other links population size with human institution designs, which in turn are affected by density pressure.

To some extent, our model in this chapter is not very different from the predator–prey dynamics of animal populations introduced in chapter 7. Indeed, when an animal population faces a situation of insufficient resources, its members often fight and kill each other until the meager resources available are enough for the smaller group of survivors in the equilibrium. So in a sense, animals can choose to be or not to be the initiator of fights. The former could be likened to bandits and the latter to peasants. It may well be that animal population growth would be more sensitive to resource pressure if they could not take the initiative to fight and were forced to share the insufficient food with others. Of course, animals do not make sophisticated utility comparisons, and human beings presumably do. But this does not constitute a significant difference; our main interest in the composition dynamics of human populations is that such dynamics correspond to meaningful and interesting interpretations. The interesting interpretation in this chapter is the interaction of population composition and the rise and fall of dynasties.

CHAPTER 10

Easterlin Cycles

Fertility and the Labor Market

10.1 BACKGROUND

I mentioned in chapter 7 that the fluctuation of human population can be summarized into three broad categories: the pretransitional, transitional, and posttransitional cycles. Among these three categories, the last one has caught the attention of most demographic economists in the past thirty years. The main reason for this unbalanced research attention is that the posttransitional cycles appear only in developed countries, where high-quality data are available for empirical research. The recent development of advanced mathematical tools also facilitates the analysis of posttransitional density-dependent population dynamics. In this chapter we will provide a summary of the theoretical and empirical analyses of the most typical population fluctuations in the posttransitional period: the so-called Easterlin cycles.

The well-known Easterlin cycles, named after the pioneer work by Richard Easterlin (1961, 1980), describe the observed two-generation-long birth cycles in the twentieth-century United States and in several other developed countries. Easterlin believed that there were two features associated with the observed cycles: they are related to the labor market, and they are more or less "self-generating" (Easterlin, 1961). The first feature implies that a complete theoretical framework should characterize how people's fertility behavior is affected by the labor market and how the labor market is affected by the fertility pattern. The second feature addresses whether the theoretical framework can generate a persistent fertility fluctuation. An ideal theoretical framework should embody both of these features, and an ideal empirical analysis should also be compatible with these features.

10.1.1 Three Previous Lines of Research

We start the background introduction by studying a Malthusian model presented by Lee (1974). Let us consider an overlapping-generation framework in which each individual lives one or two periods. The first period is childhood, the second period is adulthood, and all surviving adults will be in the labor force. Lee wrote down the following two equations:

$$W(t) = f\big(L(t)\big), \tag{10.1}$$

$$b(t) = g\big(W(t)\big), \tag{10.2}$$

where $W(t)$ is the wage rate (at time t), L is the size of the adult age group, b is the crude birth rate, and $f(.)$ and $g(.)$ are functions with $f'(.) < 0$ and $g'(.) > 0$. Because the current adult labor force is related to the previous birth rate, equation (10.1) characterizes how previous fertility patterns affect the current labor market. Equation (10.2) says that people's labor-market reward will influence their fertility.

Since the pioneer work of Easterlin, follow-up research was pursued along three distinct lines. (i) Some labor economists (such as Freeman, 1979; Berger, 1983; and Connelly, 1986) studied the impact of fertility variations on labor-market equilibrium (equation [10.1]). (ii) Several demographic economists (such as Ward and Butz, 1980) analyzed the impact of the changing economic environment on female fertility decisions (equation [10.2]). The above two approaches provided only partial analyses because they did not touch upon the self-generating cyclicity of birth, which, as we mentioned, is a key feature of the Easterlin hypothesis. (iii) The most relevant line of research has been pursued by demographic economists and mathematical biologists (such as Lee, 1974; Samuelson, 1976; Frauenthal and Swick, 1983; Tuljapurkar, 1987; Wachter and Lee, 1989; and Wachter, 1991) who took into account both features of the Easterlin hypothesis and analyzed equation (10.3) below.

Suppose that the number of children born in period t is $B(t)$ and that the mortality rate is a constant $(1 - s)$. Then $L(t) = s \cdot B(t - 1)$, and (10.1) and (10.2) can be written in the following reduced form:

$$\begin{aligned} B(t) &= g\Big(f\big(sB(t-1)\big)\Big) \cdot sB(t-1) \\ &\equiv h\big(B(t-1)\big) \cdot B(t-1), \end{aligned} \tag{10.3}$$

where $h(x) \equiv sg(f(sx))$. From (10.3) the dynamic pattern of birth can be analyzed, and the possible existence of cyclicity can be studied. Although by combining structural equations (10.1) and (10.2) the third approach has the advantage of being more comprehensive, it is not satisfactory in that some important information in (10.1) and (10.2) is lost in the reduced form

(10.3). This drawback, as we will show, has a significant impact on the analysis of Easterlin cycles.

Equation (10.3), if extended to a more refined age structure, can be written as

$$B(t) = \int_s \phi_s(\mathbf{B}(t)) B(t - s) ds$$
$$\equiv \int_s \phi(s, t) B(t - s) ds, \qquad (10.4)$$

where $\mathbf{B}(t) \equiv (B(t - 1), \cdots, B(t - n))$ is a vector of previous births, $\phi_s(\mathbf{B}(t))$ is the age-s net maternity function, and $\phi_s(\mathbf{B}(t)) \equiv \phi(s, t)$. Although equation (10.4) is general enough to characterize any lagged influence of previous birth sizes $(\mathbf{B}(t))$ on present fertility, it is too general for analytical purposes. So Lee (1974) proposed two simple and useful alternatives. The first is to assume that ϕ_s is a function of $B(t - s)$, the age-s cohort (birth) size. This was referred to as the *cohort model* in the literature, meaning that the age-s maternity is only affected by its own cohort size. The second is to assume that ϕ_s is a function of $\int_j w_j B(t - j) dj$, the weighted (by w_j) total labor force in period t. This was referred to as the *period model* in the literature. For the past two decades, these two approaches have exerted a dominant influence on the direction taken by the research on endogenous Easterlin cycles. However, empirical evidence has so far failed to back up either the cohort model or the period model in producing persistent birth cycles that fit all characteristics (such as amplitude and period).

10.1.2 Motivating a New Approach

Given that both the cohort model and the period model are simplified versions of equation (10.4), it is natural to ask the following questions: Exactly what are the simplifying assumptions (restrictions) behind cohort and period models? What is the economic interpretation of these restrictions? Is it possible that these restrictions on the model can be rejected by statistical tests? If persistent cyclicity is not compatible with the restricted cohort or period models, would it be compatible with an unrestricted framework? I will try to answer these questions later in my discussion.

Most existing research concerning Easterlin cycles focuses on deriving a threshold parametric value of bifurcation and checking whether the model in question can generate a corresponding parameter value larger than that threshold value. Technically speaking, these analyses can only confirm or deny the existence of limit-cycle solutions. The only exceptions are the studies by Feichtinger and Sorger (1989) and by Wachter (1991), where the period and/or the amplitude of limit cycles were also analyzed. Wachter concluded that it is unlikely that one could set up a framework that happens to generate birth cycles with aspects compatible with the real data. However, since the observed data period for the United States is still rather short, we are not convinced that the steady-state cycles (if they exist and will be converged to) should have an amplitude and a period similar to what we have observed in our short sample period. To answer the question of whether there *will be* persistent Easterlin cycles, it is necessary to check the *stability* of the dynamic system.

The organization of this chapter is as follows. First, I shall propose a behavior model compatible with the Easterlin hypothesis. The setup to be presented is so general that both the period hypothesis and the cohort hypothesis in the previous literature can be treated as special cases. I then use statistical methods to test which hypothesis best fits the U.S. data. Finally, the estimated parameters of the best-fitted model are adopted to check the existence and stability of the (Easterlin) periodic solution to the population renewal equation.

10.2 Theoretical Modeling

10.2.1 The Relative-Income Hypothesis

Easterlin (1980) believed that people's fertility decisions would be affected by their "relative income," by which he meant the "potential earning power relative to material aspiration" (p. 42). The aspiration of a family head of childbearing age may have been formed when she was young. Therefore, the concept of relative income is in fact a childbearing family head's intertemporal comparison of the economic condition she currently faces with a "norm" she has in mind.

As to detailed specifications, there are two popular approaches in the literature. The first is to assume that the fertility rate is affected by the size of cohorts relative to one another, as do Keyfitz (1972), Samuelson (1976), and Wachter (1991); the other is to assume that the fertility rate is a function of the present cohort sizes relative to those in the population *steady state*. The latter approach was proposed in Lee (1974) and became the mainstream approach. One advantage of comparing the current cohort size with that of the steady state is that the steady state is related to the concept of "carrying capacity"; therefore, one can connect Lee's specification of relative income with the classical Malthusian hypothesis. In what follows, we will use the steady-state value to normalize the birth-size variable.

10.2.2 Density-Dependent Renewal Equations

Following the conventional approach in the literature, we assume that the equilibrium (steady-state) birth trajectory grows at an exponential rate: $B^*(t) = B^*e^{rt}$. Substituting this in equation (10.4) and simplifying, we get

$$1 = \int_s e^{-rs}\phi(s, t)ds = \int_s e^{-rs}l_s m(s, t)ds,$$

where l_s is the proportion of births surviving to age s and $m(s, t)$ is the average number of births per surviving member aged s at time t. We shall focus upon the detrended series $B^\#(t) \equiv B(t)/e^{rt}$ and rewrite (10.4) as

$$B^{\#}(t) = \int_s l_s m(s,\ t) B^{\#}(t-s) e^{-rs} ds. \tag{10.5}$$

The trend $B*(t)$ specifies the carrying capacity of the economy, and therefore the normalized $B^{\#}(t)$ is the "excess" population, which will form a (plus or minus) density pressure.

The next step is to specify the relationship between the age-specific fertility rate and the parents' perception of relative income. Generally speaking, a typical family head's relative economic condition will be worse if the overall unemployment rate is higher, or the wage rate is lower than her perception. Because both the unemployment rate and the wage rate are determined in the labor market, it is natural for demographic economists to think of using the age-specific potential labor force to characterize the relative advantage of various age groups.

Following Lee (1974, 1978), we suppose that the age-s fertility rate is a function of the age-s welfare (or wage) relative to the steady-state level:

$$m(s,\ t) = m_s\left(W_s(t)/W_s^*\right), \tag{10.6}$$

where W_s^* is the steady-state age-s welfare. Suppose $W_s(t)$ is a function of the sizes of various age-specific normalized potential labor forces at time t, which are in turn proportional to previous age-specific births; then $m(s, t)$ in (10.6) can be written as a function of $\mathbf{B}^{\#}(t)$:

$$m(s,\ t) = m_s\left(\mathbf{B}^{\#}(t)\right)$$
$$= m_s\left(B^{\#}(t-u), \cdots, B^{\#}(t-v)\right),$$

where $B^{\#}(t-u)$ and $B^{\#}(t-v)$ are respectively the normalized sizes of the youngest and oldest workers in the labor market at time t. Thus, equation (10.5) can be rewritten as

$$B^{\#}(t) = \int_s l_s m_s\left(\mathbf{B}^{\#}(t)\right) B^{\#}(t-s) e^{-rs} ds. \tag{10.7}$$

Equation (10.7) is the density-dependent renewal equation, where the density dependency is revealed in the $m_s(\mathbf{B}^{\#}(t))$ term.

10.2.3 The Unrestricted Settings

Suppose the age-specific fertility rate is a function of the relative welfare, as specified in (10.6). Suppose further, as is typical in economic analysis, that the age-specific welfare is determined by the marginal productivity of workers of various ages. If there is an "aggregate production function" which transforms inputs of workers of all ages into the output

$$G(t) = f\left(\mathbf{L}^{\#}(t)\right) = f\left(L_u^{\#}(t), \cdots, L_v^{\#}(t)\right),$$

where $L_s^{\#}(t)$ is the normalized age-s labor-force size at time t, then we have

$$W_s(t) = \frac{\partial G(t)}{\partial L_s^\#(t)} = f_s\left(\mathbf{L}^\#(t)\right),$$

where the subscript of f indicates partial differentiation. Because a key feature of the Easterlin hypothesis is the specification of the relationship between the cohort welfare and excess (relative to the steady state) cohort labor-force sizes, researchers generally believe that it is better to use the *potential* labor-force than the *actual* labor force to characterize such a welfare impact.[1] Thus, following the common practice of previous literature, we will use the potential labor-force size $l_s B^\#(t - s)$ to replace $L_s^\#(t)$ in the $W_s(t)$ equation, and rewrite it as

$$W_s(t) = f_s\left(\mathbf{L}^\#(t)\right) \equiv f_s\left(\mathbf{l} \cdot \mathbf{B}^\#(t)\right),$$

where $\mathbf{l}$ is the vector representation of l_s's.

Now we have to specify the production functional form $f(.)$ to proceed with our analysis. Suppose $f(.)$ has the form of the generalized Leontief function (Diewert, 1974):

$$G(t) = a_0 + \sum_i a_i L_i^\#(t)^{1/2} + \frac{1}{2} \sum_i \sum_j \gamma_{i,j} L_i^\#(t)^{1/2} L_j^\#(t)^{1/2}$$

$$\gamma_{i,j} = \gamma_{j,i}, \quad i, j = u, \cdots, v. \qquad (10.8)$$

As is well known, the generalized Leontief form is an approximation of *any* production function, similar to the Translog form (Varian, 1984; Lau, 1986).[2] If age-specific welfare reflects the age-specific workers' productivity, then we can differentiate $G(t)$ in (10.8) with respect to $L_i^\#(t)$ to derive the welfare function of each age i:

$$W_i(t) = \frac{\partial G(t)}{\partial L_i^\#(t)} = \frac{1}{2} L_i^\#(t)^{-1/2} \left[a_i + \sum_{j \neq i} \gamma_{i,j} L_j^\#(t)^{1/2} \right] + \frac{1}{2} \gamma_{i,i}. \qquad (10.9)$$

Substituting equations (10.6) and (10.9) into (10.7), we have the general unrestricted version of the renewal equation.

10.2.4 Implicit Restrictions of Cohort and Period Models

Equation (10.7) is the starting point of most previous empirical and theoretical research on endogenous Easterlin cycles. For the cohort model, m_s is assumed to be affected by $B\#(t - s)$ alone:

$$m_s = \left(\mathbf{B}^\#(t)\right) = m_s\left(B^\#(t - s)\right). \qquad (10.10)$$

For the period model, m_s is assumed to be affected by the weighted total labor force, or equivalently the weighted average of previous birth sizes:

$$m_s\left(\mathbf{B}^{\#}(t)\right) = m_s\left(\int_u^v \omega_z l_z B^{\#}(t - z)dz\right), \tag{10.11}$$

where ω_z is the age-z worker's efficiency weight. Note that in Lee's original setting, there were no efficiency-weight differences, and therefore $\omega_z = 1 \ \forall j$.

Because the original assumptions are that the fertility rate should be a function of parental perception of relative welfare and that a parent's relative welfare perception is determined in the labor-market, it is logical to be curious about the implicit labor-market assumptions behind (10.10) and (10.11). Given (10.6), (10.9), and (10.10), the age-s cohort welfare in the cohort model is apparently independent of the labor-force sizes of all other age groups, and hence the implicit assumption seems to be that among all age groups there is *no substitution* in the production function $G(.)$ in (10.8). In the period model, it is the weighted average of labor force of all ages that affects the age-specific welfare, which seems to imply that there is a *perfect substitution* for $G(.)$ (with efficiency adjustment) among all age groups. In what follows, we let H_c and H_p, respectively, denote the cohort- and period-model null hypotheses, against which we can establish a statistical test. Chu and Lu (1995) proved the following theorem:

THEOREM 10.1
Given the generalized Leontief production function in (10.8), the implicit restrictions for the cohort model are

$$H_c: \gamma_{i,j} = 0, \quad \forall i \neq j, \tag{10.12}$$

and those for the period model are

$$H_p: \begin{cases} \gamma_{i,j} = \lambda_i \lambda_j, \\ \alpha_i = k\lambda_i, \quad \forall i, \end{cases} \tag{10.13}$$

for some constants λ_i, λ_j, and k.

The interpretation of (10.12) is easy: a cohort model implies that there is no cross-age interaction effect on age-specific fertility, which in turn implies that the G function in (10.8) must be additively separable. Thus, $\gamma_{i,j} = 0 \ \forall i \neq j$ must hold. Equation (10.13) is less intuitive and more complicated. Interested readers are referred to Chu and Lu (1995) for details.

10.3 ESTIMATION AND STATISTICAL TESTS

10.3.1 The Data Set

In the rest of this chapter, I use subscript a to denote a five-year cohort. Our data set includes the U.S. birth number series $B(t)$, five-year cohort population sizes $P_a(t)$, and five-year cohort fertility rates, all from 1917 to

1987, totaling 71 points. The data source is summarized by the author from the *Vital Statistics of the United States*.[3] In our analysis, the childbearing age is assumed to be in the range of 15 to 44, including six five-year cohorts, with respective subscripts $a = 1, 2, \cdots, 6$. The cohort-specific fertility rate is defined to be the number of births divided by the number of females. To facilitate our later analysis, we multiply these fertility rates by a sex-ratio adjustment term and obtain sequences of birth and population that correspond to the variable $m(a, t)$ in our previous analysis. This 71-year average adjustment term turns out to be .45944; calculation details are not presented here. The age range of the potential labor force is 15–64, including ten five-year cohorts, with respective subscripts $a = 1, 2, \cdots, 10$. Following the previous analysis, we shall use the cohort population size as a proxy for the potential labor force variable.

Let 1917 be time zero. First we fit an exponential trend for the total birth series $B(t)$ and obtain $\ln B(t) = 14.56 + .00944t + e(t)$, where $e(t)$ is the residual term. Then we calculate the normalized sequence $B^{\#}(t) = B(t)/e^{rt}$, where $r = .00944$. To normalize the $P_a(t)$ series, we perform a similar detrending procedure:

$$P_a^{\#}(t) = P_a(t) \cdot e^{-r(t-\hat{a})},$$

where $\hat{a}$ is the average age of age group a.[4]

10.3.2 Estimating the Fertility Equation

Suppose the cohort-specific fertility rate $m(a, t)$ is a function of the relative wage $W_a(t)/W_a^*$, consistent with the spirit of Easterlin's relative-income hypothesis. Lee (1978) adopted a log-linear functional specification between $m(a, t)$ and $W_a(t)/W_a^*$. But since we are going to substitute the $W_a(t)$ in (10.9), which is highly nonlinear in $\mathbf{B}^{\#}(t)$, into equation (10.6), a linear specification between $m(a, t)$ and $W_a(t)/W_a^*$ in (10.6) is sufficiently complicated to embody the potentially nonlinear relationship between $m(a, t)$ and $\mathbf{B}^{\#}(t)$. Thus, we suppose

$$m(a, t) = \theta_a + \beta_a \cdot \left(\frac{W_a(t)}{W_a^*} \right)$$

$$= \theta_a + \beta_a' \cdot W_a(t),$$

where $\beta_a' = \beta/W_a^*$. Using (10.9) and replacing the potential labor force $L_a^{\#}(t)$ by the population size $P_a^{\#}(t)$ as a proxy, we can rewrite the above equation as

$$m(a, t) = A_a + \beta_a'' P_a^{\#}(t)^{-\frac{1}{2}} \left[\alpha_a + \sum_{j \neq a} \gamma_{a,j} P_j^{\#}(t)^{\frac{1}{2}} \right], \quad a = 1, \cdots, 6, \qquad (10.14)$$

where $\beta_a'' = \beta_a'/2$, and $A_a = \theta_a + \beta_a'\gamma_{a,a}/2$.

Clearly, for each $a = 1, \cdots, 6$, one of the coefficients in (10.14) (β_a'', α_a, $\gamma_{a,j}, j \neq a$) can be normalized to be 1 in the unrestricted version. In the rest of this chapter, without loss of generality, we set $\beta_1'' = 1$. But when H_c is true, there is no overidentification, and hence the normalization is not needed. Since age-specific welfare values are all determined by the *same* aggregate production technology $G(.)$, there are interrelated coefficients among these equations (for instance, γ_{ij} will appear in all equations). Thus, we have a nonlinear seemingly unrelated regression system with coefficient constraints.

Equation (10.14) is the *unrestricted* version of the fertility model. When we estimate the cohort model or the period model, the restrictions in H_c or Hp (see [10.12] and [10.13]) must be taken into account.

Because my focus is upon model selection, I did not list the detailed coefficient estimates of each equation in table 10.1. One thing we notice is that the unrestricted model has a much smaller MAE than does either the period model or the cohort model. We also note that most estimates of β_a'', $a = 1, \cdots, 6$, are positive and significant, meaning that better age-specific relative welfare will induce higher fertility rates.[5]

10.3.3 Nested and Non-Nested Tests

Because the period model and the cohort model are restricted versions of equations (10.14), we use a *nested* test to investigate whether these restrictions are true. Because the statistic for the likelihood ratio test is much easier to derive than that of the Wald test or the LM test in our analysis, and because the dispersion among these test statistics is not significant for

TABLE 10.1. Estimation Results of (10.14) for Various Models

Age Group	MAE[a]			$\tilde{\beta}_a''^{[b]}$ of Model U	t-Statistic of $\tilde{\beta}_a''^{[c]}$
	Model C[d]	Model P[d]	Model U[d]		
15–19	.0047	.0038	.0015	1	—
20–24	.0126	.0071	.0029	6.659	1.633
25–29	.0126	.0040	.0025	1.177	7.427
30–34	.0091	.0036	.0016	−3.835	−2.048
35–39	.0074	.0058	.0010	1.290	3.935
40–44	.0036	.0036	.0003	1.129	2.084

[a] MAE $\equiv \Sigma|y_i - \hat{y}_i|/T$ is the mean absolute error, where y_i and $\hat{y}_i$ are the actual and the predicted values of the dependent variables, respectively, and T is the sample size.
[b] $\tilde{\beta}_a''$ is the estimate of β_a''.
[c] β_1'' is normalized to be 1, so that there is no associated t-statistic.
[d] C, P, and U, respectively, represent "cohort," "period," and "unrestricted."

TABLE 10.2. Nested and Non-Nested Hypothesis Testing

H_A:		H_u	H_p	H_c
H_0:	H_p	702.94*	—	0.038**
	H_c	788.66*	$5.68 \cdot 10^{-8}$**	—

Notes: H_0 represents the null hypothesis, H_A represents the alternative hypothesis, H_u represents the unrestricted version, and H_c and H_p are, respectively, cohort- and period-model restrictions. * is the x^2 value for the likelihood ratio test. ** is the Cox-test t statistic.

large sample sizes (Berndt, 1991), we present the popular likelihood ratio test result in table 10.2. We see from table 10.2 that both the period model and the cohort model are rejected.

The relationship between the period model and the cohort model is a *non-nested* one, and we perform a Pesaran–Deaton–Cox (Pesaren and Deaton, 1978) non-nested test to discriminate between them. We see from table 10.2 that neither model can be rejected. These results suggest that if we are to choose a model to perform the dynamic analysis of endogenous fertility cycles, we should adopt the unrestricted version.

10.4 ENDOGENOUS EASTERLIN CYCLES

10.4.1 Calculating Various Parameters

Because there are six fertile cohorts (15–44) and ten labor-force cohorts (15–64) in our model, I shall from now on specify the upper bounds of summation signs to avoid possible confusion. Given the survival probability l_a of age group a, and given that $P_a(t) = l_a \int_{\underline{a}}^{\bar{a}} B(t - s)ds$, we have

$$P_a^\#(t) = P_a(t)e^{-r(t-\hat{a})}$$
$$= l_a \int_{\underline{a}}^{\bar{a}} B^\#(t - s)e^{-r(s-\hat{a})}ds,$$

where $\hat{a}$ is the average age of group a and $\underline{a}$ ($\bar{a}$) is the age lower (upper) bound of group a. Let $B_a^\#(t)$ be the shorthand representation of $\int_{\underline{a}}^{\bar{a}} B^\#(t - s)e^{-rs}ds$. Substituting (10.14) into (10.7) and using the relationship between $P_a^\#$ and $B_a^\#$ characterized above, we can rewrite (10.7) explicitly as:

$$B^\#(t) = \sum_{a=1}^{6}\left\{ A_a^* B_a^\#(t) + \beta_a^* B_a^\#(t)^{\frac{1}{2}} \left(\alpha_a^* + \sum_{\substack{j=1 \\ j \neq a}}^{10} \gamma_{a,j}^* B_j^\#(t)^{\frac{1}{2}} \right) \right\}, \quad (10.15)$$

where $A_a^* = A_a \cdot l_a$, $\alpha_a^* = \alpha_a$, $\beta_a^* = \beta_a'' \cdot l_a^{1/2} \cdot e^{-r\hat{a}/2}$, and $\gamma_{a,j}^* = \gamma_{a,j} \cdot l_j^{1/2} \cdot e^{r\hat{j}/2} \forall j \neq a$.

Clearly equation (10.15) is a density-dependent renewal equation, and we want to investigate whether the $B^{\#}(t)$ sequence generated from (10.15) will give rise to persistent Easterlin-type cycles. For that purpose, we should substitute the estimated parametric values from (10.14) into (10.15) and analyze the dynamic motion of $B^{\#}(t)$ so derived. Note that previous estimations of (10.14) were based mainly on cohort and period hypotheses, which are statistically insignificant. Dynamic analyses of endogenous cycles based on these insignificant parameter estimates are certainly questionable.

But even if we leave aside the problem of parameter estimation, previous analyses of the dynamic pattern of $B^{\#}(t)$ are still incomplete. In Frauenthal (1975), Swick (1981a, 1981b), Frauenthal and Swick (1983), and Wachter and Lee (1989), the common approach is to linearly approximate (10.15) and see if the calculated density-dependent elasticity exceeds the critical value of bifurcation. If it does, limit cycles are then considered as "possible." In order to give a complete answer to the question of whether there *will be* Easterlin cycles, we must go beyond the *existence* analysis and study the *stability* of the $B^{\#}(t)$ cycle generated from (10.15), the answer to which is provided in theorem 7.4.

In chapter 7 I summarized the technical background for checking whether there is a limit-cycle solution (existence) and whether the population will converge to such a solution (stability). To analyze the existence problem, we need to check whether the estimated bifurcation parameter is larger than the endogenously determined critical value. To analyze the stability problem, we have to calculate the Floquet exponent and see if it is negative. Detailed steps can be found in Chu and Lu (1995); here we only provide a sketch. First, we use equations (10.14) to estimate the parameters; second, we substitute these parametric estimates into (10.15) to calculate the steady-state value B^*; third, we apply Taylor expansion to (10.15) around B^*; fourth, we use the parametric estimates and the B^* to calculate the (various-order) Taylor coefficients or elasticities; and finally, we use these values to calculate the various bifurcation parameters.

There are three threshold parameters that are particularly important. The first is the threshold feedback response elasticity, denoted g_0. If the estimated feedback elasticity is larger than g_0, then a limit-cycle solution exists. The second is the critical polar coordinate of the imaginary part, denoted ζ_0. If there is a limit cycle, its period length will be $p_0 = 2\pi/\zeta_0$. The third parameter is the Floquet exponent q. A limit-cycle solution will be converged to only if $q < 0$. Using the U.S. data, we present below the various parameter estimates.

10.4.2 Period Length and Limit Cycles

The U.S. data generate a threshold feedback elasticity $g_0 = 1.205$, and the actual feedback strength turns out to be $g_e = 4.858$, far larger than

g_0. Therefore, we conclude that there *exists* a limit-cycle solution for (10.15). However, the existence of a limit-cycle solution alone carries no empirical implications, since only *stable* cyclical solutions are relevant and interesting.

When $g_0 = 1.205$, we find that the corresponding period length of the limit cycle is $p_0 = 2\pi/\omega_0 = 10.63$ years, much shorter than previous analyses had found (see table 10.3 for comparison). On this point, some explanation is in order. In previous research by Frauenthal (1975), Swick (1981a, 1981b), Frauenthal and Swick (1983), and Wachter and Lee (1989), the authors all adopted a special functional form for fertility: $m(s, t) = m(s) \cdot M(\mathbf{B}(t))$. Given this special form, the elasticity $m(s, t)$ with respect to any element of the previous birth vector $\mathbf{B}(t)$ is *independent of s*. Thus, the implicit restriction of the separable functional specification of $m(s, t)$ is that the feedback elasticity of all groups is the same, which in turn implies that it is impossible for previous birth numbers to have *conflicting* age-specific feedback effects on the fertility behavior of different age groups. This also explains why all previous researchers only had to run a single regression equation (normally NRR or TFR with respect to previous births).

Given that the elasticities of $m(s, t)$ with respect to a birth size are restricted to being the same for all s, we would normally expect this

TABLE 10.3. Previous Results on Easterlin Cycles (EC)

Source	Threshold Parameter	Period Length	Estimated Parameter	Existence of EC
Cohort Models				
Lee (1974)	—[a]	—	0.954	No
Frauenthal and Swick (1983)[b]	2.30	52	3.376	Yes
			2.795	Yes
Wachter and Lee (1989)	2.30	52	1.72	No
Period Models				
Lee (1974)	4.0	38	7.724	Yes
Wachter and Lee (1989*)[c]	2.64	106	8.05	Yes
Wachter and Lee (1989**)[d]	2.58	98	9.567	Yes
Wachter (1991)	2.4†[e]	95	3.5†[e]	Yes
Relative Size Model				
Wachter (1991)	2.3	52	1.9†[e]	No
Cascade Model				
Wachter (1991)	1.2†[e]	42	1.3†[e]	Yes

[a] There was no threshold value in Lee's (1974) analysis because he used spectrum analysis instead of the bifurcation approach.

[b] Two sets of explanatory variables were used by Frauenthal and Swick, so two estimated parameters were generated.

[c] * corresponds to the case where the 1930 data are assumed to be the steady-state values.

[d] ** corresponds to the case where the 1981 data are assumed to be the steady-state values.

[e] † indicates approximation values obtained by observation.

elasticity to be negative, denoting the Malthusian density-dependency (or crowding) effect. But in the labor market, workers of different age groups sometimes *complement* each other. For instance, a large older and more experienced labor cohort aged 65 may complement the young and inexperienced labor cohort aged 25; whereas a large cohort aged 35 may have a crowding effect on the cohort aged 25. Thus, it is possible that a larger-than-equilibrium cohort labor force may have a *negative* impact on total fertility when the cohort labor force in question is aged 35 but a *positive* impact when the cohort labor force in question is aged 65. None of the previous modeling is compatible with such mixed impacts of different age cohorts.

When the above-mentioned cross-age substitute or complementary effect in the labor force is taken into consideration, as in our general model with an unrestricted aggregate production function, the overall feedback strength of population density is the composite of all age-specific feedback elasticities. It is difficult to derive an analytical relationship between period length and the substitutability of age-specific labor force, but it is relatively easy to understand that the period length we obtain may be quite different from the previous ones.

We should also note that, although our 10.63-year period length, like many of the strange period lengths obtained in previous research (see table 10.3), is not compatible with the two-generation cycles observed in the United States, there is no real conflict either. The period length obtained corresponds to the limit-cycle solution in the *steady state*, which may not be stable, and need not have anything to do with the *current* U.S. data.

After calculating p_0, g_0, and g_e, we need to calculate the Floquet exponent q. It turns out that the U.S. data generate a positive $q = 1.81 \times 10^{-15}$. Such a positive estimated Floquet exponent implies that the system is a *subcritical* one, and hence the corresponding limit-cycle solution is unstable. This is a major distinction between the analysis here and the ones in the previous literature. In all the analyses listed in table 10.3 and elsewhere,[6] the focus was upon the existence or nonexistence of a limit cycle or a complex solution for the models they analyzed. Although Tuljapurkar (1987) proposed the method of checking stability for nonlinear population models, so far as we know no one has applied it to the analysis of Easterlin cycles as we have. The Floquet exponent being positive tells us that although there exists a limit-cycle solution, our real-world data *will not converge to it*. This finding suggests that to discuss the limit-cycle solution without knowing its stability is not meaningful, a conclusion similar to Samuelson's correspondence principle.

But given that the limit-cycle solution is not stable, where will the U.S. $B^{\#}(t)$ series go? Indeed, the dynamic motion of a subcritical system is very unpredictable. According to Lorenz (1989), given that $g_e > g_0$ and $q > 0$, the equilibrium is not stable and no orbits exist. So all we can conclude is that the U.S. birth series will neither converge to the equilibrium B^* nor plunge into a limit cycle.

10.5 ALTERNATIVE EXPLANATIONS OF EASTERLIN CYCLES

A premise of our analysis in previous sections is that there is a *unique* equilibrium or *attractor* for the dynamics of the population, and we test whether the cyclical data we observe is consistent with the possible cyclicity of this unique equilibrium. However, as Chesnais (1992) pointed out, the number of cycles observed in various series for the Western countries is actually only one, which makes the very existence of a cyclical attractor doubtful. He argued that no tests of Easterlin's hypothesis have ever proved convincing. Chesnais's comment has led mathematical demographers such as Bonneuil (1989, 1990, 1992) to search for other possible explanations for the so-called Easterlin cycles.

In fact, the possible misinterpretation of cyclical series also appears in the study of other population data. As Bonneuil (1990) pointed out, because of the noise inherent in biological as well as demographic systems, localizing attractors is usually difficult in many empirical studies. Very often, observed fluctuations most likely represent an orbit which was at least twice periodic with noise superimposed. The contribution of Bonneuil is to extend the traditional definition of population attractors to the stochastic case and to provide a different interpretation for the observed fertility fluctuations.

Let $N_{t,a}$ be the number of women aged a in period t, ϕ_a be the age-specific fertility rate in the absence of any contraception, B_t be the total birth in period t, and I_t^f be the overall Coale index:

$$I_t^f = \frac{B}{\sum_{a=15}^{49} N_{t,a}\phi_a}.$$

Bonneuil used the reconstructed data of Pays de Caux (for the years 1589–1700) to calculate the I_t^f time series and to draw the series in the I_t^f/I_{t-1}^f two-dimensional space. It turns out that the evolution of I_t^f looks irregular and nonlinear because of sudden bursts at irregular time epochs. The trajectory looks as if it is confined alternatively in two given zones, looping in each of them for a while but sometimes jumping between the two when there is a sufficiently strong perturbation. Moreover, the jumps between the two confining zones appear discontinuous, and if we look at these jumps and returns *alone*, we may be misled into believing that the trajectory is cyclical. Bonneuil's finding therefore provides us with an alternative idea of equilibrium, which is totally different from the one proposed by Easterlin. Besides the numerical example given above, Bonneuil (1992) also provides a rigorous analysis of the extended notion of confiner and attractors. This analytical definition can be applied to other data sets.

If the U.S. fertility series reveals a switching-confiners regime owing to exogenous shocks, then the behavioral hypothesis proposed by Easterlin is really redundant. In that case, economists should allow statisticians to analyze the fertility time series. However, we need data for a longer time series to be able to see which of the two competing hypotheses (Bonneuil vs. Easterlin) is true.

CHAPTER 11

Demographic Transition and Economic Development

11.1 BACKGROUND

Demographic transition refers to a shift in reproductive behavior from a state of high birth and death rates to a state of low birth and death rates. This transition takes place because of advances in agricultural technology and medical science or improvement in hygiene environment, all of which result in corresponding declines in the mortality rate.[1] In this first phase of the demographic transition, population growth rises because the decline in mortality rate has not been coupled with any significant change in parents' fertility decisions. Then, in the second phase of the transition, parents begin to reduce their fertility as they realize that their ideal number of children can be more easily achieved with fewer births. The widespread use of contraceptive techniques facilitates parents' attempts to reduce fertility, which in turn causes a decline in the population growth rate. Eventually, the population growth rate converges to a new level, which may be higher or lower than in the pretransitional stage.[2]

To facilitate comparison, we can use figure 11.1 to characterize the time and process of the transition. In figure 11.1, T_α marks the apparent starting point of a continuous decline in mortality. T_β, which normally occurs later than T_α, refers to the time at which the fertility rate begins to decline. T_γ is the point of lasting return, with an average rate of natural increase equal to or less than that of the period preceding the date of T_α. The convention is to define $D = T_\gamma - T_\alpha$ as the duration of the transition period.

Chesnais (1992) separated the observations of world demographic transition into several types. The first type includes developed countries in Europe and Japan; the second type consists of countries with immigrant European populations, such as the United States, Australia, and Argentina;

131

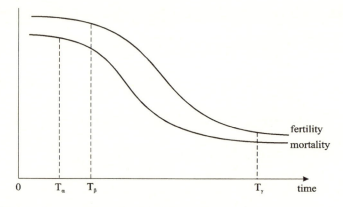

FIGURE 11.1 The stages of demographic transition.

late-developing countries, such as India, South Korea, and Jamaica, belong to the third type. For countries of the first type, the mortality decline process is closely related to the development of medical technology, which was gradual and spread out over time; hence, the demographic transition is also long. Late-developing countries and those with large immigrant populations were able to adopt the already-developed medical technology from the advanced countries at one time. Therefore, their mortality rates could drop sharply, thereby shrinking the duration of the demographic transition. As Chesnais summarized it, the duration of the demographic transition for Nordic countries can be as long as 150 years, whereas it is 64 years for the United States and as short as 50 years for Taiwan. Of course, the duration of the transition period also hinges upon how fast the fertility rate declines. India is expected to have a very long transition period because its fertility rate remains very high a long time after mortality rates declined.

Despite the fact that the natural growth rate of the population returns to a low level after the time T_γ, the age structure may still undergo significant changes after that time. At T_γ, the population usually contains a large proportion of middle-aged individuals who were born when the fertility rate was still high. As this large group of people grow older, the population age structure also gets older, which is called *population aging*. In fact, this is a problem faced by many countries at the end of the twentieth century.

Although the demographic transition is typically characterized by a decline in the mortality rate followed by a decline in the fertility rate, human economic decisions do make the impact of such a transition rather complicated. First, the reduction in child mortality rates makes parents more willing to invest in children (a quantity–quality tradeoff). This facilitates the overall accumulation of human capital, which in turn is believed to be the key reason for the positive correlation between demographic transition and economic development. Second, the transition also causes population aging. In a democratic society where intergenerational transfer policies are determined by majority voting, we expect that all kinds of unfunded pension systems that compensate the old at the expense of the young are going to appear. We also expect that, given a pension system with fixed tax and benefit rates, the pension deficit should increase as the population ages.

Third, in the transition process, the relative proportion of all age groups changes. If extended families are widespread, and if income inequality differs for different age groups, then, along with the transition, the family income inequality index will also change. Finally, at different stages of the transition process, the proportion of dependent population (young and old) is different, which may be a factor explaining the changing aggregate savings rate of the economy. In later sections of this chapter, I shall provide analyses of all these economic problems.

11.2 DEMOGRAPHIC TRANSITION AND ECONOMIC GROWTH

Ever since Kuznets (1965), economists have noticed the synchronized pace of demographic transition and economic development. Early-developed countries in western Europe, the United States, Canada, and Japan have all experienced the transition stage from high fertility/mortality to low fertility/mortality. Recent development evidence has also shown that fast-growing countries (Taiwan, Singapore) are those that went through the demographic transition smoothly, whereas slow-growing countries (India, Mexico) are those that could not get out of the high-fertility trap. Therefore, a natural question to ask is whether there exists a theoretical relationship between demographic transition and economic development. But research in this direction has not been successful under the neoclassical growth model of Solow (1956), for it typically predicts a converging steady-state growth rate of per capita income, which is incompatible with the diverging development paths among countries we have observed over the past 50 years.

Other than the above-mentioned unrealistic "converging growth path" prediction, Solow's model is also weak in predicting the relationship between income growth rate and population growth rate. It is well known that in Solow's model, the steady-state level of per capita income is a decreasing function of the population growth rate. The reasoning is that higher population growth dilutes the accumulation of per capita capital, which in turn reduces per capita income. Although this prediction gets some empirical support in areas such as China and India, such a reasoning is narrowly restricted to the dilution of *physical* capital, and is not broad enough to be compatible with general development experience, which may be related to the accumulation of *human* capital.

Recent advancement in the new growth theory has provided an alternative possibility for explaining the correlation between economic development and endogenous fertility decisions. In this section, I will introduce two typical models in this area. Notice that here I emphasize the role of population in the transitional stage (from primitive agricultural to advanced industrial) of modern economic development. I am reluctant to put much weight on the long-run analysis, which will be the focus of the discussion in chapter 14.

11.2.1 The Becker–Murphy–Tamura Model

The key idea of a paper by Becker, Murphy, and Tamura (1990, hereafter BMT) is that there is an increasing return in the human-capital production technology, so that when the human-capital stock is abundant, the rate of return on human-capital investments in children (*quality*) is high relative to the rate of return on the number (*quantity*) of children. As a result, a society with low (high) human-capital stock tends to have more (less) births and less (more) human-capital investment. These two scenarios will generate two extreme stable steady states, which correspond to the advanced and underdeveloped economies in the world.

Specifically, BMT considered a young/old overlapping-generation model and assumed that at period t a representative parent has the following utility function:

$$V_t = u\!\left(c_t\right) + \delta\!\left(m_t\right)m_t V_{t+1}, \qquad (11.1)$$

where V_t and V_{t+1} are the utilities of parents and each child, $u(c_t)$ is parental utility flow from consumption c_t, and m_t is the number of children. $\delta(m_t)$ is the between-generation discount rate determined by parental altruism toward each child. BMT assumed that $\delta' < 0$, meaning that the discount rate declines as the number of children increases.

Besides the preference specification, parents face three technological or budget constraints. The first has to do with the production technology of human capital for each child:

$$H_{t+1} = Ah_t\!\left(H^0 + H_t\right), \qquad (11.2)$$

where H^0 is the initial endowment of H, A is a constant, and h_t is the amount of time spent to teach one child at period t.

Let l_t be the time spent by every adult producing consumption goods at period t and D be the productivity of this sector; then the total output is $Dl_t(H^0 + H_t)$, which is to be spent on adult consumption and child rearing. This constitutes the second constraint of the parent:

$$c_t + fm_t = Dl_t\!\left(H^0 + H_t\right), \qquad (11.3)$$

where f is the unit of goods needed for rearing each child.

Finally, suppose rearing a child also requires v amount of time and that the parent has total time T; then the parent's time constraint is

$$T = l_t + m_t(v + h_t). \tag{11.4}$$

Faced with the constraints in (11.2)–(11.4), the parent chooses m_t and h_t to maximize (11.1).

BMT then adopted the following functional specification:

$$\delta(m) = am^{-\varepsilon}, \quad u(c) = \frac{c^\sigma}{\sigma}.$$

Given the above specification, they showed that there are two possible solution paths. The first is the "underdevelopment trap" case, where the parent voluntarily chooses a corner solution $h_t = 0\ \forall t$, and hence $H_t = 0\ \forall t$. This will be the case when producing children is inexpensive, and the children are well endowed with earning power. Thus, a sufficiently high rate of return from bearing children induces parents to have many children and discourages any investments in children's human capital. This may be a characterization of the situation of some less developed countries.

The second possible solution path is an interior solution for both m_t and h_t. It turns out that the optimal solution for h_t in this case is stationary:

$$h^* = \frac{\sigma v}{1 - \sigma - \varepsilon}, \tag{11.5}$$

and the solution for m_t is implicitly defined by

$$a(m^*)^{-\varepsilon}(T - vm^*) = A^{-1}(1 + g^*)^{1-\sigma}, \tag{11.6}$$

where g^* is the steady-state growth rate of c_t and H_t defined by[3]

$$g^* = \frac{\sigma v A}{1 - \sigma - \varepsilon} - 1. \tag{11.7}$$

From equations (11.6) and (11.7), we see that the fertility and the steady-state rate of growth in per capita income may be positively or negatively correlated across countries. If g^* differed because the productivity of human capital investments (A) differed, then the fertility rate and the growth rate would be positively related. If g^* differed mainly because the cost of children (v) differed, then the fertility rate and the growth rate would be negatively related. This is a theoretical prediction about the relationship between fertility rate and economic growth rate, which is quite different from the prediction of a neoclassical growth model. BMT also showed that the fertility rate should be negatively related to the level of the current stock of human capital, which is believed to be consistent with reality.

The BMT model uses the hypothesis of increasing return on human capital to characterize the parental tradeoffs between the quantity and quality of children. One phenomenon not explained by the BMT model is the relationship between economic growth and the demographic *transition*, initiated by the decline of mortality rates.[4] This gap was filled by Ehrlich and Lui (1991), as explained below.

11.2.2 The Ehrlich–Lui Model

Instead of assuming that parents are altruistic, as in the case of the BMT model, Ehrlich and Lui (1991) considered the case of selfish parents who raise children just to provide support for their own old-age expenditure. This kind of "child-as-old-age-support" argument is more compatible with much of the literature in development economics.

Ehrlich and Lui (1991) assumed a human-capital production function similar to (11.2) and a time constraint similar to (11.4), except that T was assumed to be 1. The key difference is their setting of the parental utility function. Individuals are assumed to live one or two or three periods, depending on the realization of the mortality uncertainty. The first life period is called childhood; children have p_1 probability of surviving to the middle life period, becoming a young parent. A young parent has p_2 probability of surviving to the third life period, called old parent. It is assumed that children accumulate human capital and do not consume, and a person's lifetime utility is specified to be

$$
u_t = \left(\frac{1}{1-\sigma}\right)\left\{\left[c_1(t)^{1-\sigma} - 1\right] + \delta p_2\left[c_2(t+1)^{1-\sigma} - 1\right]\right.
$$
$$
\left. + \left[c_3(t+1)^{1-\sigma} - 1\right]\right\},
\tag{11.8}
$$

where c_1 and c_2 are young and old parents' consumptions, respectively, and c_3 is the "companionship" enjoyed by the old parent.

Ehrlich and Lui (1991) argued that a young parent will form an implicit contract with each child, which states that the parent should receive from a grown-up child an amount of old-age support proportional to that portion of the child's future income that is associated with H_t. This proportion is denoted w_t at period t. Similarly, the current young parents will be willing to support the old parents with a proportion of the young generation's income. Ehrlich and Lui argued that such a contract will be voluntarily honored by each person, and is therefore time-consistent.

Suppose a young parent at period t decides to have m_t children and to spend h_t amount of time in educating each child and that the period-t stock of human capital is $H_t + H^0$. Then the parent's income available for consumption is

$$
c_1(t) = \left(H_t + H^0\right)\left(1 - vm_t - h_t m_t\right) - p_2 w_t H_t,
$$

where $p_2 w_t H_t$ is the expenditure supporting the old parent.[5] The old parent cannot work anymore, and his or her old-age consumption comes completely from the transfer of their children: $c_2(t + 1) = m_t p_1 w_{t+1} H_{t+1}$. Finally, the companionship function is assumed to be[6] $c_3(t + 1) = C(p_1 m_t)^b H_{t+1}^a$, where C, a, and b are three constants.

The parents' decision is divided into two stages by Ehrlich and Lui (1991). In the first stage, they take H_t, w_t, and w_{t+1} as given and choose the optimal m_t and h_t. In the second stage, parents choose the optimal contract w_{t+1}. Ehrlich and Lui proved the following *demographic transition* theorem:

THEOREM 11.1 *(Ehrlich and Lui, 1991, p. 1043)*
If the economy is initially in a stagnant equilibrium and if $0 < a, b < 1$ holds, then a once-and-for-all increase in p_1 will cause the human-capital stock to increase over time, either converge to a higher steady state or grow without bound. In the initial phase following the increase in p_1, m_t may increase or fall, although it will eventually start to decline to its minimum level. An increase in p_2 has a qualitatively similar impact except that m_t must increase in the initial phase.

The intuition behind the above theorem is as follows. An increase in p_1 increases the return on the parent's investment on both m_t and h_t, and hence initially it is not clear whether parents will decide to increase m_t or to increase h_t. But as the stock of human capital gradually accumulates, the increasing return property associated with the production of H_{t+1} (see [11.2]) eventually makes the return to h_t dominate that of m_t. In contrast, because by assumption old parents have to rely on support from their children, an increase in p_2 will increase the young parent's incentive to have more children to increase his own expected old-age support. Thus, m_t will increase in the initial phase after p_2 increases.

Theorem 11.1 is a nice characterization of the economic impact of a reduction in mortality rate, with the corresponding reduction in fertility rate as a result of the parent's decision. In the scenario posited by Ehrlich and Lui (1991), parents will try to increase their offspring's income, because they know that a fixed proportion of this income will be transferred to themselves. Ehrlich and Lui argued that although people are selfish, such transfers will be prevalent as an implicit contract between the parent and the children.

The BMT (1990) and Ehrlich and Lui (1991) models have different specifications about parental preferences, but they share the common feature that the increasing return property of human-capital production is the key factor that induces parents to reduce the quantity and increase the quality of their children. This is a crucial element that connects individual fertility decision with aggregate economic development.

11.3 DEMOGRAPHIC TRANSITION AND PUBLIC PENSION

Although the 100-year transition stage was relatively short in human history, the institutional changes during this period have been quite significant. In the preindustrial economy, the family was a tighter unit than it is now, and most parents could expect to receive old-age support from their children. But along with the demographic transition, the fertility size of each family decreases (as we showed in the previous section); the finer division of labor and improved transportation facilitate some children moving out of their families; and the children, who have abundant *human* capital, are also more independent than before, when their parents controlled most of the *physical* capital. All these changes have made parents realize that children are no longer reliable sources of their old-age support. Of course, parents can save when they are young and spend their savings when they are old, and the financial market could certainly absorb some of the demand for such cross-generation self-support saving plans. But sometimes the demand for old-age support has been revealed in the political market rather than in the economic market, and that often causes significant changes in government policies. This situation is what we want to study below.

11.3.1 The Majority-Voting Model

Many government policies, including the presently prevalent pay-as-you-go pension system, involve transfers of resources across generations. Because in a democratic society government policies are made by the public, in many cases by the rule of majority voting, the rise of pension systems is itself endogenous. Along with the demographic transition, the age structure of the economy changes, and hence the relative number of beneficiaries in an across-generation transfer scenario also changes. Thus, the majority-voting rule may favor generating a particular transfer scenario in the economy. This is the research focus of Browning (1975), Hu (1982), Boadway and Wildasin (1989), and Tabellini (1990). This subsection will concentrate on the model of Boadway and Wildasin, which is itself a modification of the work of Hu and Browning.

Boadway and Wildasin considered a continuous-time overlapping-generation model with perfect certainty. Each person works from period 0 to R, which represents retirement, and dies at n. Suppose the benefit and tax flow of a pension are respectively β and τ. Given a constant discount rate δ, the government's balanced-budget constraint can be written as

$$\tau \int_0^R e^{-\delta s} ds = \beta \int_R^n e^{-\delta s} ds, \quad \text{or} \quad \tau = \eta \beta,$$

where $\eta \equiv (e^{-\delta R} - e^{-\delta n})/(1 - e^{-\delta R})$. Given the above balanced-budget constraint, there is only one free policy variable for the government, which is assumed to be β. In a democratic society, β is not exogenous but to be determined by majority voting. A key assumption made by Boadway and Wildasin is that they consider a situation which is either in the steady state or has infrequent voting, so that each voter chooses a *scalar* value β (instead of all future β_t's) for the rest of his remaining life.

Suppose the current time is t, and suppose the preexisting β is β^0. An individual wants to solve the following problem:

$$\max \int_t^n e^{-\delta(s-t)} u(c_s) ds$$
$$\text{s.t.} \quad \dot{A}_s = w_s + \beta_s - \tau_s + rA_s - c_s, \quad t \le s \le n. \tag{11.9}$$

In the above expression, A_s is the stock of assets and is assumed to be nonnegative with an initial value depending on β^0, and w_s is the exogenous wage flow. $\beta_s = \beta$ is positive for $s > R$ and is 0 for $t \le s \le R$, and τ_s is positive for $t \le s \le R$ and is 0 for $s > R$. For any given β and β^0, we can form a Hamiltonian, calculate the first-order condition, and derive the optimal solution for c_s and A_s. Substituting these optimal solutions into the original objective function, we have the indirect utility function as a function of β and β^0, denoted $V_t(\beta; \beta^0)$.

Boadway and Wildasin then considered several cases, depending upon whether the *benefit constraint* or the *liquidity constraint* is binding. The former case refers to the situation in which individuals cannot borrow against future social security benefits, and the latter case refers to the situation in which individuals cannot borrow against future wages. In an economy with public pensions and mature financial markets, it is normally the case that the benefit constraint is indeed binding, but the liquidity constraint is not necessarily so.

Boadway and Wildasin then showed that V_t is concave in β, and hence is single-peaked over β. Therefore, a majority-voting scenario will generate a well-known "median-voter" equilibrium (Black, 1958). Let d be the median age and β_d^* be the median-age person's corresponding optimal social security. Boadway and Wildasin proved the following theorem:

THEOREM 11.2 (*Boadway and Wildasin, 1989, p. 324*)
Suppose the benefit constraint is binding but the liquidity constraint is not. If $\beta_d^* \ge \beta^0$, then the median-age voter's optimal β_d^* will be the majority-voting equilibrium level of β. If $\beta_d^* < \beta^0$, then the median voter in general is not the median-age voter, and the majority-voting equilibrium level of β is less than β^0.

As we argued in the previous paragraph, the condition of a binding benefit constraint and a slacking liquidity constraint (in theorem 11.2) is roughly compatible with reality. I will show in the next chapter that, as the fertility rate declines along with the demographic transition, the age structure of the economy will undergo a first-order stochastic dominance shift, so that the median age of the society will decline as the fertility rate increases. But because most social security schemes have an age-invariant tax rate and benefit schedule, as a person ages, his tax payment period shrinks and the benefit receiving period remains the same. This fact certainly increases his preference for higher β. Thus, theorem 11.2 predicts that, along with the demographic transition, an older population age structure tends to generate a higher level of social security, which seems to be an intuitively appealing result.

11.3.2 Tabellini's Approach

One obvious drawback of the Boadway and Wildasin model is their assumption of infrequent voting; that is, in their voting scenario, they rule out the possibility that future generations can "revote" to change the previous voting result. This is certainly an unreasonable assumption, for future voters can never be counted on not to repeal the original social security system. In terms of game theory, the majority-voting result should at least be *renegotiation-proof*. Moreover, most social security programs have both the function of intergenerational transfers and intragenerational redistribution. The latter redistributive function will affect the attitudes of rich and poor voters differently, thereby affecting the majority-voting equilibrium. The model by Tabellini (1990) is an effort to adapt to these two considerations. The formal model Tabellini considered is as follows.

Consider a 2-period overlapping-generation structure. Suppose every parent has $(1 + m)$ children, where m is the rate of population growth. There is mutual altruism between parents and children in the following sense. The utility function of the ith child in period t is assumed to be:

$$J_t^i = \max\left[\frac{\gamma}{1 + m} H_t^i + u\left(c_t^i\right) + E_t H_{t+1}^i\right],$$

where c_t^i is the consumption of the ith child in period t, with $u(c_t^i)$ the corresponding utility flow; E_t is the expectation operator; H_t^i is the indirect utility function of the period-t parent in the ith household; and γ characterizes the degree of the child's altruism. The utility of the period-t parent in the ith household is:

$$H_t^i = \max\left[d_t^i + \delta\left(1 + m\right)J_t^i\right],$$

where d_t^i is the consumption of the ith parent in period t and δ is the degree of the parent's altruism.

The ith child receives an endowment $w_t(1 + e_t^i)$ at the beginning of his life, where e_t^i is an individual-specific, mean-zero random variable characterizing the child's ability and w_t is the aggregate endowment random variable. Each child pays τ_t proportion of his income as social security tax and saves s_t^i amount. So his budget constraint can be written as

$$w_t\left(1 + e_t^i\right)\left(1 - \tau_t\right) \geq c_t^i + s_t^i.$$

For the tth-period parent, his or her income comes from the old-age endowment k, saving returns $R_{t-1}s_{t-1}^i$, and social security benefit g_t. This income is to be spent on consumption. So the budget constraint becomes

$$k + g_t + R_{t-1}s_{t-1}^i \geq d_t^i.$$

Taking the tax rate τ_t as given, the government budget constraint is $g_t = (1 + m)\omega_t\tau_t$, which determines g_t.

Each person treats τ_t as given and maximizes his or her utility function, taking into account the budget constraint. Since there are no outside assets, the aggregate savings of all people must sum to zero in an *economic* equilibrium ($\Sigma_i s_t^i = 0$), which determines the equilibrium interest rate R_t. Then each person can derive his or her indirect utility function as a function of τ_t and vote for the most preferred tax rate through the majority-voting rule. Tabellini (1990) showed that since the social security tax is proportional to earnings, the higher the child's earnings, the lower is the preferred social security tax rate for both children and parents. But parents always prefer a larger social security tax than their children do because it would benefit the older generations. Thus, in a voting scenario, it is the old group and the poor young group that prefer a larger social security tax. Tabellini then formulated the condition of a majority voting *political* equilibrium. For my purposes, I only list his most relevant result:

THEOREM 11.3 *(Tabellini, 1990, p. 12)*
The social security tax rate under a majority-voting political equilibrium is a decreasing function of m.

The above theorem, together with the Boadway and Wildasin result, tells us that during the demographic transition process, when the age structure becomes older or when the fertility rate declines, a general voting democracy indeed tends to provide more social security than would have been the case in a stable population structure. In fact, in an aging economy, the social security transfer is just one kind of transfer from the young to the old; other institutional designs also have the same kind of impact. In the next section, we will discuss the *measurement* of such wealth transfers during the demographic transition.

11.4 INTERGENERATIONAL TRANSFERS AND LIFE-CYCLE CONSUMPTION

Aggregate wealth can be separated into two broad categories: real wealth and transfer wealth.[7] The transfer wealth can be further separated into family transfers (bequests, education, and other child-rearing expenses), public sector transfers (pension and health care), and market transfers (individual borrowing and lending). Although the sums of transfers made and received at any moment of time must be zero, many (especially public) transfers can obligate future generations to make transfers to members of the current generation. Therefore, the sum of transfers across all living generations may be negative or positive.

Lee (1994a, 1994b) studied the impact of fertility decline on intergenerational transfers. Specifically, he wanted to analyze how a change in population growth rate affects the present value of life-cycle consumption across golden-rule steady states. Lee's analysis presents three major results. First, he showed that in an economy with golden-rule capital accumulation and stable population growth, the proportional effect on the present value of life-cycle consumption can be written as:

$$\int_0^n e^{-rx} l(x) \left[\frac{\partial c(x)}{\partial r} - \frac{\partial y(x)}{\partial r} \right] dx = \frac{c}{b}(A_c - A_y) - \frac{K}{m}, \qquad (11.10)$$

where n is the upper bound of human life, r is the steady-state population growth rate, $c(x)$ and $y(x)$ are per capita consumption and earning profiles, c is the original steady-state level of per capita consumption, A_c and A_y are the mean ages of consumption and earnings, m is the crude birth rate, and K is the original capital size. The interpretation of (11.10) is very much the same as that in chapter 3: the first term on the right-hand side is the age-structure effect, and the second term is the capital-dilution effect.

Lee's second result uses transfer accounting to show that the right-hand side of (11.10) can be rewritten as

$$\frac{c}{b}(A_c - A_y) - \frac{K}{m} = \frac{T}{m},$$

where T is the size of total transfer wealth. The third of Lee's results shows that the *stock* of transfer wealth can be estimated through a multiplication of *flow* and the difference of transfer ages:

$$T = \tau^+ (A_{\tau+} - A_{\tau-}),$$

where τ^+ is the size of the average transfer flow and $(A_{\tau+} - A_{\tau-})$ is the mean age difference of receiving and making transfers.

Lee then estimated the respective mean age and flow size of different kinds of transfers in the family and in the government sector. Applying the above formulas, we can get an estimate of the effect of population aging on steady-state consumption. Using the data from the United States, Lee showed that with a 1% reduction in the population growth rate (r), the U.S. social security transfer has caused an annual loss of $910 per household to be made up in reduced transfers or increased taxes.

Lee's calculation can serve as an estimate of the impact of a public transfer system. As one may already see, however, there are several assumptions behind such a calculation that we should keep in mind. The first is the stable population assumption. Demographic transition almost by definition is about the *transitional* stage instead of the steady state of a population. Hence Lee's calculation may be described more accurately as a comparative *static* result, rather than an estimate of the impact of *aging*, which is itself a phenomenon in the transitional stage. Second, the golden-rule assumption of capital accumulation is a rather strong one. This assumption is necessary for calculation, for otherwise the interest rate will not equal the population growth rate, and the analysis will be rather messy. But unfortunately it is difficult to appraise how far away we are from the golden rule. Finally, the impact of a social security transfer is not independent of the attitude of the household. If the Barro (1974) assumption is right, then families will make efforts to offset what the government has been doing. But if the Feldstein (1974) assumption is right, social security will reduce the size of capital significantly, which in turn will reduce labor productivity and earnings.

11.5 Composition Distortion of Inequality Measurement

So far our discussion has been focused upon either the institution or the size of resource transfers during the demographic transition. In this section, we will study the measurement problems associated with the demographic transition period. Our focus, of course, is restricted to topics with economic interpretation or implications.

Because a demographic transition process typically starts with a large proportion of young people and ends when these people are old, one way to view the transition process is to think of this changing population age structure as a "migration" process from the young age group to the old one. Thus, if we randomly draw a family sample in a society with widespread extended families, we are likely to have one with more young members at the beginning and more old members at the end of the demographic transition. For variables with family-based measurements (such as family incomes, savings, and assets), since the variable dispersion is usually different for different age-specific groups, the "age migration" process during the demographic transition certainly implies distinct family inequality measures of the variables in question during various stages of the transition. In this section, I will focus upon the inequality measurement of a typical family variable, family *income*; but the analysis certainly applies to other variables as well.

11.5.1 Decomposing Family Income

To study the impact of the demographic transition on income inequality, I separate the income earners of an extended family into age groups and treat each age-specific earner as an income-generating "source".[8] Following the general practice of national income accounting, I divide family incomes into four categories: 1) wage earnings, 2) property income, 3) owner-operator income, and 4) other incomes. In practice, only wage earnings can be accurately affiliated with age-specific family members, and family income inequality in many countries can be largely attributed to wage dispersion. In the analysis of this section, therefore, I shall decompose the family wage income into age-specific parts.

Suppose our economy is composed of N families, each with total income $Y^j, j = 1, 2, \cdots, N$. Each family's income is composed of the above-mentioned four sources. We shall denote $Y_i^j, i = 1, 2, 3, 4$, the source-i income of the jth family, y^j the share of family j's total income in the society, and y_i^j the share of family j's source-i income in the society. These N families in the economy can be ranked according to its y^j in ascending order. We denote $r(y^j)$ the rank of family j. The rank function $r(y_i^j)$ according to y_i^j can be defined similarly. We shall let a variable without a superscript denote the N vector of all families. For instance, $(y_i^1, \cdots, y_i^N)$ is denoted y_i.

Let $G(Y)$ and G_i be, respectively, the Gini coefficient of Y and Y_i. Let $Si \equiv \Sigma_j Y_i^j / \Sigma_j Y^j$ be the share of source-i income in total income in the society and $R_i \equiv cov(y_i, r(y)) / cov(y_i, r(y_i))$ be the rank correlation between Y_i and Y. Since family income is composed of four sources, by applying the decomposition technique of Fei et al. (1979), we can write the Gini coefficient of total income as $G(Y) = \Sigma_{i=1}^4 S_i R_i G_i$. Similarly, the family wage income can be further decomposed into A age groups: $G_1 \equiv G(Y_1) = \Sigma_{a=1}^A S_{1a} R_{1a} G(Y_{1a})$, where $G(Y_{1a})$ is the Gini index of age-a wage income, and R_{1a} and S_{1a} are similarly defined.

11.5.2 Marginal Comparison

Suppose that at some point in time during demographic transition process, the number of age-m earners increases from b_m^j to $b_m^j(1 + u_m)$ for each family j. This, according to Stark et al. (1986), is a reasonable approximation for small changes in age structure. Under some regularity conditions, Stark et al. showed that the change in b_m^j will cause a marginal change in the source-m wage income of each family by the same percentage u_m. Stark et al. proved the following theorem:

THEOREM 11.4
The elasticity change of $G(Y_1)$ with respect to u_m is as follows:

$$\frac{\partial G(Y_1)/\partial u_m}{G(Y_1)} = \frac{S_{1m}R_{1m}G(Y_{1m})}{G(Y_1)} - S_{1m}. \qquad (11.11)$$

According to the above theorem, whether an increase in the size of the m-age group will increase or reduce the Gini coefficient of aggregate earnings will be determined by the relative size of the two terms on the right-hand side of (11.11). The first term is the contribution of age-m wage to total wage inequality, and the second term measures the share of age-m wage in total wages. Analogously, one can derive the impact of changing b_m on $G(Y)$, the Gini index of total income. The interpretation is similar and can be found in Chu and Jiang (1997).

11.5.3 Global Comparison

Besides the above-mentioned marginal analysis, one can also examine whether the changing population structure during the demographic transition has any overall impact on the Lorenz curve. Using the data of Taiwan, Chu and Jiang (1997) compared the actual Lorenz curve with one adjusted by a base-year population and tested whether the demographic transition had caused any significant shift in the Lorenz curve. Their idea was adapted from Bishop et al. (1994), and the comparison process is as follows. First, they calculate the yearly growth rate of aggregate age-specific family members relative to the numbers of a base year. Then they construct a series of adjusted family earnings by dividing the age-specific earnings of each family in each year by the age-specific member growth rate. Finally, they add other incomes to these adjusted earnings to obtain a series of adjusted family incomes.

Let $\{I_k \mid k = 1, \cdots, K\}$ be the set of target incomes corresponding to the population quintiles of Y. Let us denote the actual income Y_1 and the adjusted income Y_2. For each year, we can construct a series of actual Lorenz ordinates, denoted $\{O_1(I_k; Y_1) \mid k = 1, \cdots, K\}$, and a series of adjusted Lorenz ordinates, denoted $\{O_2(I_k; Y_2) \mid k = 1, \cdots, K\}$. $O_1(I; Y_1)$ represents the accumulated share of actual income received by families with income less than I, and $O_2(I; Y_2)$ is the accumulated share of adjusted income received by these families. The vector of the difference between O_1 and O_2, denoted $(\Delta(I_1), \cdots, \Delta(I_K))$, characterizes the impact of the changing age composition on the Lorenz curve. According to Bishop et al. (1994), the difference vector $(\Delta(I_1), \cdots, \Delta(I_K))$ is asymptotically normal. The test statistic for the difference at any ordinate is $Z_k = \Delta(I_k)/(V_{kk}/N)^{1/2}$, $k = 1, 2, \cdots, K$, where V_{kk} is the variance of $\Delta(I_k)$ and N is the sample size. To test whether O_1 and O_2 are different, Bishop et al. showed that we should compare Z_k with the critical value in the Student Maximum Modules (SMM) table.

The null hypothesis to be tested is that the actual and the adjusted ordinates are equal. It if turns out that each of the adjusted Lorenz ordinates is significantly smaller (larger) than its corresponding actual Lorenz ordinates, then we can conclude that the demographic transition has a significantly advantageous (disadvantageous) effect on measured income inequality. Using the data from Taiwan, Chu and Jiang (1997) performed the above-mentioned test. They showed that between 1978 and 1993 the adjusted Lorenz curve lies below the actual Lorenz curve of the respective year except during the 1979–1980 subperiod. The increase of inequality is particularly significant at the end of the observation period. This result is reasonable, since the effect of the changing age structure has been *accumulating* throughout the whole period of the demographic transition. The evidence tells us that the changing population structure in Taiwan has significantly hidden the seriousness of its increase of income inequality in the past several years. In 1992, for instance, the actual G_t is .292 and the adjusted $\hat{G}_t$ is .318, so that the changing age structure has caused a superficial 8.77% undervaluation of Taiwan's Gini coefficient, revealing a strong composition effect due to changes in the age structure.

11.6 DEMOGRAPHIC TRANSITION AND THE SAVINGS RATE

In the neoclassical growth model of Solow (1956), capital accumulation is the engine of economic growth. Because capital accumulation comes from individual savings, it is interesting to investigate whether the fertility decision of the parents has any direct impact on household savings behavior. The answer to this question is also crucial to understanding whether a slow pace of development in countries such as India has anything to do with a fast population growth rate. We put the discussion of this issue in the last section of this chapter because the evidence, as Mason (1987) puts it, "is far from universally accepted."

There are three major hypotheses that link aggregate savings with changing population growth rates. The first is the *dependency-rate hypothesis* proposed by Leff (1969), who argued that when the youth or old dependency ratio is high, the working generation has a heavier family consumption burden, and therefore the family savings rate will be low. Although Leff's conjecture was appealing, his empirical formulation and estimation drew so much criticism that no definite conclusions could be obtained.

The second is the *old-age security hypothesis* proposed in Neher (1971) and Lewis (1983). They believe that children, particularly in developing countries, are substitutes for savings or alternative ways that parents prepare for their retirement. In countries where parents are willing to have more children, their old-age support is quite sufficient so that it is not necessary for them to save much. There is also some rough empirical evidence that supports this conjecture.

The third is the *life-cycle hypothesis*, which emphasizes the composition effect of population age structure on aggregate savings. Although each person does not accumulate net savings over his life cycle, with savings in productive years offset by lack of savings in childhood and old age, aggregate savings in the economy need not be zero because the age-specific composition in a society is usually uneven. When the age structure reaches a peak in the productive years, the positive savings of these productive people will more than offset the negative ones of the children and old people, hence generating positive savings purely because of the age-composition effect. Mason (1987) applied the techniques we introduced in section 11.4 and showed that, under some technical assumptions, the logarithm of one minus the saving ratio can be written as:

$$\ln\left(1 - s\right) = a + \left(A_y - A_c\right)g,$$

where a is a constant, A_y and A_c are the mean ages of earning and consumption, and g is the rate of growth of the national income. Mason used international cross-sectional data to estimate the above equation and derive different results in different areas.

Although Mason concluded that his evidence supports the proposition that a higher dependency ratio leads to lower savings, we are not strongly persuaded by the empirical evidence so far. One weakness of Mason's analysis, as in the analysis in section 11.4 above, is that he assumed a golden-rule steady-state per capita income growth rate and a stable population age structure; this is clearly inconsistent with the real-world situation in all developing countries, which his data points cover. Deaton and Paxson (1997) recently used pseudo-panel data (the time series of cross-sectional data) to analyze savings behavior in Taiwan, Thailand, Britain, and the United States. They found that the data can support a life-cycle interpretation of consumption and savings but cannot support a significant relationship between savings and the population growth rate. Higgins and Williamson (1997), however, showed that falling mortality and lagging declines in fertility have had a profound impact on Asian savings over the half-century pince 1950.

In fact, the existing literature has not provided a formal characterization of the demographic transition, and most analyses confuse comparative statics with comparative dynamics. In the next chapter, we will provide a formal demography for population aging, distinguish comparative statics and aging dynamics, and analyze some related issues.

CHAPTER 12

Age-Distribution Dynamics During Demographic Transitions

12.1 BACKGROUND

Everyone knows that *population aging* refers to the phenomenon of a growing proportion of old people. This may happen 60 years after a "baby boom", as the "baby boomers" begin to reach their old age. Population aging may also be a natural consequence of demographic transitions, for we know that the proportion of old people will increase as the fertility rate declines.

Although there have been numerous economics research papers on topics related to population aging, the focus of most of these research projects has not been on the process and dynamics of population aging but rather on the various problems of the elderly (such as housing, pension, medical care, savings, and retirement) that will grow as the population ages. The typical example is the series of research projects on the economics of aging undertaken by the National Bureau of Economic Research. These research reports were edited by David Wise into several books on aging. In order to make some policy suggestions, however, we must be able to derive the future dynamic pattern of the age distribution, so that the macro level prediction of some age-related variables can be arrived at analytically instead of numerically. Unfortunately, little analytical work has been done along these lines.

The purpose of this chapter is to derive the analytical pattern of the age distribution dynamics, which not only helps us calculate the aggregate value of age-related variables but also gives us some insight into finding reasonable aging indexes. Previous researchers often adopted the common measure of population aging, "the proportion of the population older than a critical age,"[1] which is called the "head-count ratio" of the aged. As the head-count ratio of the aged rises above 10%, by instinct one

148

may realize the seriousness of the aging problem. But since we know little about either the formal dynamics or the economic implications of population aging, we do not even know whether the head-count ratio is an appropriate index for characterizing the seriousness of the aging problem. We will show in later sections how information on age distribution dynamics helps us identify reasonable indexes of population aging.

12.2 COMPARATIVE DYNAMICS OF POPULATION AGING

Population aging by definition is a dynamic phenomenon, which has had various causes in the past and also shows a somewhat predictable pattern for the future. As is well known, the aging problem today is a natural result of a fertility or mortality decline in the past. Furthermore, for many countries in the world, population aging will be a more worrisome problem in the future than it is today. Indeed, many researchers have to rely on simulation or population forecasting to predict the pension deficit or the old-age housing shortage in the future.[2] Because in most countries aging is caused by declines in fertility or mortality rates, any simulation or forecasting basically involves multiplying the current population figures by some life-table parameters. Instead of comparing the year-by-year aging indexes numerically, it would be helpful if we can formally derive the changing *pattern* of future population age structures.

12.2.1 Previous Research

Adopting the notation from chapter 3, let $B(t)$ be the births at instant t, $l(a)$ be the proportion of those born surviving to age a, and $m(a)$ be the average number of births per surviving member aged a. We have the following well-known accounting identity:

$$B(t) \equiv \int_0^n B(t-a)l(a)m(a)da. \tag{12.1}$$

The density of age group a at time t, denoted $g(a, t)$, is therefore

$$g(a, t) = \frac{B(t-a)l(a)}{\int_0^n B(t-s)l(s)ds}, \tag{12.2}$$

with the corresponding distribution function

$$G(a_0, t) = \int_0^{a_0} g(a, t)da = \frac{\int_0^{a_0} B(t-a)l(a)da}{\int_0^n B(t-a)l(a)da}.$$

When the population reaches a steady state, which is called the *stable population structure* in chapter 3, $B(t) = B_0 e^{rt}$, where r, the growth rate of the stable population birth size, is such that

$$1 = \int_0^n e^{-ra} l(a) m(a) da. \tag{12.3}$$

Under a stable population structure, the age density and distribution functions are time-invariant but will depend on r. We denote them, respectively, $g(a; r)$ and $G(a; r)$.

In general, there are several age-related economic variables associated with a person's life cycle. For instance, each person has a life-cycle income path $\{i(a)\}_{a \in [0,n]}$; a life-cycle consumption path $\{c(a)\}_{a \in [0,n]}$; a pension-tax payment path $\{\tau(a)\}_{a \in [y,R]}$, where y and R are the time in and out of the labor market; and a pension benefit path $\{b(a)\}_{a \in [R,n]}$. A simple definition of pension deficit at time t is

$$D(t) = \int_0^n \left[b(a) - \tau(a) \right] g(a, t) da.$$

In the steady state, replacing $g(a, t)$ by $g(a; r)$, the deficit can be rewritten as

$$D(t) = \int_0^n \left[b(a) - \tau(a) \right] g(a; r) da.$$

Similarly, if we define an age-specific savings function as $s(a) = i(a) - c(a)$, then the aggregate saving in the steady state is

$$S(r) = \int_0^n s(a) g(a; r) da.$$

Lee (1980, 1994), Mason (1988), Willis (1988), and Lee and Lapkoff (1988) analyzed the sign of $dD(r)/dr$, $dS(r)/dr$, and studied other slightly variant problems.

12.2.2 Consequences of Changing Fertility Rate

Let the age-specific fertility function be characterized by $m(a, \theta)$. m is affected by θ in such a way that $\partial m(a,\theta)/\partial \theta \geq 0$ $\forall a$, with strict inequality for a positive measure of a. Without loss of generality, suppose $\theta = 0$ when $t \leq 0$ and that the population is stable at $t = 0$. If there is no change in the parameters, $B(t) = B_0 e^{rt}$ $\forall t > 0$. Suppose from time 0 on, θ increases permanently from 0 to $\theta > 0$. Then the population will eventually converge to another stable structure with a larger growth rate $r' > r$. But during the transitional stage, the changing pattern of the age structure may be predictable. This is what we are trying to find out: we want to study how such an increase in θ changes the dynamic evolution of the age distribution.

Let us rewrite the birth function in (12.1) as

$$B(t, \theta) \equiv \int_0^n B(t - a, \theta) l(a) m(a, \theta) da, \tag{12.1'}$$

in which we characterize the influence of θ. Chu (1997) proved the following lemma:

LEMMA

$$\frac{B(t+s, \theta)}{B(t, \theta)} > e^{rs} = \frac{B(t+s, 0)}{B(t, 0)}, \quad \forall \ t, s > 0. \tag{12.4}$$

$$\frac{d^2}{d\theta ds}\left(\frac{B(t+s, \theta)}{B(t, \theta)}\right) > 0. \tag{12.5}$$

The above lemma says that after θ increases, the growth rate of birth increases with time and is always higher than r.

Next we use the results in (12.4) and (12.5) to derive the comparative dynamic result of the age structure. Let $g(a, \theta, t)$ be the population density of people aged exactly a at time t, given that the parameter in the fertility function is θ. For any age b, dividing both the numerator and the denominator of $g(b, \theta, t)$ in (12.2) by $B(t - b, \theta)$, we have

$$g(b, \theta, t) = \frac{l(b)}{\int_0^b \frac{B(t-a, \theta)}{B(t-b, \theta)}l(a)da + \int_b^n \frac{B(t-a, \theta)}{B(t-b, \theta)}l(a)da}.$$

Differentiating $g(b, \theta, t)$ with respect to θ yields

$$\frac{dg(b, \theta, t)}{d\theta} = -\frac{g(b, \theta, t)^2}{l(b)} \cdot \left[\int_0^b \frac{d}{d\theta}\left(\frac{B(t-a, \theta)}{B(t-b, \theta)}\right)l(a)da\right.$$

$$\left. + \int_b^n \frac{d}{d\theta}\left(\frac{B(t-a, \theta)}{B(t-b, \theta)}\right)l(a)da\right].$$

In the square brackets above, the first integral term is positive and the second integral term is negative by (12.4). When b increases, by (12.5) the absolute value of the integrand in the first (second) integral term increases (decreases). Furthermore, the range of the first (second) integral increases (decreases) as b increases. Thus, if $dg(b, \theta, t)/d\theta > (<) \ 0$ for some b, it must be true that $dg(a, \theta, t)/d\theta > (<) \ 0$ for $a < (>) \ b$.

Besides the above information, we also know that when $b = 0$, the first integral term vanishes, so that $dg(b, \theta, t)/d\theta > 0$. Similarly, when $b = n$, the second integral term vanishes, and hence $dg(b, \theta, t)/d\theta < 0$. Combining these results, we see that $dg(b, \theta, t)/d\theta$ changes sign only once, and therefore we have

THEOREM 12.1
There exists a critical age a*(t) such that (see figure 12.1)

$$\frac{dg(a,\,\theta,\,t)}{d\theta} \geq (<)\,0 \quad if\ a \leq (>)\,a*(t). \tag{12.6}$$

Theorem 12.1 is a comparative *it dynamic* result; it holds for every $t > 0$ after the parameter θ increases at time $t = 0$. The demographic transition period after T_β (when the fertility rate starts to decline; see figure 11.1) in fact corresponds to a reduction in θ in the above analysis. Theorem 12.1 provides a complete prediction about the dynamic pattern of population age density for $t > T_\beta$. As $t \to \infty$, the population converges to another stable age structure, and our result certainly remains true. Thus, theorem 12.1 is clearly an extension of the previous comparative *statics* on stable population structure. This can be shown as follows.

In the steady state, $B(t,\theta) = B_0 e^{r(\theta)t}$, so

$$g(b,\,\theta,\,t) = \frac{e^{-br(\theta)}l(b)}{\int_0^n e^{-ar(\theta)}l(a)da}.$$

Thus,

$$\frac{d\log g(b,\,\theta,\,t)}{d\theta} = (-b + \bar{a})\frac{dr(\theta)}{d\theta},$$

where

$$\bar{a} \equiv \frac{\int_0^n ae^{-ar}l(a)da}{\int_0^n e^{-ar}l(a)da}.$$

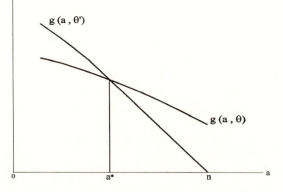

FIGURE 12.1 The change of $g(a,\theta)$, $\theta' > \theta$.

is the mean age of the population. This is consistent with the conventional result of the mathematical population in Coale (1972).

Unless otherwise specified, in the rest of this chapter I shall skip the time variable t in the age density and distribution functions, with the understanding that a change in $g(a, \theta)$ or $G(a, \theta)$ refers to a change in the whole path of $g(a, \theta, t)$ or $G(a, \theta, t)$.

12.2.3 Extensions

As we can see from figure 12.1, theorem 12.1 essentially predicts a "pivoting" of the population age density for all t. As $t \to \infty$, we have a comparative static result exactly the same as the one in Arthur (1984). In the steady state, Arthur proved that the pivotal point is the mean age of the population; however, this result cannot be established in the transitional period between two steady states. Arthur's (1984) analysis was a comparative static one; but the change in fertility he considered is a *functional* change, more general than the conventional partial differentiation considered in Coale (1972). In fact, theorem 12.1 can also be extended to functional changes in m. To shorten my presentation, here I provide only a sketch.

Consider a general change in the m function from $m(a, 0)$ to $m(a, \theta) = m(a, 0) + \theta k(a)$ along an arbitrary direction $k(a)$. We denote the differential δm. It can be shown that, with such a functional change in m, the following inequality is crucial to reestablishing our lemma (and hence theorem 12.1):

$$\int_0^\omega e^{-ra} l(a) \delta m(a) da > 0.$$

The above inequality, similar to the one given in Arthur (1984), provides a condition for sustaining the result of density pivoting for more general shifts in the fertility function. It says that as long as the *weighted average change in fertility* is positive, the density-pivoting result remains true. In reality, there are widespread *intertemporal substitutions* in female fertility decision making when women's opportunities in the labor market change through time. Such intertemporal substitution concerns may increase the female fertility of some age groups while the overall trend of fertility is declining. In this case, the fertility change is not monotonic, and the above inequality is helpful in checking whether the density-pivoting result remains true.

It is particularly important to note that the range of a was not specified in theorem 12.1. Specifically, in the proof of theorem 12.1, all we have used is the changing pattern of the relative number of births ($B(t - a, \theta)/B(t - b, \theta)$) with respect to a change in θ; the range of $[0, n]$ is arbitrarily given. Thus, if we restrict our attention to a subregion of age $[a_1, a_2] \subset [0, n]$, then we are looking at an age distribution that is *conditional* on $[a_1, a_2]$. For instance, for the social security system, a_1 refers to the age of entrance into the labor market (when the person starts to pay some social security taxes), and a_2 is the time when all benefits cease. It is easy to see that the following theorem must also hold.

THEOREM 12.2
Within any age range $[a_1, a_2] \subset [0, n]$, let the conditional age density be

$$h(b, \theta) \equiv \frac{B(b, \theta)l(a)}{\int_{a_1}^{a_2} B(a, \theta)l(a)da}, \quad a_1 \le b \le a_2.$$

There exists a critical age $\tilde{a} \in [a_1, a_2]$ such that

$$\frac{dh(a, \theta)}{d\theta} \ge (<) \, 0 \, if \, a \le (>) \, \tilde{a}.$$

Since $g(a, \theta)$ is a density function, $\int_0^n \dfrac{dg(a, \theta)}{d\theta} da = 0$ must hold. Thus, theorem 12.1 implies that when θ increases, the new population age distribution first-order stochastically dominates (FSD) the original one, that is,

$$G(a, \theta_1) > G(a, \theta_2) \, \forall a \in [0, n), \quad \theta_1 > \theta_2. \tag{12.7}$$

Thus, (12.6) is stronger than (12.7), and the former can be called a *conditional stochastic dominance* relation, similar to the one proposed in Chu and Koo (1990).

12.2.4 Consequences of Changing Mortality Rate

If γ is a parameter in the mortality function ($l = l(a, \gamma)$), then the formula of $dg(a, \gamma)/d\gamma$ involves terms such as $d\left(\dfrac{l(a, \gamma)}{l(b, \gamma)}\right)\Big/ d\gamma$, the sign of which cannot be assured. But there is one important class of examples where the changing pattern of the age density is predictable. Suppose there is a proportionally equal reduction in $l(a)$, that is, $d\log[l(a, \gamma)]/d\gamma$ is constant. Such a mortality decline is called a *neutral* mortality change, similar to the one defined in Preston (1982). In this case, $l(a, \gamma)/l(b, \gamma)$ remains unchanged as γ changes. Then, applying the same analysis, it is easy to establish the following result.

THEOREM 12.3
Let $g(a, \gamma)$ be the age density when the mortality parameter is γ. Suppose the mortality decline is it neutral, in the sense that $d \log[l(a, \gamma)]/d\gamma$ is constant; then there exists a critical age $\hat{a}$ such that

$$\frac{dg(a, \gamma)}{d\gamma} \ge (<) \, 0 \quad if \, a \le (>) \, \hat{a}.$$

Although the above-mentioned neutral pattern of mortality change is analytically convenient, it may not work out empirically for *gradual* declines in mortality, particularly in developed countries. As Lee (1994) argued, when mortality is high, it is more likely that reductions in death rates are greatest for the youngest ages; when the mortality rate becomes low, reductions in mortality are greatest for the oldest ages. Consequently, in countries that have experienced gradual declines in mortality, the initial declines led to an increase in the youth of their populations, rather than to the monotonic aging effect suggested here. Thus, our analysis of the case of mortality declines is a qualified one. For developing countries that experienced a sudden inflow of modern medicine and hygienic knowledge, mortality decline was more likely to fit the neutrality assumption of Preston (1982). In those cases, theorem 12.3 provides a prediction about the changing pattern of the age density during the demographic transition period after T_α (see figure 11.1).

Notice that all the comparative dynamic results listed in the above theorems are derived from a comparison of the time path of age distributions before and after the parameter change. Specifically, we are comparing $g(a, \theta_1, t)$ with $g(a, \theta_2, t)$ for $t > 0$. The dynamics are not comparing $g(a, \theta, t)$ with $g(a, \theta, t + s)$, which refers to analyzing the *converging path* of a new regime. Readers who are familiar with mathematical population theory should know that the birth renewal equation in (12.1) can easily have a complex eigenvalue, so that the converging path will be cyclic. This tells us that there will be no definite pattern of changes between $g(a, \theta, t)$ and $g(a, \theta, t + s)$.

12.3 Applications of the Density-Pivoting Results

In the beginning of section 12.2, I mentioned several theoretical analyses that compare the economic variables of two *stable* population structures with different growth rates. With the help of our theoretical analysis in section 12.2, we are able to provide alternative answers to the previously raised questions in the literature.

12.3.1 Pay-As-You-Go Pension Deficit

Consider an intergenerational transfer system similar to the one studied in Lee (1980, 1994) and Keyfitz (1988). Let y be the age of entering the labor market and R be the age of retirement. Suppose there is a mandatory social security system that requires every working person aged $a, a \in [y, R]$, to pay $\tau(a)$ dollars at age a as a social security tax payment and that pays the person $b(a)$ dollars in return after retirement, that is, when his or her age is in the range $(R, n]$. At time t, the total tax revenue is $\int_y^R \tau(a)B(t - a, \theta)l(a)da$, and the total outlet is $\int_R^n b(a)B(t - a, \theta)l(a)da$. Before the change in θ, the social security budget is assumed to be balanced, that is,

$$\Delta(\theta) \equiv \int_y^R \tau(a)B(t - a, \theta)l(a)da - \int_R^n b(a)B(a, \theta)l(a)da = 0.$$

Within such a simple social security scenario, we want to study whether the societal budget would improve or deteriorate after θ increases.

As far as the comparison of the *stable* population is concerned, Lee (1980) showed that the sign of $d\Delta(\theta)/d\theta$ hinges upon the difference between the *mean age of tax payment* $\bar{a}_\tau$ and the *mean age of benefit receipt* $\bar{a}_b$. The definitions of these mean ages are, respectively,

$$\bar{a}_\tau = \frac{\int_y^R ag(a, \theta)\tau(a)da}{\int_y^R g(a, \theta)\tau(a)da},$$

$$\bar{a}_b = \frac{\int_R^n ag(a, \theta)b(a)da}{\int_R^n g(a, \theta)b(a)da}.$$

For the social security example examined above, the taxes are all collected before the payment of the benefit; therefore, without having to proceed with any calculation, it should be clear that $\bar{a}_b > \bar{a}_\tau$ must hold. So, applying Lee's theorem (1980), we know that as θ decreases there will be a budget deficit in the *steady state*.

For the transitional period in which population aging really takes place, however, the stable population mean age is not relevant. It is our analysis in section 12.2 that should apply. Below we shall demonstrate the seriousness of the case where the budget deficit worsens while the *process* of population aging is occuring.

Dividing $\Delta(\theta)$ by $B(t - R, \theta)$, we have

$$\frac{\Delta(\theta)}{B(t - R, \theta)} = \int_y^R \tau(a)\frac{B(t - a, \theta)}{B(t - R, \theta)}l(a)da$$

$$- \int_R^n b(a)\frac{B(t - a, \theta)}{B(t - R, \theta)}l(a)da = 0.$$

Differentiating the above equation with respect to θ yields

$$\frac{d\dfrac{\Delta(\theta)}{B(t - R, \theta)}}{d\theta} = \frac{1}{[B(t - R, \theta)]^2}\left[-\Delta(\theta)\frac{dB(t - R, \theta)}{d\theta} + B(t - R, \theta)\cdot\right.$$

$$\left.\left(\int_y^R \tau(a)\frac{d}{d\theta}\left(\frac{B(t - a, \theta)}{B(t - R, \theta)}\right)l(a)da - \int_R^n b(a)\frac{d}{d\theta}\left(\frac{B(t - a, \theta)}{B(t - R, \theta)}\right)l(a)da\right)\right].$$

Because the budget was originally balanced, we have $\Delta(\theta) = 0$, so the first term in the square bracket is zero. Furthermore, equation (12.4) tells us that $d[B(t - a, \theta)/B(t - b, \theta)] > (<) 0$ as $a < (>) b$. Thus, the second term in the square bracket is positive. Therefore, the above expression is positive, and hence $\Delta(\theta)/B(t - R, \theta)$ is increasing in θ. Since

$$\frac{d \dfrac{\Delta(\theta)}{B(t - R, \theta)}}{d\theta} = \frac{\Delta(\theta)}{B(t - R, \theta)} \left[\frac{\dfrac{d\Delta(\theta)}{d\theta}}{\Delta(\theta)} - \frac{\dfrac{dB(t - R, \theta)}{d\theta}}{B(t - R, \theta)} \right] > 0,$$

$\Delta(\theta)$ must be increasing in θ at a rate faster than $B(t - R, \theta)$. In summary, we have the following:

THEOREM 12.4
Suppose the social security budget is balanced originally. If the fertility function is shifted down at time 0, then there will be a budget deficit $\forall t > 0$. Moreover, such a deficit grows at a rate (with respect to θ) faster than $B(t - R, \theta)$.

12.3.2 Age-Specific Income Inequality

Lam (1984) considered an age-specific distribution of income and discussed the impact of changing the steady-state population growth rate on the income inequality index. The particular inequality index he studied was the coefficient of variation. It turns out that, as the population growth rate changes, the sign of the resulting change in the coefficient of variation depends on the "mean age of the variance of income," which is not easy to interpret. We will now propose another approach to evaluate the change in age-specific income inequality when the fertility rate increases.

Let y be the age when a person's income becomes positive, and let the age density conditional on $a \geq y$ be $h(a, \theta)$, where θ is the parameter in the fertility function. According to theorem 12.2, we know that for any subrange of $[0, n]$ and for $\theta > 0$, there is an $\tilde{a}$ such that

$$h(a, 0) < (\geq) h(a, \theta) \quad \text{iff } a > (\leq) \tilde{a}.$$

The usual age-specific income profile is as shown in figure 12.2, where R is usually the age of retirement. For the time being, suppose we are studying the income inequality of the working group, that is, $a \in [y, R]$. Then the income $i(a)$ is likely to be increasing in a for the full range of $[y, R]$: $i'(a) > 0 \; \forall a \in [y, R]$. One can interpret the inequality studied for the age range of $[y, R]$ as the inequality of *earnings*.

Atkinson (1970) argued that every inequality measure has a particular social welfare function imbedded in it and that it would be better to make an inequality comparison without any restrictive welfare specification.

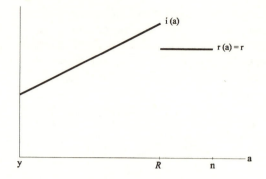

FIGURE 12.2 Lifetime income before and after retirement.

Atkinson also showed us that societal income stochastic dominance is useful for inequality comparison. In our context, we can write the social welfare function on the age domain $[y, R]$ as:

$$W(\theta) = \int_y^R u(i(a))h(a, \theta)da, \tag{12.8}$$

where $u(i)$ is the indirect utility function of a person with income i. It is well known (see Hadar and Russell, 1969, theorem 1) that, as long as $u'(.) > 0$ (so that $du(i(a))/da = u' \cdot i' > 0$), if $H(a, 0)$ first-degree stochastically dominates $H(a, \theta)$, then $W(0) \geq W(\theta)$. In this sense, we can establish the inequality impact of increasing θ. In summary, we have:

THEOREM 12.5
If the age-specific social welfare function is as shown in (12.8) with $u'(.) > 0$, then population aging caused by a reduction in θ increases $W(\theta)$.

When we are considering the income inequality of the whole range of ages $[y, n]$, then there will be definite analytical results only in qualified situations. The following analysis is an example. Suppose the before-retirement income is $i(a)$ for $a < R$, which increases with age at a constant rate. Let the after-retirement income be a fixed pension payment $r(a) = r$ for $a \geq R$. Then the social welfare is

$$W(\theta) = \int_y^R u(i(a))h(a, \theta)da + \int_R^n u(r)h(a, \theta)da.$$

Differentiating W with respect to θ, integrating by parts, and using the identity[3]

$$H_\theta(y, \theta) = H_\theta(n, \theta) = 0,$$

we get

$$W'(\theta) = [u(i(R)) - u(r)]H_\theta(R, \theta) + \int_y^R -u'(i(a)) \cdot i'(a)H_\theta(a, \theta)da.$$

Since $i'(.) > 0$, we know that the second term of the above equation is negative. Furthermore, $i(R) > r$ is likely to be true (see figure 12.2). So the sign of W' depends on the relative sizes of these two terms. In the above expression, $u(.)$ is specified by the researcher, $i(z)$ and $i'(.)$ can be estimated, and $H_\theta(., \theta)$ can be calculated from the life table. Making such a comparison seems to be a more intuitive job than checking the mean age of income variance, as was done in the previous literature.

In reality, if elderly people have during their working lives made good investment plans which ensure that their pension income does not shrink much after retirement, then the difference between $i(R)$ and r is likely to be small, and hence $W'(\theta) \leq 0$ will hold.

12.4 ALTERNATIVE AGING INDEXES

12.4.1 Problems with the Head-Count Ratio

Most demographers seem to have been used to the usual measure of population aging: the proportion of the population older than some critical age, which, as we mentioned at the beginning of this chapter, is referred to as the "head-count ratio" of the aged. But as Sen (1976) pointed out in a different context, the head-count ratio is in general a very crude index for capturing the information in the right tail of a distribution. Sen's original focus was the measurement of poverty, corresponding to the left-tail population of an income distribution. In this section I shall show that the issues and methods used for the measure of poverty can be applied to the study of age structure and can help us improve the measurement and characterization of population aging.

Sen's main criticism of the head-count ratio index is that this index is completely insensitive to the information *within* the tail distribution. Taking the measurement of aging as an example, the head-count ratio index cannot reveal the "distance" between particular groups of the elderly and the critical age point. Specifically, a 15% head-count ratio (over 65) may correspond to either a population with 15% of people mostly in the range [65,69], or a population with 15% mostly in the range [75,79]. Moreover, the head-count ratio is also insensitive to the relative proportions of various age groups among the old, and any change in the age density within the right tail cannot affect the head-count aging index.

12.4.2 Some Desirable Axioms

The research of Sen (1976), Foster and Shorrocks (1988), and Foster et al. (1984) gives us some insight into finding a better aging index. Sen and Foster et al. proposed several axioms to motivate their generation of the *poverty* index. We adapt the relevant interpretation to our context and restate them below.

- *Monotonicity Axiom* (MA): Other things being equal, an increase in age of a person older than the critical age (say 65) must increase the aging index.
- *Transfer Axiom* (TA): Other things being equal, a pure marginal transfer of age from a person older than the critical age to anyone younger than the critical age must reduce the aging index.
- *Transfer Sensitivity Axiom* (TSA): If a marginal transfer $t > 0$ of age takes place from an aged person with age a_i to another aged person aged $a_i - d$ ($d > 0$), then the magnitude of the reduction in the aging index must be smaller for smaller a_i.

One should keep in mind that the above-mentioned "transfer" of age cannot be understood literally. A transfer of age from a person in the age-a group to a person in the age-b group is essentially a small variation in the age density around point a and a corresponding variation in the age density around point b. Intuitively this is not so different from our usual understanding of the transfer of incomes. In the monotonicity axiom, there is no transfer of ages, and so only the density around the old-age region in question is changed.

The head-count ratio index does not satisfy any of the above three axioms. It violated MA because it cannot characterize the "distance" between a particular old age group and the critical age (65). Nor does the head-count ratio satisfy TA or TSA, for it is completely insensitive to the "transfer" of ages above 65.

12.4.3 Theoretical Structure

Let $G^{-1}(p) \equiv \inf\{s \geq 0 | G(s) \geq p\}$ for $p \in [0, 1]$. Given an age distribution function $G(.)$ and a critical age z, with the same insight as that in Foster and Shorrocks (1988), we define the following aging indexes:

$$I_1(G; z) \equiv 1 - G(z),$$

$$I_2(G; z) \equiv \frac{1}{(n - z)} \int_{G(z)}^{1} [G^{-1}(p) - z] dp,$$

$$I_\alpha(G; z) \equiv \frac{1}{(n - z)^{\alpha-1}} \int_{G(z)}^{1} [G^{-1}(p) - z]^{\alpha-1} dp, \quad \alpha \geq 3.$$

As one can see, I_1 is the conventional head-count ratio. I_2 is a weighted proportion of the old, which weights the proportion older than the critical age z by the difference between z and their corresponding ages. In other words, I_2 is a normalized sum of the proportion of the old group. I_α, $\alpha \geq 3$, is a similar weighted sum except that we give more weight to the group that is particularly aged (those with age much larger than z). Evidently, $I_1, I_2,$ and I_α are all in the [0,1] range. Furthermore, Foster et al. (1984) proved

THEOREM 12.6 *(Foster et al. 1984, p.763)*
I_α satisfies the monotonicity axiom for any $\alpha > 0$, the transfer axiom for any $\alpha > 1$, and the transfer sensitivity axiom for $\alpha > 2$.

Thus, the I_α index defined above is closely connected with the desirable axioms.

For an arbitrary age distribution function $G(a)$, let $G_1(a) \equiv G(a)$, and for $\alpha = 2, 3, \cdots$, let G_α be defined iteratively by

$$G_\alpha(s) = \int_0^s G_{\alpha-1}(a)\,da.$$

Similarly, we can define F_α for another age distribution $F(.)$. We then characterize the α-degree stochastic dominance relation as follows. We say that $F(a)$ α-degree stochastically dominates $G(a)$ if and only if

$$F_\alpha(s) \leq G_\alpha(s) \quad \forall s > 0$$
$$F_\alpha(s) < G_\alpha(s) \quad \text{for some } s > 0.$$

Foster and Shorrocks (1988) proved a slightly different version of the following theorem which applies to all positive integers α.

THEOREM 12.7
F α-degree stochastically dominates G if and only if

$$I_\alpha(F, z) \geq I_\alpha(G, z) \quad \forall z$$
$$I_\alpha(F, z) > I_\alpha(G, z) \quad \text{for some } z.$$

Theorem 12.7 says that there is a one-to-one correspondence between stochastic dominance and the ranking of aging indexes. It is well known from Fishburn (1980) that an α-degree stochastic dominance implies an $\alpha + 1$ degree stochastic dominance. We have shown in equation (12.7) that the age distribution $G(a, \theta_1)$ first-degree stochastically dominates $G(a, \theta_2)$ for $\theta_1 < \theta_2$. Thus $G(a, \theta_1)$ also α-degree stochastically dominates $G(a, \theta_2)$ for $\alpha = 2, 3, \ldots$. Applying theorem 12.7, we know that

$$I_\alpha(G(., \theta_1), z) \geq I_\alpha(G(., \theta_2), z) \quad \forall z$$

must hold, with strict inequality for some z. Thus, applying the Foster and Shorrocks result to our aging discussion, we establish the theorem below.

THEOREM 12.8

Suppose population aging is caused by a reduction in θ in the fertility func-
tion m(a, θ). Suppose θ starts to decrease at time t = 0. Then for any given
z, the aging index I_α (., z) increases for all α > 0 for all t > 0.

If the population aging is caused by a downward shift in the mortality
function, and if such a shift is *neutral*, as defined in the previous section,
then by theorem 12.3 we still have a first-degree stochastic dominance
change in the age distribution, and hence the changing pattern of the aging
indexes I_α can still be predicted.

Theorem 12.8 is important and useful for the following reasons. The I_α
indexes give us some refined aging measures which describe with finer
detail the right tail of the age distribution. As α increases, I_α assigns more
weight to the oldest old, and this information is useful for some purposes.
For instance, if the societal resource demand for old-age medical care is a
high-degree polynomial function of the old people's age, then I_α with a
larger α clearly carries more information than I_1. Second, as long as the
aging phenomenon is caused by a decline in the fertility or mortality function, theorem 12.8 tells us that the changing pattern of the aging index I_α is
predictable, along with the demographic transition. When α = 1, theorem
12.8 is a formal characterization of Coale's (1957) proposition about the
relation between fertility levels and the proportion of young and old population. Finally, for different application purposes, the critical age z may be
chosen differently; but theorem 12.8 also tells us that as θ changes, the
dynamic pattern of change of the I_α indexes would be mutually *consistent*
for any α and any choice of z.

12.4.4 Calculating the Aging Indexes

We proposed in the previous section several aging indexes other than the
head-count ratio to characterize the general phenomenon of population
aging. In table 12.1 we list three aging indexes for eight typically aging countries. The data set is from *Sex and Age Distribution of the World Popula-*
tion, published by the United Nations. The advantage of these indexes has
been discussed in the previous section; we now list a few interesting points.

If we look at the columns for Japan in 1990 and Italy in 1980, we see
that in terms of the I_1 index, Italy is older; whereas in terms of the I_3 index,
Japan is older. Evidently, Japan in the 1990s has more oldest old than did
Italy in 1980. If Japan is to refer to the policy experience of Italy in 1980,
the head-count ratio may carry misleading information. In another instance,
if we compare the I_1 indexes of Japan and Italy in 1970 and 1990, we see
that the I_1 index grew 33% in Italy and 69% in Japan. However, we see that
the I_3 index grew 56% in Italy but 122% in Japan. This shows that the population size of the oldest old in Japan grows much faster than in Italy, and
hence these two countries are experiencing different patterns of aging.

TABLE 12.1. Aging Indexes of Eight Countries

Country	1990			1980			1970		
	I_1	I_2	I_3	I_1	I_2	I_3	I_1	I_2	I_3
United States	.1252	.0484	.0274	.1129	.0418	.0231	.0981	.0355	.0191
Canada	.1122	.0419	.0232	.0939	.0338	.0183	.0786	.0285	.0155
Italy	.1448	.0550	.0311	.1315	.0462	.0242	.1089	.0379	.0199
Netherlands	.1283	.0497	.0282	.1151	.0430	.0236	.1016	.0357	.0188
Japan	.1199	.0444	.0244	.0904	.0307	.0157	.0707	.0225	.0110
Taiwan	.0621	.0192	.0093	.0428	.0124	.0057	.0292	.0283	.0038
S. Korea	.0500	.0157	.0077	.0381	.0113	.0053	.0330	.0100	.0047
Singapore	.0606	.0211	.0111	.0472	.0141	.0066	.0337	.0095	.0044

Source: *Sex and Age Distribution of the World Population* New York: United Nations (Department of International Economic and Social Affairs), various years.

Finally, it is obvious from table 12.1 that the Newly Industrial Countries all had much faster aging processes than the developed ones. This is also consistent with the faster speed of their demographic transition.

12.5 SUMMARY OF RESULTS

Readers are referred to figure 12.3 for a summary of the results we have derived so far. In this figure, we see that, along with the aging process after θ decreases, both the age density and the aging indexes satisfying desirable axioms have predictable changing patterns. The stochastic dominance shift in age densities can also help us make better welfare judgment on policies that involve intergenerational transfers.

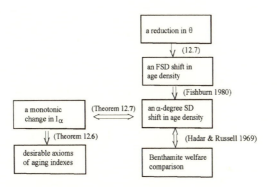

FIGURE 12.3 Consequences of a reduction in θ.

Population Dynamics in the Past and in the Future

CHAPTER 13

Population Size and Early Development

13.1 BACKGROUND

13.1.1 Various Stages of Economic Growth

The Malthusian theory hypothesizes that the natural environment imposes various capacity constraints on human population growth and that population size has been and will be checked by these constraints. In such a classical theory, which was presumably motivated by observations of the ancient world, population might be the most important dynamic variable, although its role is rather passive: population is a variable that would be affected by, but would not affect, the environment. Boserup (1981), however, sees the role of population in the development of human economy as more consequential. She gave many persuasive examples that showed that, at least for the period up to the mid-twentieth century, population size might be a variable which actively spurred technological progress. This is also the viewpoint held by Lee (1986) and Pryor and Maurer (1982).

After the Industrial Revolution, the role of population in economic dynamics, along with the reduction of mortality fluctuations and the increasing control of female fertility, evidently became secondary. The key variable that dominates the analysis of economic dynamics in the neoclassical growth theory along the lines of Solow (1956) is capital (or per capita capital). In Solow's growth model, the role of population is minimal in the steady state: neither the *level* nor the *growth rate* of the steady-state per capita consumption has anything to do with the *size* of a population; only the steady-state per capita income level will be affected by the population *growth rate*.[1]

The growth pattern in the latter half of the twentieth century is markedly different. A key feature of our recent growth experience is the rapid innovation of new technologies. Modern growth theory has embraced the concept of increasing returns to explain such a unique growth pattern. However, various versions of the theory of increasing returns turn out to be necessarily linked to population. The hypothesis of *learning by doing* implies that growth in productivity is an increasing function of aggregate production, which is itself positively related to the size of population. The *human capital approach* to the theory of growth assumes that the total stock of human capital has an external effect on production, which thereby causes a positive relationship between population and aggregate output. Theories that emphasize the *nonrivalry* property of knowledge suggest that larger populations generate greater public access to knowledge and thus an increasing return on technological growth.[2]

The three hypotheses to the theory of increasing returns discussed above (learning by doing, human capital, and non rivalry production factors) approach the problem of growth from different directions. They all arrive at the same conclusion, however, which is that there is a scale effect (Backus et al., 1992) in growth: quite simply, large countries grow faster. Most economists have tried to preclude population as a scale variable, citing the counterexamples of Bangladesh, China, and India. Many have dealt with this problem by changing the variable that enters the equation of increasing returns in such a way as to remove the influence of population. Rivera-Batiz and Romer (1991), for example, showed that the steady-state growth of income was an increasing function of population. A slightly different approach was taken by Romer (1990), in which the functional setting of the technological-change equation is altered. In this way, the growth of income depends not on population size but rather on human capital. Similarly, Kremer (1993) showed that small changes in the setting of the law-of-motion equation of technology generate widely different predictions in the steady-state relationship between population and economic growth over the past "one million years."

13.1.2 Conflicts Between Theory and Evidence

But these attempts, for reasons given below, were never satisfactory. First, although we might be able to generate some plausible implications by trying out all possible analytical settings of the technological-change equation, such a mechanical trial-and-error approach is obviously *ad hoc*, and even the best-fit model will be hard to interpret. Second and more important, empirical observations have not been motivating factors in the above-mentioned mechanical changes in the functional relationship between population and technology. For instance, the abundant persuasive evidence contained in the well-received work of Boserup (1965, 1981), which covers both the ancient period and the two most recent centuries after the Industrial Revolution, has not received sufficient attention in previous modeling.

Mechanically altering the setting of the technological-change equation, as was done by many researchers, is unlikely to produce a model that is an abstraction of reality. Third, although *a scale* effect might be established empirically in specific industries over a certain period of time, casual observations (India vs. Belgium) and countrywise empirical work (Barro and Sala-i-Martin, 1995) both deny any definite long-run relationship between economic growth and population size or growth. But theories equipped with a population-technology functional equation will always generate an either (weakly) positive or negative relationship between population and growth, as one can see from all the papers cited above. This kind of (either positive or negative) one-way prediction is certainly not compatible with the variations of the empirical evidence in different historical epochs.

Contemporary observations in India (high density/low growth) and Belgium (high density/high growth) might tempt one to dismiss the hypothetical relationship between population and economic growth mentioned above and argue that population has *no relation* with economic growth. However, the strong evidence provided by Boserup (1981) appears to imply *some relation* between economic growth and population size in most areas and most periods of human history. Given such conflicting viewpoints, a compromise conjecture might be that there is some *equivocal* (not one-to-one) relationship between population and technological growth. The questions then are, What is this equivocal relationship and how do we embody such an equivocal relationship in an analytical model?

Lee (1986, 1988) and a few others have attempted to define such an equivocal relationship by introducing population into the technological-change equations in a nonlinear fashion, so as to generate multiple analytical "regimes" in the dynamic phase diagram. These regimes then correspond either to the Malthusian case or to the Boserupian case, and varying the initial values of parameters may lead to different dynamics under different regimes. However, this method seems to have weak predictive power. Definite analytical solutions to the regime-separation border on the phase diagram can be difficult to derive, making it problematic to classify countries into various regimes.

Bonneuil (1994) argued that population size does not drive technological changes in a mechanistic manner; it only gives an indirect pressure. Assuming that technological changes need time and effort, Bonneuil showed that a larger population size reduces the time left for human beings to avoid an undesirable situation. My theory in this chapter provides a macro prediction compatible with that of Bonneuil's; however, I put more emphasis on the decision-theoretical foundations at the individual level.

13.1.3 Population as a Passive Support

I believe that there does not currently exist a unified theory that can explain the relationship between economic growth and population size throughout all periods of human history. The roles of population in early primitive development and in modern industrial development are in fact quite different. In a primitive economy, the size of population is important for the development of cities and markets, which in turn facilitates a finer division of labor. But for modern economies, the engine of economic growth is the continuous advance of technological innovation, which has no direct relationship to population size.

I also believe that, even in ancient times, there is no one-to-one relationship between population size and economic growth. A detailed reading of the evidence in Boserup tells us that population is never a variable that *actively* enters the law of motion equation of technology; rather, it is a variable that *passively* supports the technology advancement. Kuznets (1960), Simon (1977, 1981), and Ng (1986) all argue that a large population size spurs technological change because it increases the number of potential inventors or because it reduces the per capita cost of invention. However, this thinking is not entirely consistent with Boserup's (1981) evidence. In her book, Boserup repeatedly argued that only with a large population could an economy support the development of various infrastructures, which are usually very labor-intensive. These infrastructures improve the overall transaction efficiency, which in turn facilitates the division of labor and economic growth. Any attempt that characterizes Boserup's idea should not ignore the special feature of infrastructure that connects the size of population with the finer division of labor.

Consider this hypothetical example, which illustrates the dependence of technology on population. Suppose we reduce the population of the earth to only half a million and consider the dramatic impact this would have on existing transportation technologies: most transportation infrastructure would become unnecessary. It is likely that there would be no more need for mass-transit trains, for example. Not only would production be halted, but related technological innovation would also cease. The extensive computer reservation systems used by all kinds of transportation facilities would no longer be needed to support the reduced number of passengers, and it is doubtful that the tax base of such a small number of people could possibly be sufficient to support the train system. It may even be argued that the available labor force would be too small to maintain any advanced technology. Without a sufficiently large population, the economy is simply insufficient to support and sustain, much less invent, modern transportation infrastructure and related technology.

Notice that the implications in the above example are not the same as those of the existing theories in which population size appears on the right-hand side of the law-of-motion equation of technological change or human capital accumulation. Those models imply that between technological change and population size there is an *active, if-and-only-if* relationship. But my hypothetical example above says that population is no more than a *passive support* for technological changes.

That a large population automatically generates advancements in technology is an argument that is unsupported historically. It is obviously undesirable for economic models to make predictions that are incompatible with reality, but that is exactly what happens with models which place population on the right-hand side of the technology law-of-motion equation.

13.1.4 Transition Stages Versus Steady States

The above discussion also suggests that population does not play a role in the *steady state*; rather it is a key variable that facilitates either the *static* division of labor or the transition of economic development. As Lee (1986) noted when he summarized Boserup's theory, "The Smithian advantage to a finer division of labor is a static nature, and not to be confused with the present argument that the division of labor encourages technological progress through *learning by doing* (italics added), and through other indirect ways" (p. 102). Thus, to accurately characterize the role of population on technological growth, in this chapter I ignore the continuous, dynamic version of the model of division of labor and concentrate upon the static case. I will establish models that connect population, infrastructure, and the division of labor and discuss the transition from primitive to modern economy. The model in section 13.3 discusses the transition from primitive to modern technologies. Sections 13.4 and 13.5 are based on stylized facts observed from Boserup (1981) and are intended to provide an explanation for early economic development. The role of population in contemporary and future economic growth will be discussed in the next chapter.

13.2 SOME STYLIZED EVIDENCE

Every economist worth his or her salt can cite Ester Boserup's (1981) book on population and technological change. In fact, in recent literature on the subject, this book is referenced quite frequently. Often, the implications obtained are not very compatible with empirical observations. We believe that this is a result of a failure to appreciate many key but abstract features of her work. This failure can be remedied by a careful rereading of her text.

Boserup's observations span the globe: from America to Europe, African and Arab countries, the Oceania islands, and Southern and Eastern Asia. The levels of technologies she surveys range from hunter–gatherer societies to the mid-twentieth-century industrial world. Even various types of technology are studied in detail: agricultural, industrial, urbanization and transportation technologies are all covered. She treats the relationship between population and technological changes as being not dissimilar to the relationship of population to economic growth.

The stylized modern observations of Romer (1994) are very much in accord with Boserup's research on technological change preceding the mid-twentieth century. Romer (pp. 12–13) noted that "Technological advance comes from things that people do. . . . When more people start prospecting for gold or experimenting with bacteria, more valuable discoveries will be found." Boserup similarly finds (p. 4) that "there is a link between the motivation for invention and the amount of invention . . . such a link existed even before the time of organized scientific research." This motivation for invention, Boserup conjectured, was strongly related to population, for technology could never become widespread unless it was commercialized. Research and development have always been stimulated by the possibility of future returns on investment, which of course depends on commercialization. It is less obvious, but no less true, that not only the dissemination but also the invention of new technologies is a result of commercialization, potential or realized. Jones and Wolf (1969) found that fertilizer, in one example, could not possibly be utilized on a large scale until the development of a railway network. Likewise, Boserup noted (p. 116) that "large scale imports of food and fodder had to await the steamship." As we shall see shortly, transportation technologies are particularly sensitive to population dynamics.

Romer suggests that "Discoveries differ from other inputs in the sense that many people can use them at the same time" (p. 12). Lee (1986) and other demographic economists have reached similar conclusions. As previously stated, this property of technology can be thought of as nonrivalry in general, although Boserup explicitly links this property to transportation technologies. Before the Industrial Revolution, her argument goes, the main advantage of a dense population was "the better possibilities to create infrastructure" (p. 129). Irrigation technology, the building and maintenance of roads, digging canals, and the development of a railway are all cited as examples of projects that are quite impossible without a sufficiently large population. She notes that the sixth-century A.D. construction of a canal system in China required a labor force of more than a million dedicated workers. The canals facilitated the convenient long-distance transportation of large quantities of foodstuffs and other products. Such a labor-intensive project could never have been undertaken by a sparse population. Lee (1986) did not miss this point, as he said that "the larger the population engaged in non-food producing activities, the greater the possible division of labor, and the greater the possibilities for technological advance" (p. 102).

It is important to note that this is a passive advantage of a large population, in contrast to the active role of population in the models developed by Ng (1986) and Simon (1981). It is historically evident that large populations can support infrastructure innovations, but it does not follow that this leads to the spontaneous generation of new inventions.

Peasant families before the Industrial Revolution did not toil in the field from sunup until sundown. Indeed, Boserup asserts that family members must have spent a considerable amount of time producing tools and other equipment, making clothing, and repairing dwellings. Agriculture was almost certainly only a part-time occupation in light of these additional responsibilities. The Industrial Revolution resulted in these good and services becoming widely available through specialized individuals or factories. Such specialization is facilitated by a large population for three primary reasons. First, mass production only becomes profitable when an economy (market) is large enough. Second, as mentioned earlier, an extensive transportation infrastructure is completely contingent upon population size. This infrastructure obviously increases transaction efficiency and encourages the increasing division of labor. Third, as noted by most economic historians, the development of a transportation infrastructure is crucial to urbanization. This is an important point when one considers that most urban workers are not involved in the production of food, and that food must therefore be transported, sometimes great distances, from the source to the consumers. This point is illustrated throughout Boserup's book in many examples. Because it is easily demonstrated that a large population is a precondition for an extensive transportation infrastructure, it follows that it is also a requirement of urbanization.

Romer (1994) also includes one further observation that was not mentioned in Boserup's earlier work. This is the concept of ownership of invention, or, as Romer puts it, "Many individuals and firms have market power and earn monopoly rents on discoveries" (p. 13). Although this may be thought of as a counterexample to nonrivalry, the scope of Boserup's book, extensive though it is, does not cover the most recent technological innovations. Such a counterexample does not preclude the important link between population and technology from being extended into modern times, hoeever, as our mass-transit train example illustrated. Population size is, at a minimum, an important variable in the transformation of a primitive economy into one of advanced technology.

Summarizing the above discussion, there are three observations which motivate our modeling in the next two sections.

1. The most important advantage of a large population size is its greater potential to support more advanced infrastructure, which has the nonrivalry property.
2. The most important infrastructure in early economic development is transport technology. When this technology improves, the transaction efficiency of food, fertilizer, clothing, and other products is enhanced, which in turn facilitates the division of labor.
3. An ever-finer division of labor enables some people to specialize in agriculture and some in the industrial sector. The economy of specialization fosters increases in output in both sectors.[3]

13.3 From Primitive to Market Economy: The Role of Population Size

Goodfriend and McDermott (1995, hereinafter GM) divided the history of economic development into three epochs separated by two transitions: from primitive economy to preindustrial market economy and from preindustrial to industrial economy. Their model provided a rough picture of the role of population size in the *transition* of technologies in economic history.

GM assumed that each household is endowed with a primitive production technology with diminishing returns:

$$Y_p = B\ln(1 + e_p m), \tag{13.1}$$

where Y_p is the output, e_p is the fraction of time that each household member works in the primitive sector, and m is the number of family members. From (13.1) we see that the marginal productivity of e_p,

$$\partial Y_p / \partial e_p = \frac{Bm}{1 + e_p m},$$

is decreasing and convex in e_p.

Besides the above primitive technology, there is a market-based production technology that uses a large number of intermediate goods:

$$Y = \left(e_y hN\right)^{1-\alpha} \int_0^M \left[x(i)\right]^\alpha di, \tag{13.2}$$

where $0 < \alpha < 1$; N is the number of workers (population) in the economy, each of whom has human capital h and devotes e_y fraction of his time to the production of final goods; $x(i)$ is the quantity of intermediate input indexed by i; and M is the upper bound of the continuous index measurement of i. If e_k is an individual's total fraction of time spent in the *market* sector, then given e_y, $e_k - e_y \equiv e_I$ is the fraction of time spent in the production of the intermediate goods. Notice that equation (13.2) is the Ethier (1982) production function that has an intrinsic increasing return in the variety of intermediate goods.

GM solved their model as follows: Each final good producer chooses labor hours and intermediate inputs to maximize profit, taking output prices as given. This maximization generates a demand price function for labor and intermediate goods. The intermediate-good producers are monopolistically competitive; they take the above-mentioned demand prices as given and choose the optimal output $x(i)$. The market sector will be in equilibrium if the following conditions are satisfied: (i) all firms maximize their profits; (ii) intermediate- and final-good producers all have zero profits; (iii) labor supply and demand of all sectors are equal. It turns out that in equilibrium the *degree of specialization*, denoted M, is determined by

$$M = \alpha^* e_k hN, \tag{13.3}$$

where α^* is a constant related to α. As one can see from the above equation, the degree of specialization is an increasing function of e_k, h, and N, which are all variables related to the scale or efficiency of the market sector but unrelated to the primitive sector (see [13.1]).

GM also showed that the reduced-form final output from the market sector in equilibrium can be shown to be $Y = A(e_k h N)^{2-\alpha}$. Since $2 - \alpha > 1$, the above equation shows that the final-good production exhibits increasing return to effective labor $e_k h N$. The wage in the market sector can be written as

$$w = Ah^{2-\alpha}\left(e_k N\right)^{1-\alpha},\tag{13.4}$$

which is increasing and concave in e_m.

As we compare the market-sector wage function in (13.4) with the marginal productivity of e_p ($\partial Y_p/\partial e_p$) from the primitive sector, we can see the role of population size in economic transition. Notice that $\partial Y_p/\partial e_p$ is independent of N, but the market wage will decrease as N increases. If both the primitive sector and the market sector exist, then in equilibrium w and $\partial Y_p/\partial e_p$ must be equal for some N. When N is small, w is longer than $\partial Y_p/\partial e_p$, so the equilibrium is a primitive autarky.[4] When N increases, the market sector begins to appear, and eventually as N is sufficiently large, the primitive sector shrinks to its minimum. In short, GM (1995) proved the following theorem:

THEOREM 13.1
The transformation from a primitive economy to a market economy is possible only when the population size is sufficiently large.

GM also discussed the increasing return property of the evolution of human capital. As the economy develops to a certain stage, individuals find it more profitable to spend some fraction of their time accumulating human capital. The accumulation of human capital triggers the *Industrial Revolution* and continuous technological advancement later on. After the Industrial Revolution, improved hygienic and medical knowledge increases the size of population significantly. So the population size today far exceeds the level necessary for support of most of the invented infrastructure or other nonrivalry goods. It has been a consensus of modern growth theorists that the size of population is not an important variable for explaining the research-and-development-oriented technological changes of recent years. That is why the role of population diminishes.

13.4 INFRASTRUCTURE AND THE DIVISION OF LABOR

The model by Goodfriend and McDermott (1995) that I reviewed in the previous section has given us a rough idea of the role of population size in supporting a market economy. But as far as the role of population size is concerned, their theory has several drawbacks. First, Boserup (1981) gave a clear exposition in various places in her book of the idea that the connection between population size and the finer division of labor was established through the development of the *infrastructure* sector. Evidently, the G&M model has not captured such a feature. Second, it is important to notice that the macro size of labor specialized in the infrastructure sector is a result of each individual's micro job decision. Furthermore, when an individual is "specialized," his or her job decision is in fact a corner solution. The scenario Boserup described is a process of an ever-finer division of labor, from the nonexistence of the infrastructure sector to the existence and advancement of this sector. Because such a process involves switches from one (job) corner decision to another, it is natural to resort to the corner equilibrium framework of Yang and Ng (1993) to proceed with our analysis.

In the following section, I will present a model that is compatible with Boserup's observations. The model, developed by Chu and Tsai (1995), posits that: (i) a publicly accessible transportation system exists; (ii) such technology is more advanced when labor is more specialized; (iii) improved transportation technology naturally leads to improved transaction efficiency, which in turn facilitates a finer division of labor; and (iv) because the division of labor involves an economy of specialization, a finer division of labor can lead to an increase in per capita income. Chu and Tsai's major implication mirrors Boserup's main hypothesis: improvement in economic welfare is only possible when a population is sufficiently large, but the reverse of this may not be true.

13.4.1 Preferences and Technology

Chu and Tsai (1995) considered an economy with N identical individuals and one commodity for consumption Y^c. Without loss of generality, each individual's utility function is assumed to be $U(Y^c) = Y^c$. One's net consumption is composed of two parts: $Y^c = Y + kY^d$, where Y is the quantity one produces by oneself and Y^d is the amount bought from the market. There is $1 - k$ proportion of goods lost in the process of transaction, and so we premultiply Y^d by k. Thus, $k \in [0,1]$ can be treated as the transaction efficiency coefficient of the consumption good.

We simplify the production process in the GM model and assume that there is only one intermediate good Z. Each individual has one unit of labor time available, which will be devoted to the production of either Y or Z. Let l_y and l_z be the respective time inputs; then we have $l_y + l_z = 1$. Chu and Tsai suppose that only labor is used to produce Z, and the production function is

$$Z + Z^s = l_z^a. \tag{13.5}$$

In (13.5), it is assumed that $a > 1$, which means that there are "economies of specialization."[5] The prouced intermediate output will either be sold in the market (Z^s) or used for one's productio (Z).

Let Y be the self-provided amount of final goods, Y^d and Y^s be the final good bought and sold, respectively, and r be the transaction efficiency of the intermediate good. Following Yang and Ng (1993), the production of final output is assumed to be Cobb–Douglas:

$$Y + Y^s = \left(Z + rZ^d\right)^\alpha \left(l_y^a\right)^{1-\alpha}, \qquad (13.6)$$

where $\alpha \in (0,1)$ is a parameter. $Z + rZ^d$ in (13.6) is the total amount of intermediate goods used, together with labor, to produce the total consumption output $Y + Y^s$. This output is to be either self-consumed (Y) or sold (Y^s). In (13.5) and (13.6), if one chooses to have $l_z = 1$ or $l_y = 1$, we say that one is "specialized."

13.4.2 The Infrastructure Sector

To embody the influence of transportation technology on transaction efficiency, which is Boserup's insight, it is assumed that the transaction efficiency coefficient k is determined by $k = \tilde{k}\,(I,\theta)$, where I is the level of infrastructure construction. θ in this $\tilde{k}$ function is a vector of other variables, such as literacy ratio, cultural background, and government attitude (Boserup, 1981). To simplify the analysis, the possible influence of I on r is ignored in the analysis.

The level of infrastructure construction is assumed to be a function of the amount of labor units devoted to this sector, denoted N_I. Thus the transaction efficiency function can be explicitly written as

$$k = \tilde{k}\left(I\left(N_I\right),\ \theta\right) \equiv k\left(N_I,\ \theta\right).$$

It is assumed that the infrastructure sector has positive but diminishing marginal productivity:

$$\frac{\partial k}{\partial N_I} > 0, \quad \frac{\partial^2 k}{\partial N_I^2} < 0.$$

13.5 POPULATION SIZE AND THE DIVISION OF LABOR

There are three goods in the model we just introduced: Z, Y, and I. Individuals who are specialized in the production of $i = Y, Z, I$ are called i-specialists. Yang and Ng (1993) showed that there are only three possible equilibria in the above model: (i) an autarky equilibrium in which each individual produces both Y and Z, and there is no infrastructure construction; (ii) an equilibrium with both Y-specialists and Z-specialists, and there is no infrastructure construction; (iii) an equilibrium with all three kinds of specialists and infrastructure construction.

All producers of Y and Z are price takers, and their incomes come from the sale of their production in the market. We assume that there is a benevolent dictator who collects taxes from all users of the infrastructure and uses this tax revenue to pay the wages of the *I*-specialists. In equilibrium, the demand and supply of all produced goods must be equal. Furthermore, since each individual is assumed to be identical *ex ante*, the freedom of choosing jobs will impose the condition of equal indirect utilities in the equilibrium.

Let a subscript *A* indicate the first equilibrium scenario (autarky), *D* indicate the second scenario (division of labor without the infrastructure sector), and *I* indicate the third scenario (division of labor with the infrastructure sector). Chu and Tsai (1995) showed that the indirect utility of a typical individual corresponding to each of these three scenarios is as follows:

$$U_A = \alpha^{\alpha\alpha}\left(1-\alpha\right)^{\alpha(1-\alpha)},$$

$$U_D = \alpha^{\alpha}\left(1-\alpha\right)^{1-\alpha} r^{\alpha} k_0^{\alpha},$$

$$U_I = \alpha^{\alpha}\left(1-\alpha\right)^{1-\alpha} r^{\alpha} k\left(N_I,\ \theta\right)^{\alpha}.$$

The number of *i*-specialists ($i = Y, Z, I$) in these three scenarios can also be calculated. Through straightforward comparative static analysis, Chu and Tsai proved the following theorems:

THEOREM 13.2
In scenario three, the equilibrium number of individuals devoted to the infrastructure sector, denoted N_I, increases as the total population size (N) increases.

THEOREM 13.3
U_I is an increasing function of the total population size N.

By comparing the relative size of U_A, U_D, and U_I, the following result can also be derived:

THEOREM 13.4
In an economy with a larger population size, it is more likely that scenario three will appear.

Boserup's idea that a larger population size can support a more advanced infrastructure sector is formally characterized in theorem 13.2. Several authors of previous research argued that a larger population size can support more public infrastructure projects because the per capita cost of supporting each public project is less. But such an argument is flawed. In a market economy with the freedom to choose jobs, the number of people in the infrastructure sector is *endogenously* determined; it is each individual's job-choice micro decision that determines the overall size of each sector. Without the result in theorem 13.2, the relationship between N and N_I cannot be predicted with certainty.

Theorem 13.3 says that the utility level under the third scenario is an increasing function of N. We also notice that the utilities of the other two scenarios (U_D and U_A) are independent of N. That is why a larger population size can possibly sustain a higher utility level and support a more refined division of labor, as stated in theorem 13.4.

Theorem 13.3 above is consistent with most of the observations in Boserup's book. Notice that the role of population is just a passive support of possibly better welfare. When N is larger, it is more likely that the maximum utility *achievable* is larger; but there is no definite mechanism that can lead to such a maximum. For instance, if the change in population size is not significant enough, then the economy may remain in the old scenario with a primitive division of labor; hence, the utility level is insensitive to the small change in population size. Furthermore, if there is a fixed area of land, then the usual assumption of diminishing return to land may even reduce individual welfare, which is what the Malthusian theory would predict. To give another simple example, let us suppose that the dictator of a country may not be at all "benevolent." In this case, even if the change in population size is large enough, there is really no way for the economy to move to a high-utility scenario.

13.6 Discussion

In the previous sections we have shown how a large population size can *make possible* the advancement of the infrastructure sector, improved transaction efficiency, a finer division of labor and specialization of workers, and the resulting enhancement of economic welfare. Chu (1997) extended the above analysis to the case with many intermediate-good sectors and found that the results are essentially the same as described in theorems 13.2–13.4. These results are also consistent with Boserup's analysis of why Japan was a country more suitable for industrialization than China and India in the nineteenth century, despite the fact that China, India, and Japan all had fairly large population sizes. Boserup pointed out that government attitude, as well as other natural and historical conditions, had dominated the adaptation pattern of industrialization in these Asian countries. This again shows that population size is merely a passive support for further economic development.

The focus of this chapter is on the role of population size in the transition from primitive to market economy. As to the role of population in modern research-and-development-generated technological changes, I have no quarrel with the prevalent view that it is the size of human capital, not the physical number of people, that matters. But I have reservations concerning the common prediction of the growth theory, which is that the economy will converge to a steady-state balanced growth path with continuously improving welfare and possibly continuously growing population. To many economists, the classical Malthusian capacity-constraint hypothesis may have become out of date. But if we consider a wider perspective, it is not at all clear that human beings can enjoy a growth path without threat. In the next chapter we will provide a different viewpoint about long-term environmental constraints.

CHAPTER 14

Population Dynamics
in the Very Long Run

14.1 BACKGROUND

In the last chapter we reviewed the role of population in early economic development. In that ancient period, mortality was significantly affected by exogenous shocks such as famines, epidemics, floods, droughts, and various other direct or indirect environmental uncertainties, and parents' preferences for children were by and large checked by natural constraints. Not until the last three centuries have human beings been able to make significant progress in hygiene and medical knowledge, progress which has facilitated the recent sharp increase in human population.

In the twentieth century, the life expectancy of human beings in many areas of the world has more than doubled compared to the numbers two hundred years ago. Moreover, advanced radar facilities have been able to forecast extreme weather conditions, satellites are able to detect the locations of natural resources accurately, advanced agricultural technology makes barren land cultivable, and computers have also made possible many complex jobs. All these technological advances have increased the welfare of human beings and appear to have pushed back the exogenous constraints we face. As I mentioned in chapter 13, with the support of a sufficiently large population size, the division of labor becomes ever finer, and more and more labor can be devoted to the research and development sector, which in turn facilitates the various technological advances. These advanced technologies are *endogenously* determined by entrepreneurs, in sharp contrast to the situation in ancient times when the existing technology constituted the natural *exogenous* limit to population growth.

As Romer (1990) pointed out, since knowledge has the nonrivalry property, the societal production technology (which embodies the available knowledge frontier) may naturally have the property of increasing returns with respect to physical resource inputs. As a result, the natural-resource carrying capacity constraint becomes relatively inessential. Then it seems that infinite economic growth can be compatible with any size of population without ever being restricted by exogenous checks.

Some environmental economists have challenged the above optimistic prediction. They argue that economic development in fact has gradually damaged the environment and eventually will hurt the economy.[1] Those challenges, however, have never been serious enough to fully counter the above-mentioned infinite-growth argument. As many economists have argued, environmental changes are usually gradual, and therefore the price mechanism should reveal the gradually rising costs associated with environmental degradation, thereby causing adjustments in economic activities. For instance, when a production activity causes environmental damage, it is believed that an imposition of a Pigouvian tax or other government intervention should induce research and development activities to invent a damage-free substitute or damage-reducing machinery and shift the original inefficient solution to an efficient one.

The above argument has two serious flaws: it oversimplifies the relationship between technological advances and environmental changes and it also implicitly assumes away the costs associated with the *process* of technology advances. These flaws will become obvious as we broaden our perspective and consider the problem from the angle of biology and evolutionary ecology.

In the next section, I first review the work of Nerlove (1991, 1993), who studied the evolutionary relationship between population size and the environment, and show under what circumstances there exists a steady-state evolutionary path. Nerlove's definition of environment is different from that in Arrow et al. (1995). The former model is more appropriate for area- or country-specific environments, whereas the latter deals with global ecology and is beyond the policy control of any particular government. Furthermore, the interaction between population and ecology involves a much longer time span and is subject to considerations very different from those of ordinary economic decisions. In section 3, I move on to consider the general interaction between population and ecology. Then, in section 4, I set up a mathematical model and briefly discuss the various possible population dynamics in the long run.

14.2 Nerlove's Model

Nerlove (1991, 1993) published two papers concerning the relationship between population size and environmental quality. The central idea behind his model, which was first put forward by Hardin (1968), was that the unpriced or underpriced character of environment or natural resources normally does not enter into parents' cost/benefit analysis of childbearing.

Moreover, since life expectancy in environmentally adverse circumstances is low, parents in such an adverse environment have stronger incentives to bear more children in order to offset the expected high mortality rate. The more children they bear, however, the worse environmental quality they face, which induces an even worse life-expectancy rate. The environmental quality and the population size may evolve in such a way that a vicious circle develops, which evidently becomes a kind of "tragedy of the commons," as mentioned in Hardin (1968).

14.2.1 Formulation

Let the population size and the environmental quality be two state variables in the dynamic system. Nerlove wanted to discover when there would exist a stationary state for the population and environment and how government tax and subsidy policies could avoid the possible occurrence of the tragedy of the commons and bring about Pareto-improving results.

Specifically, Nerlove (1991, 1993) considered a one-sex overlapping-generation model in which people live either one or two periods. The first period is childhood, and people who survive to their second period of life all become parents. Let Z_t denote the state of environmental degradation and N_t the number of children alive at the end of period t, who will instantly become parents at that moment. Nerlove considered the following equation for the dynamic movement of Z_t:

$$Z_t = g(Z_{t-1}, N_{t-1}), \tag{14.1}$$

where $\partial g / \partial Z_{t-1} > 0$ and $\partial g / \partial N_{t-1} > 0$ are assumed. The inequality $\partial g / \partial Z_{t-1} > 0$ characterizes an autocorrelative property for environmental quality, which appears reasonable. The inequality $\partial g / \partial N_{t-1} > 0$ states that the population size affects the environment unfavorably.

The population-growth equation Nerlove proposed is:

$$\frac{N_t}{N_{t-1}} = h(Z_{t-1}). \tag{14.2}$$

Nerlove believed that good environmental quality (i.e., smaller Z_t) makes parents willing to substitute child quality for quantity and reduces childbirth, which represents the case of developed countries, and that poor environmental quality (i.e., larger Z_t) induces childbirth, which represents the situation of developing countries. But as Z_t gets even larger, it is likely that the increasing environmental deterioration raises the death rate. As such, Nerlove argued that h' should change sign just once, with h' being positive (negative) when Z_t is small (large). The shape of the h function is shown in figure 14.1.

A stationary population is characterized by $N_t = N_{t-1} = \overline{N}$, which corresponds to a level of environmental degradation $\overline{Z}$ such that

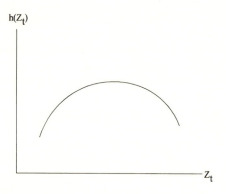

FIGURE 14.1 The shape of $h(.)$.

$$1 = h(\overline{Z}). \tag{14.3}$$

A $\overline{Z}$ satisfying (14.3), however, is not necessarily a sustainable equilibrium; the corresponding stationary population size $\overline{N}$ must also satisfy $\overline{Z} = g(\overline{Z}, \overline{N})$.

Specifically, equations (14.1) and (14.2) constitute a so-called planar system, in which the trajectory of $S_t \equiv (Z_t, N_t)$ is determined given any initial value S_0. Let $(\overline{Z}, \overline{N})$ be any stationary point, and let the various elasticities evaluated at $(\overline{Z}, \overline{N})$ be defined as

$$\xi_z = \frac{\partial g}{\partial Z} \cdot \frac{\overline{Z}}{\overline{Z}}, \quad \xi_N = \frac{\partial g}{\partial N} \cdot \frac{\overline{N}}{\overline{Z}}, \quad \eta_z = h' \cdot \frac{\overline{Z}}{\overline{N}}.$$

Nerlove proved the following result: a stationary point $(\overline{Z}, \overline{N})$ satisfying (14.1) and (14.2) is unstable if $\eta_z > 0$, that is, the rate of change of population responds positively to environmental degradation. If $\eta_z < 0$, then the system (14.1)–(14.2) is stable if and only if $\xi_z - \xi_N\eta_z \leq 1$.

The first part of the above result is intuitive: there can be a stable population only if the population size stops growing as the environment deteriorates. As to the second part of this result, given that $\eta_z < 0 < \xi_z, \xi_N$, the inequality $\xi_z - \xi_N\eta_z \leq 1$ will hold if all these elasticities are small in absolute value. If one of these elasticities is large in absolute value, then the state variable may become so sensitive that the restriction $\xi_z - \xi_N\eta_z \leq 1$ may be violated. In such a case, an oscillatory spiral trajectory may occur. Since the private and social marginal costs of reproduction are not the same, Nerlove (1991) then showed how social interventions in the form of taxes or subsidies can be used to induce a specific birth rate corresponding to a socially desirable stationary state.

If we treat the environment as an organic "prey" population and human beings as predators, then the model in (14.1) and (14.2) can also be viewed as a nonlinear predator–prey model. On the one hand, the environment has its own recovery (from outside shocks) speed when there are no predatory activities by human beings, and the speed of such recovery lessens as the size of the predator population increases. On the other hand, since human beings have to rely on the environment to survive, their reproduction rate is in general a function of the environmental quality. In the predator–prey framework, as we explained in chapter 7, various solutions are possible. The attractor may well be a limit cycle, and there is no reason to expect an equilibrium with a stationary population. The contribution of Nerlove is to provide a reasonable specification of the relationship between environment and population and to show that a desirable equilibrium with a stationary population may be achieved through policy intervention.

14.2.2 Some Alternative Ideas

Nerlove's articles were the first rigorous attempts to study the analytical dynamic interaction between population size and environmental quality. In a sense, Nerlove's framework is a modern version of the Malthusian model: the index of carrying capacity in the Malthusian theory is replaced by the environmental quality variable, and human reproduction is assumed to be related to environmental quality in a nonlinear way. The scope of environment with which Nerlove was concerned, however, has a relatively "local" content. In modern times, tragedies of the commons remain a true concern, but, as Arrow et al. (1995) pointed out, the so-called environmental problems have shifted from local land degradation to the global sustainability of the "earth environment," the ecosystem. Furthermore, given the prevalence of medical services and food aid made possible by advanced transportation and communication technology, local land degradation is unlikely to cause a serious decline in population size. If population dynamics are affected by environmental factors, these factors are more likely tied to the resilience of the *global* ecosystem rather than the sustainability of the local environment.

According to Arrow et al. (1995), the loss of ecosystem resilience as related to economic development has some special features. First, the loss of ecological resistance because of economic development can seldom be anticipated. Neither is it likely that the market or the State can respond to such unexpected ecological shocks.[2] For instance, the damage CFCs (chlorofluorocarbons) and CO_2 inflict on the atmosphere did not catch the attention of scientists until the 1970s, many decades after various greenhouse gases had been extensively emitted (Shaw and Stroup, 1990). But since CFCs are highly stable and can remain in the atmosphere for as long as fifty years, it is already very late now to remedy the economy's previous faults even if we chose to do so.

The second feature of the loss of ecological resilience, also mentioned by Arrow and his associates (1995), is that damage is usually discontinuous and irreversible. Such a discontinuous change in the ecological system may cause a sharp decline in the size of the population. These two features of environmental damage are clearly not in Nerlove's model.

Another comment concerning Nerlove's analysis relates to the policy proposals he made. For a local degradation problem, it is relatively easy for the local government to tax or subsidize to overcome the discrepancy between the public and private cost/benefit calculation. But global ecological problems are by definition international problems; therefore, it is very difficult for any single government to effect a remedy. The resolution of such ecological problems requires international coordination. As long as countries are dominated by their individual concerns, there may be *international* tragedies of the commons.

Given the above observations, it seems necessary to set up an alternative analytical model that more closely reflects the dynamic relationship between population and global environmental characteristics. In the next section, I first review the relevant literature on ecology and ethnology to identify the abstract elements that affect human population dynamics. In the section which then follows I formulate the mathematical model and describe its dynamic implications.

14.3 Ecology, Ethnology, and Economic Activities

14.3.1 The Decline in Biodiversity

A basic principle of ecology, according to Harvey and Hallet (1977), is that natural complex systems are generally stable and are able to return to their equilibrium state after a disturbance. But it appears that this basic principle may be ruined by massive human interventions of unprecedented scale.

As Smith (1996) pointed out, the internal complexity of an ecosystem is positively related to its stability. If an ecosystem has experienced a large shock that has eliminated many of its species, the remaining species are critical to the system's integrity. A full complement of species can give the ecosystem a "buffering capacity" against large random shocks. Smith argued that the biodiversity of a region may be the best measure of ecological resilience.[3] When the ecological resilience is seriously damaged, an exogenous random shock may create an irreversible ecological change. This will cause human beings (and many other species) to find themselves in an unfamiliar environment and seriously reduce the size of the human population (Arrow et al., 1995). The question is, will economic development necessarily (or likely) cause biodiversity declines, and if so, why?

The first reason why human economic development may cause a decline in biodiversity is that human beings are largely ignorant of the ecological effects of their economic behavior until the damages are too great to reverse. As we mentioned in the previous section, many industries have been emitting CO_2 for more than one hundred years and $CFCs$ for several decades, but it was not until recently that the impact of greenhouse gases on global warming could be confirmed by scientists. The impact of global warming, according to Shaw and Stroup (1990), includes forests shifting northward; sealevels rising, inundating wetlands, beaches, and coastal cities; rainfall patterns changing; air pollution worsening; and catastrophes such as fires, insect plagues, floods, and droughts. Evidently, these disasters will significantly reduce the number of species that do not successfully adapt themselves to these changes, and hence reduce biodiversity. Furthermore, after several hundred years of industrial development, the emission of CO_2 seems to be unavoidable for many production activities and products (such as cars). It is now difficult to alter all these technologies and products to significantly lessen the emission of greenhouse gases, even if alternatives exist. This is a special case of the lock-in effect mentioned in Arthur (1989).

The second reason why economic development may cause biodiversity decline has to do with the modern technology *diffusion* process involved in many economic activities. As Swanson (1995) pointed out, human society now relies upon only four forms of crops (maize, wheat, potato, rice) for most of its subsistence needs, and only a very small number of high-yielding varieties of these four plants are utilized. But it is estimated that humans have used 100,000 edible plant species over their history. It is then natural to ask what has caused such a decline in edible plants. The answer to this question hinges upon the path-dependence property of the technology diffusion process.

Swanson argued that there are three kinds of increasing returns in the process of economic development. Take the development of agriculture as an example. (1) Given automatic machinery, modern agriculture shows increasing returns with respect to the land factor. Most modern agriculture needs a large area of land and uniform plant size (i.e., single species) to practice mechanical cultivation. To exhaust the advantage of this modern machinery, on every piece of cultivated land, all forests, grassy plants, and other species have to be removed. Swanson (1995) reviews many recent examples of converting natural habitat to single-species agriculture. The average percentage change of land from forest to cultivated area turned out to be as high as 37% in the past two decades in many developing countries. (2) When a limited number of crops happened to be grown in some early-developed countries, the capital goods used in planting these species were also invented and improved. With the help of these capital goods, these species become the "successful" (high-yielding) ones. With the extensive development of international transportation and trade, these capital goods were exported to other developing countries and facilitated the growth of these successful species in agricultural production there. (3) With more experience of planting specific species, the corresponding phytopathology is further developed, which in turn increases the incentive to grow these disease-free species.

The latter two kinds of increasing returns in agricultural development have the feature of path-dependence discussed in Arthur (1989) and again create a lock-in effect in a very few species. This lock-in path-dependence effect, as Arthur forcefully emphasized, is not limited to agriculture and is prevalent in other industries as well.

14.3.2 Genetic Specialization

The disadvantage of genetic specialization can be clearly seen in the following example, discussed in Gould (1977).

As is well known, the antlers and horns of elks are essentially visual-dominance symbols. The most important function of antlers is not for combat, but for conferring high status and for access to females. Because elks with large antlers have a higher probability of mating with females, the large-antler genes reproduce themselves more easily. In the long run, natural selection leads to the flourishing of deer with larger and larger antlers. In ethnology, this is called the "specialization" of adaptation.

The Irish elk, famous for their huge antlers, existed only in the period from 12,000 to 11,000 years ago. The elk lived in a stable environment without major challenges. Because the size of the antler was then the most important criterion of genetic selection, after several hundred years, the existing Irish elk all had very large antlers. It has been estimated that these antlers could reach as much as ninety pounds in weight and twenty feet in width. These Irish elk were very well adapted to the grassy, sparsely wooded, open country of the Alleröd epoch. However, after the final retreat of the ice sheet, evidently the Irish elk could not adapt either to the tundra or to the later heavy forestation. It is believed that many Irish elk were easily trapped by low branches. The major reason was that their antlers were too big to allow free movement.

The general message here, as Gould pointed out, is that "the Darwinian evolution decrees that no animal shall actively develop a harmful structure, but it offers no guarantee that useful structure will continue to be adaptive in changed circumstances. The Irish elk was probably a victim of its previous success" (p. 90). When a species is overadapted and specialized, it becomes more and more dependent upon other factors or species in the environment. When nature initiates a random shock that attacks one species of the mutually dependent specialized group in an originally stable environment, this group may experience serious population decline. The disadvantage of genetic specialization applies not only to the Irish elk but also to many other species. Gould argued that this adaptation–specialization–extinction pattern is "rather commonplace" in biological history.

14.3.3 Culture Adaptation versus Genetic Adaptation

One seldom-noticed problem faced by human beings in fact may precisely be a product of our extreme success in adaptation. As most ethnologists have noted, the unique feature in the evolution of mankind is that its biological evolution has transcended itself by replacing organic evolution with cultural evolution.[4] Most mammals have adapted to cold climates by growing warm fur, but man alone has achieved the same end by wearing fur coats. The former is organic evolution, while the latter is cultural evolution. As Dobzhansky (1961) argued, culture is by far the most potent adaptive mechanism that has emerged in the evolution of life. Its potency is due to its being learned, taught, and changed much faster than genes can evolve.

The general observation of species evolution is that well-adapted species are able to respond to natural shocks if these shocks, whether foreseeable or not, are moderate. But just as in the case of the Irish elk, if the natural environment significantly changes, it is often the best-adapted species that will experience the toughest time. Would this observation be a rule that applies to human beings as well?

In the previous subsection, we mentioned that species living in a stable environment for a long period of time may become less adaptive to an unexpected or unfamiliar environment. A recent article by Ng (1995) suggested that the cultural evolution of human beings necessarily tends to develop a stable environment. These two propositions combined imply that human beings are inclined to adapt specialized lifestyles and may have difficulties in facing erratic exogenous shocks that lead to an unfamiliar environment.

Ng (1995) separated animals into two types: the impulse-response hard-wired type that reacts mechanically to outside shocks and the conscious rational soft-wired type that can make choices as they face outside shocks. But because there are so many kinds of outside shocks, even sophisticated species such as human beings are unable to program a shock-response choice function with zillions of possible shocks in the domain.

A simplified choice-function design, according to Ng (1995), is to develop a hard-wired *learning* system that can generate soft-wired flexible choice functions. For human beings in particular, the consciousness affects the activities of the individual by influencing his or her choice through a reward/punishment system. By and large, activities that benefit the survival of our species will be rewarded with a sense of "happiness," and those that hurt our survival will be punished with a sense of "sadness." With such a reward/punishment mechanism design, human beings tend to improve upon the environment surrounding them, so that they can receive more rewards more often. For instance, our efforts to invent heaters, air conditioners, cars, medicines, telephones, and so forth can all be attributed to a desire to enhance the rewards. The reward/punishment system improves along with the development of human civilization, and the environment becomes increasingly comfortable (stabilized), so that we are less vulnerable to outside shocks. But as mentioned in the previous subsection, such a stabilized environment could make us less adaptive to an unexpected or unfamiliar environment.

Let us consider the following simple example of human beings. We are now almost sure that an asteroid in the Cretaceous period caused the extinction of dinosaurs and the loss of many other species. If a meteorite even one-tenth the size of that asteroid hit the earth today, it is very likely that most public utilities, transportation, and other infrastructures would be destroyed. It is doubtful how many days people living in a high-rise in a city or metropolis, who are used to tap water, gas cooking, and electricity, could survive with the malfunction of all these services. On the other hand rural peasants or aborigines, who are less adapted to modern culture and live a less "specialized" life, stand a better chance of survival. The adaptive specialization in human beings are certainly different from the genetic specialization of other species but the potential negative impact appears to be similar.

Such crises of overspecialization, however, often escape the perception of human beings. Again, the reason hinges on the fact that the disadvantage of overspecialization is likely to become evident only after a very long period of time and therefore is unlikely to be sensed by individuals in their short lifespans.

The point here is that human economic development usually leads to a stabilization of the environment and a specialization of individual lifestyle, which in turn lead to a deterioration in the ability of human beings to adapt to large random shocks. This is by no means an idle concern, for, as we mentioned in the previous subsection, human economic development has caused significant biodiversity declines, which in turn increase the probability of facing an major natural shock.

14.4 Toward a Mathematical Formulation

14.4.1 Three Epochs of Economic Development

We follow Goodfriend and McDermott (1995) and divide the history of economic development into three epochs. The first is the premarket period that preceded the appearance of cities. In this *primitive* epoch, the family was the production unit meeting most consumption needs, and there is no formal, regular transaction of goods. This period started 5,000 to 6,000 years before the present and lasted until cities became important. The second epoch is the period of preindustrial market development before the Industrial Revolution. In this *preindustrial* epoch, the population size gradually increased, which facilitated the ever-finer division of labor (Chu, 1997; Chu and Tsai, 1995); however, the environment had not yet reached the point where human capital accumulation was desirable. The third epoch, called the *modern* epoch, starts with the Industrial Revolution in the eighteenth century. In this period, various production technologies, abstractly characterized as "knowledge," were invented, accumulated, learned, and passed on. Because of the nonrivalry property of knowledge, an increasing-return production technology became possible, which in turn rendered possible the rapid growth of output and population.

Let N_t be the number of workers (or population), W_t be the real wage, H_t be the stock of human capital, and M_t be the number of intermediate products, characterizing the degree of the division of labor. A discrete-time version of the model of Goodfriend and McDermott (1995) can be written as follows.[5]

$$M_t = K \cdot H_t \cdot N_t, \tag{14.4}$$

$$W_t = A \cdot H_t^{1+a} \cdot N_t^{\alpha}, \tag{14.5}$$

$$H_{t+1} = c_L \cdot H_t^{1-\gamma} \cdot M_t^{\gamma} + \left(1 - \omega\right)H_t, \tag{14.6}$$

where $c_L, A, K, \alpha \in (0,1), \gamma \in (0,1)$ are all constants and ω is the depreciation rate of H_t.

Equations (14.4)–(14.6) apply to all three epochs of economic development; however, in the former two epochs, some of these equations have a degenerated pattern. In the primitive epoch, the size of human capital is fixed and assumed to be a constant: $H_t = H_0$. The real wage and the number of intermediate goods are also constants: $M_t = M$ and $W_t = W$. In the preindustrial epoch, H_t still remains constant H_0, but the division of labor begins to be refined and the real wage begins to rise. The dynamic system in the second epoch becomes

$$M_t = K \cdot H_0 \cdot N_t,$$
$$W_t = A \cdot H_0^{1+a} \cdot N_t^{\alpha}, \tag{14.7}$$
$$H_t = H_0.$$

In the third epoch, all three equations in (14.4)–(14.6) apply. In what follows, I shall write the logarithm of M_t, W_t, and N_t, respectively, as m_t, w_t, and n_t.

14.4.2 Human Reproduction and Survival Probability

The law of motion of N_t is assumed to be

$$N_t = \eta\left(W_{t-1}\right)f\left(m_{t-1}, X_t\right)N_{t-1}, \tag{14.8}$$

where η is the human reproduction rate, f is the survival probability, and X_t is a random variable characterizing the environmental state. The specifications of η, f, and X are further explained below.

The familiar quantity–quality tradeoff argument tells us that the fertility rate will decline when the real wage and the opportunity costs are sufficiently high. The discussion in Kremer (1993) showed us that there are two critical values of the W's (say W^* and W^{**}) such that (i) $\eta'(W_{t-1})$ is positive when $W_{t-1} \leq W^*$, and (ii) $\eta'(W_{t-1}) = 0$ when $W_{t-1} > W^{**}$. Case (i) usually refers to earlier periods of human history, and case (ii) applies only to the postindustrial epoch.[6]

We explained in the previous section that, in a modern economy, the stablized environment and the over-adaptation of agents adversely affects their adaptability to disadvantageous unexpected random shocks. Notice that a finer division of labor in fact increases the survival probability of each individual when the environmental state is "within a reasonable range"; people's survival probability will decrease only when the environmental state is sufficiently poor. Suppose x_t is the realization value of X_t, and let $x_t = 0$ be the critical value of the environmental state. Specifically, $x_t \geq 0$ means that the environmental state is favorable, or unfavorable but within a reasonable range, for human survivorship; $x_t < 0$ means that the environment is disastrous. Assuming $m_t < m_t'$, we adopt the following survival probability function:

$$f(m_t, x_t) \begin{cases} < f(m_t', x_t) & \text{if } x_t > 0; \\ \geq f(m_t', x_t) & \text{if } x_t \leq 0. \end{cases} \tag{14.9}$$

Equation (14.9) says that when the environment is tolerable ($x_t > 0$), a more advanced technology, characterized by the finer division of labor (larger m_t), increases the survival probability. When the environment is poor ($x_t < 0$), a highly refined division of labor, and hence a highly specialized lifestyle, may suffer from the disadvantage of specialization, which causes an exaggeration of the disastrous environmental state (see figure 14.2).

Finally, we also explained in the last section why economic development reduces the biodiversity of the ecosystem, which in turn decreases the resilience of the environment and hence changes the pattern of natural

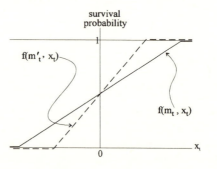

FIGURE 14.2 The shape of $f(m, x)$, $m_t' > m_t$.

random shocks. Thus, we expect that the mean of X_t, denoted μ_t, and the variance of X_t, denoted σ_t, are both increasing functions of the m_t.

14.4.3 Potential Crisis of the Modern Epoch

From the discussion in chapter 13, we know that a large population size is necessary for a finer division of labor; this is also revealed in equation (14.4). From (14.6), we see that, because a higher level of knowledge can be produced and sustained only when N_t is sufficiently large, the population size is also indispensable for knowledge accumulation. With the setup in (14.4)–(14.6) and (14.8)–(14.9), Chu and Tai (1997) calculate the survival probabilities in the three epochs. These probabilities are evidently random variables, and hence any comparison of these probabilities must be in a stochastic sense. Under reasonable assumptions, Chu and Tai proved the following results: Suppose the economy is as specified in equations (14.4)–(14.6) and (14.8)–(14.9). Then (i) when the level of the division of labor is sufficiently high, the variance of the survival probability is positively related to the level of the division of labor; (ii) the probability of a drastic decline in population size, in the sense that the survival probability is smaller than a specific number, is higher when the level of the division of labor is higher; (iii) the probability of shifting from the modern epoch to the primitive epoch is higher than that of shifting from the preindustrial epoch to the primitive epoch.

Notice that which epoch the economy belongs to is endogenously determined. Economic agents compare the welfare level (W_t) in each epoch and decide the degree, as well as the extent, of the division of labor. If the size of population drops drastically, people in the modern epoch may realize that it is not efficient to maintain an extensive division of labor; neither is it beneficial to accumulate human capital. Thus, a drastic drop in population size may trigger a major setback in economic development, forcing us to return to the primitive epoch. This is the intuition behind part (iii) of the above result. In the process, there is no further accumulation of knowledge, and the original stock of knowledge is gradually lost or forgotten (depreciated). The process, if and when it happens, could be disastrous.

This scenario may have a low probability of occurring, but the point is that the probability *increases* along with the development of the modern economy. There are two aggravating factors. The first is that the expansion of human activities unavoidably involves biodiversity decline, which increases the probability of experiencing an irrecoverable environmental change. The second factor is that modern economic development "stabilizes" the environment, which makes human beings less adaptive to an unfamiliar environment. Specifically, the first factor decreases the ability of our environment to absorb exogenous shocks, and the second factor decreases the adaptability of individuals to exogenous shocks. These factors combined make human beings more vulnerable to natural ecological shocks, and hence an increased probability of a drastic population decline. This explains the intuition behind parts (i) and (ii) of Chu and Tai's result.

The above analysis is clearly sensitive to the mathematical formulation specified. Indeed, our current knowledge of the ecological system does not allow us to check whether our specification in (14.7)–(14.8) is reasonable. What is presented here is the possible negative impact of biodiversity decline and the cultural specialization of adaptation on population dynamics. If our argument that the probability of a sharp population decline increases with economic development is valid, then this argument appears to be a *modern Malthusian theory*. In a sense, this theory says that even in the modern economic epoch, there is still a "natural" constraint on human development. This constraint is no longer characterized by the availability of resources or the technological frontier; rather, the constraint is characterized by the ecological balance of the universe.

CHAPTER 15

Epilogue

One of the most striking features of the topics analyzed in the previous chapters is the breadth and depth of the economics involved in the analysis of population dynamics. The conventional perception that "demographic movements were largely exogenous to the economic system, and were to be left to sociologists and other non-economists" (Samuelson, 1976, p. 243) may be based on a conventional understanding of demography itself. Once we realize that modern individual fertility decisions may be affected by many *economic* variables, we can understand why demographic movements may be correlated with various economic indexes of the society. Once we shift our focus from the size and growth rate of the population to its economic characteristics, we realize that there is an abundance of topics for research and analysis. Moreover, once we perceive that the characteristic composition of the population is usually an aggregate result of various decisions by individuals, we find that our analysis is not confined to fertility-related economic variables. Thus, we are able to use the general framework to study the income distribution (chapters 4, 5), the attitude composition (chapter 8), the occupation structure (chapter 9), and the aggregate savings and pensions (chapters 11, 12) of the population.

The methodology adopted in this book is quite consistent: I emphasize the impact of individual decisions on the aggregate dynamics of demographic characteristics. As far as the steady state or dynamic fluctuations are concerned, the theory of stochastic processes is the basic tool necessary for the analysis. Other than the possible technical difficulty, there is nothing conceptually difficult in the modeling. But very often, the aggregate variables in question may feed back and influence individual decisions. In chapters 8 and 9, we see how the aggregate custom or occupational composition in the previous period affects individual decisions in the current period. These are in fact special cases and are easily dealt with. For many other economic variables, the micro–macro interaction involved is rather complex. There are several variables that may affect and also be affected by individual decisions. For instance, if fertility is a function of parental income, then, as I showed in chapter 4, the societal income distribution, as well as income mobility, will be affected by the specification of the income-fertility function. But we also know from chapter 5 that income mobility may induce poor parents to concentrate their resources on fewer children in order to raise their social position. Thus, there is an obvious interaction between individual fertility decisions and the existing mobility conditions. A theoretical characterization of the above interaction, as we can imagine, is rather difficult and deserves further research in the future.

For another instance, in section 11.3, I introduce the branch of the literature that explains why the age composition of the economy during demographic transition tends to induce a public pension system. Because the demographic transition in many countries is a result of fertility decline, the conclusion in section 11.3 can also be viewed as a theoretical influence of the fertility rate on pension decisions. On the other hand, from the "child-as-old-age-support" hypothesis, we also predict that parental fertility rates should fall when their old-age support has already been provided by an extensive public pension system. The long-run development of pension and fertility patterns should therefore be dynamically interrelated, and an equilibrium should embody the above two channels of influence. Modeling the above interaction is a more involved task than is the analysis in chapters 8 or 9, although the job does not appear to be overly formidable.

Perhaps the most uncomfortable and uncertain result I present concerns human population in our own *future*. I am not convinced by the argument made by Simon (1981) on his cover page that "the primary constraint on our national and world economic growth is our capacity for the creation of new ideas and contributions to knowledge. The more people alive who can be trained to help solve the problems that confront us, the faster we might remove the obstacles..." The question unavoidably becomes a philosophical one: Are natural obstacles or constraints completely *removable*?

Even if we can continually progress in technological knowledge, even if the knowledge is nonrivalrous and makes increasing returns in production possible, and even if modern technologies can produce and transport sufficient food to poorer developing countries, can an infinite growth path, with a positive or even a stationary population growth rate, be sustained? This seems to be a question that should be addressed simultaneously by demographers, ecologists, economists, and biologists. Economists study how technologies, which improve the environment for human development, are invented, diffused, and improved by human beings. Ecologists analyze how the environment changes in response to the activities of human beings. Demographers figure out the changes in vital rates in response to environmental and economic changes. And biologists study how human beings evolve in tandem with their environment in the long run. Ignoring the active decisions of human beings will lead us to view human development as very passive. Ignoring the biological or ecological angles will lead us into delusions of infinite growth. Obviously, neither prejudice is acceptable. It is not the sole responsibility of economists to provide a long-run forecast of the human population, but it seems to be rather irresponsible for economic theorists to ignore the environmental and ecological impact of economic development and propagate the fantasy of *unbounded* economic and population growth.

Our observations from the past two hundred years are in fact insufficient for us to have a general understanding of the pattern of knowledge diffusion, the way new knowledge affects economic production, and, more important, the cost and constraint of knowledge accumulation. Fogel (1994) emphasized the need for economic theorists to study economic history in order to understand the dynamic processes of social phenomena. But so far much of the discussion on the future pattern of human population growth or the relationship between population and technological changes has often jumped to a "knowledge law-of-motion equation" and launched into the dynamic analysis there, without paying much attention to the generality or historical support of such a mechanical equation. As Fogel pointed out at the end of his Nobel lecture (p. 389), "uncovering what actually happened in the past requires an enormous investment in time and effort. Fortunately for theorists, that burden is borne primarily by economic historians." But still economic theorists "need to spend the time necessary to comprehend what the historians have discovered. A superficial knowledge of the work of economic historians is at least as dangerous as a superficial knowledge of theory." This final remark by Fogel serves as the best caveat to researchers in population dynamics.

Notes

1. As Schultz (1981) put it, one supposition of Malthus is that fertility rates within marriage are essentially uncontrolled by conscious individual behavior.

2. Becker's (1991) reputable *Treatise* contains an excellent summary of various kinds of family decisions. See also the review article by Bergstrom (1997).

CHAPTER 2

1. Analysis of the cases of continuous time and state spaces is similar but involves more advanced probability theory. Interested readers can go to Mode (1971, chapters 6 and 7) for further information.

2. When there is density-dependency or other kinds of decision interactions, supposition (ii) will be violated. Density-dependent models will be discussed in chapters 8 and 9.

3. Recall that we assumed in subsection 2.1.2 that **B** is a bounded subset, so n is a finite number here.

4. See Parlett (1970).

5. The growth rate ϱ is called the *intrinsic rate of population increase*.

6. Because a type-i agent can remain the same type for an uncertain number of periods.

CHAPTER 3

1. Recall that β is assumed to be the upper bound of human population so that $m_a = 0 \ \forall a > \beta$.

2. A simple and more heuristic proof can be found in Arthur (1982).

3. There may be more than one solution to the above equation. See Coale (1972) for further analysis.

4. $r \equiv ln \varrho$.

5. Equation (3.2) may hold without the steady-state presumption; it can be obtained by making only the assumption that the population growth rate and the age structure are constant.

CHAPTER 4

1. This assumption is reasonable given our suppressed two-period life structure.

2. The Inada condition requires that $u'(x,.) \to 0$ as $x \to \infty$ and $u'(x,.) \to \infty$ as $x \to 0$. The same definition applies to $f(.,.)$ and $L(.)$.

3. Daley's (1968) work is in fact an extension of Kalmykov (1962).

4. For economic examples of comparative static analysis of the Markov processes, see Danthine and Donaldson (1981).

5. See Anand and Kanbur (1993) for a recent survey.

6. The reason Chu and Koo (1990) proposed an assumption stronger than Kalmykov's SM condition is simple: there exist counterexamples that show that the SM condition is not sufficient to warrant even the simplest comparative static analysis.

7. As pointed out by Atkinson (1970), every inequality comparison has some kind of implicit social welfare criterion behind it. The above-mentioned direct ranking of income distribution, which does not rely on detailed functional specifications of social welfare, is a better alternative to conventional comparisons of various inequality measures.

8. A static sample can also be used to estimate $M_{i,f}$ if the person being interviewed can specify detailed income status of his parents 25 years ago, which is quite unlikely in reality.

9. For more details, see Atkinson (1981) and Adelman et al. (1994).

10. The estimation, of course, has to take into account the constraints such as $\Sigma_{i=1}^{n} \tilde{M}_{i,j} = 1 \ \forall j$. There are also other behavioral assumptions needed to estimate elements of **M**. For instance, since completed fertility is usually unavailable from family survey data, Cheng and Chu (1997) had to assume some kind of age-specific dynamic pattern for life-cycle fertility in order to calculate the completed fertility rate from the survey data. Readers are referred to their article for further details.

CHAPTER 5

1. Further analysis will be presented in chapter 9.

2. If $h_i(.)$ first intersects the 45° line from below, then the first intersection is not a stable fixed point. This implies that starting with some $\zeta_{0,i}$, the eventual extinction probability $\zeta_{\infty,i}$ would not be the first intersection, contradicting Theorem 5.2 above.

3. This assumption is not necessary and is made purely to simplify our later presentation.

4. When bequests are in the form of human capital investment fund, imagine that b_M is the resource needed to support one child through high school. By assumption, this equals the amount needed to support two children through junior high

school (b_L). Similarly, b_H is the resource needed to support one child through college, which by assumption equals two shares of b_M.

Chapter 6

1. See Caswell (1990), chapter 10.
2. The inequality $u_{i,j}(x, y) \leq x, y$ implies that the number of matings cannot exceed the available number of males or females. This certainly rules out the possibility of polygamy or polyandry.
3. A function $h(x)$ is homogeneous of degree r if $h(\lambda x) = \lambda^r h(x) \; \forall \lambda > 0$.
4. When a divorced parent remarries, it is assumed that his or her original children will not affect the fertility decision of the new union. Thus, all new unions are assumed to have $n^+ = n^+ = 0$ for simplicity of presentation.
5. Together with a set of purely technical conditions.
6. See Bennett (1983) for discussion of the legal issues involved in the common-law doctrine.
7. See Ross (1983) for details.
8. Here $W(0)$ has been normalized to be zero.
9. Several other technical conditions needed to sustain this theorem are omitted. Interested readers are referred to Leung's paper for detailed discussion.
10. The earliest discussion of the equilibrium sex ratio of a species goes back to Fisher (1958). The research along that line, however, emphasized the mechanism of genetic selection over a very long period of time. The focus of this chapter is different.
11. Because some of the individual-specific characteristics of girl (or boy) producers, such as hormone level or follicular phase length, are unlikely to go through frequent changes, we do not expect a mother to switch frequently between being a girl producer and a boy producer over her fertile period.
12. They also redo the regression by using the men's indexes, and the results are essentially the same.
13. See Hsiao, 1986, chapters 3 and 8.
14. In general there is no one-to-one relationship between the multiple regression coefficient (β) and the coefficient of correlation between $m_{i,t}$ and $r_{i,t}$. But in (6.11), the country effect and the time effect are essentially added to normalize the birth-rate series, and hence β can be treated as the coefficient of a simple regression $m'_{i,t} = \alpha_0 + \beta r_{i,t} + \epsilon_{i,t}$, where $m'_{i,t} \equiv m_{i,t} - \alpha_i - \gamma_t$ is the normalized birth rate.
15. These two types were first mentioned by Blinder (1973). But since there was no explicit two-sex structure in Blinder's setup, his analysis was confined to some restrictive cases.

Chapter 7

1. The formula is well defined between vectors containing zero entries only if the locations of the zeros coincide.
2. Detailed analysis of the above definition can be found in Lorenz (1989).
3. See Tuljapurkar (1987) for more details.
4. Some preliminary results can be found in Chu and Lu (1997).

Chapter 8

1. In his discussion of the number of seminar participants, Schelling (1978) assumes that people use the number who attended last week as an expectation of attendance this week.

2. If $x_1^* \neq x_2^*$, then the evolution of p_t will become slightly more complicated, but the insight remains the same.

3. See Boldrin (1988) for more detailed explanations.

4. See Cooter and Ulen (1988), chapter 12, for explanations.

Chapter 9

1. Before Chao and Hsieh (1988), the most extensive study, by Ho, was limited to the fourteenth to twentieth centuries. Durand (1960) made an effort to trace Chinese population history back to the first century. Other related piecemeal research includes Hartwell (1982) and Kuan (1980).

2. Sketchy evidence of this phenomenon can be seen in figure 9.1. More precise numbers are to be found in C&H.

3. Natural fertility is the fertility level that occurs in the absence of conscious effort to control completed family size.

4. This assumption is the same as the one made in section 8.3.

5. In Chinese history, there were numerous instances of severe disruptions of agriculture as dikes were ruptured or bridges were burned during revolutionary wars. But in general this happened only in "large-scale wars." On the other hand, historians would record these instances only when their attendant political or economic costs were high. Thus, it seems that $\{R_t\}$ is a good proxy variable of the damage to agriculture. I will discuss this further in the next section.

6. C&H provided detailed reasoning for such a three-ladder division, which will not be repeated here.

7. See book 3, chapter 8, of the volume by the "father of war," Carl von Clausewitz (1976).

8. Here we skip the usual caveat that there may be stable period-3 cycles. More detailed discussion can be found, for example, in David Kelsey (1988).

Chapter 10

1. See Lee, 1974, p. 579, for a detailed explanation.

2. The Translog form has the computational advantage when cost share is the variable to be estimated. In our analysis, it turns out that the Translog form is too cumbersome to program, and so the generalized Leontief formula is adopted in its place.

3. The data are on a compact disk, which is available from the author on request.

4. Observant readers may notice that Wachter and Lee (1989) applied a different growth equation to detrend their population data when they analyzed the period model. They did so because the growth rate of the U.S. population may be different from the birth rate due to immigration. Their approach is straightforward because in their period model only the total population size is used as the explanatory variable in the fertility regression, whereas in my regression I use all age-specific population sizes as explanatory variables.

5. Since we normalize β_1'' to be 1, the absolute value of β_a'', a = 2, ..., 6, is not meaningful. Although it is not my purpose to explain the negative relationship between $W_a(t)$ and $m(a, t)$ for the 30–34 age group, I suspect that this negative coefficient may be related to the fertility timing decision of females. For instance, if the opportunity cost of bearing a child is highest for a female aged 30–34, she would probably prefer to postpone or give up childbearing if her economic perspective looks good. This may create a negative relationship between relative economic welfare and fertility rate for this group. See Ward and Butz (1980) for a more detailed analysis.

6. See, for example, Day et al. (1989), Feichtinger and Dockner (1990), and Feichtinger and Sorger (1989).

CHAPTER 11

1. A more detailed discussion of how the diffusion of new agricultural technology and new crops can set off a demographic transition can be found in Nerlove (1996).

2. Because the focus of this chapter is upon the interaction between population and the economy, I ignore some details of the definition and characterization of a demographic transition.

3. It is implicitly assumed that the right-hand side of (11.7) is greater than zero.

4. Other comments about the BMT model can be found in Nerlove and Raut (1997).

5. It is assumed that there exists a perfect insurance market, so that each person receives the expected value of the child's supporting fund, which equals the product of surviving probability p_2 and the size of transfer $w_t H_t$.

6. This setting is in fact problematic, for there is unlikely to be a "child survival insurance" market for old-age companionship, and hence it should not be the *expected* number of children that appears in the c_3 term in the utility function.

7. There is also financial wealth in the form of debt and credit. But since total debt or credit must sum to zero, we can ignore this part for our purposes.

8. Since the seminal work by Fei et al. (1979), most researchers have decomposed family-income inequality according to income sources, economic sectors, or income-determining characteristics, while overlooking the role population composition might have played.

CHAPTER 12

1. In Stolnitz (1992), aging is measured by the proportion of people aged 60 and over. In Kart (1994), the critical age is 65. A similar definition has been adopted by the World Health Organization (WHO).

2. See, for instance, Manton et al. (1994) and Keyfitz (1988).

3. This is because $H(y, \theta) = 0 = 1 - H(n, \theta)$ $\forall \theta$.

CHAPTER 13

1. Solow's theory also predicts that unbounded economic growth is compatible with an unbounded population growth, implying that the exogenous environment

is no longer a constraint to human population. We will come back to this point in the next chapter.

2. Romer (1990) and some other researchers have focused on the public access to knowledge when it is used. Others, notably Arrow (1962) and Ng (1986), have shown that the cost of inventing new technology is constant, and therefore the cost per capita of creating knowledge is inversely related to population size. In any case, the connection between technological growth and population size remains strong.

3. What Boserup described was just a general pattern; there are certainly cases in human history where improvement in infrastructure did not increase per capita output significantly, as Fogel (1964) showed in his well-known example. Also notice that, although our observation involves an outflow of labor from the agricultural sector to the industrial sector, the scenario here is different from the traditional "excess labor" argument of development.

4. To see this, notice that $\partial Y_p/\partial e_p$ is greater than the market wage for any $e_k \geq 0$ (point E is higher than F, say); hence, there is a tendency for market-sector workers to transfer to the primitive sector.

5. See Yang and Ng (1993) for details.

Chapter 14

1. See Meadows et al. (1992).

2. Meadows et al. (1992, p. 184) argued that "the market is blind to the long term and pays no attention to ultimate resources and sinks, until . . . it is too late to act."

3. *Biodiversity* refers to the diversity of living organisms. More comprehensive discussion can be found in Hammer et al. (1993).

4. Some ethnologists call human culture "the out-body organ".

5. My formulation is a discrete rewriting of Goodfriend and McDermott's equations (10), (12), and (14). Their $1 - \alpha$ is replaced by α here.

6. The Malthusian theory tells us that, in the ancient period, when the population size is close to the carrying capacity, the food support may be less than sufficient, and successful reproduction would be a decreasing function of the existing population size. But this is not crucial to our analysis here.

References

CHAPTER 1

Arthur, W. Brian, and McNicoll, Geoffrey. 1978. "Samuelson, Population and Inter-generational Transfers." *International Economic Review* 19:241–246.

Becker, Gary S. 1960. "An Economic Analysis of Fertility." In *Demographic and Economic Change in Developed Countries*, ed. Richard Easterlin. Princeton, NJ: Princeton University Press.

———. 1991. *A Treatise on the Family: An Enlarged Edition*. Cambridge, MA: Harvard University Press.

———, and Lewis, H. Gregg. 1973. "On the Interaction Between the Quantity and Quality of Children." *Journal of Political Economy* 81:S279–S288.

Bergstrom, Theodore. 1997. "A Survey of Theories of the Family." In *Handbook of Population and Family Economics*, ed. M. R. Rosenzweig and O. Stark. Amsterdam: North-Holland.

Chesnais, Jean-Claude. 1992. *The Demographic Transition: Stages, Patterns, and Economic Implications*. Oxford: Clarendon Press.

Coale, Ansley J. 1972. *The Growth and Structure of Human Populations: A Mathematical Approach*. Princeton, NJ: Princeton University Press.

Dasgupta, Partha. 1995. "The Population Problem: Theory and Evidence." *Journal of Economic Literature* 33:1879–1902.

Kalmykov, G. I. 1962. "On the Partial Ordering of One-Dimensional Markov Processes," *Theory of Probability and Its Applications* 7:456–459.

Keyfitz, Nathan. 1968. *Introduction to the Mathematics of Population*. Reading, MA: Addison-Wesley.

Leslie, P. H. 1945. "On the Use of Matrices in Certain Population Mathematics." *Biometrica* 33:183–212.

———. 1948. "Some Further Notes on the Use of Matrices in Population Mathematics," *Biometrica* 35:213–245.

Leung, Siu Fai. 1991. "A Stochastic Dynamic Analysis of Parental Sex Preferences and Fertility." *Quarterly Journal of Economics* 103:1063–1088.

Lotka, Alfred J. 1939. "A Contribution to the Theory of Self-Renewing Aggregates, with Special reference to Industrial Replacement." *Annals of Mathematical Statistics* 10:1–25.

Malthus, Thomas R. [1783] 1970. *An Essay on the Principle of Population*, ed. Anthony Flew. Baltimore: Penguin Books.

Nerlove, Marc, Razin, Assaf, and Sadka, Efraim. 1987. *Household and Economy: Welfare Economics of Endogenous Fertility*. Orlando, FL: Academic Press.

Pollak, Robert A. 1990. "Two-Sex Demographic Models." *Journal of Political Economy* 98:399–420.

Razin, Assaf, and Sadka, Efraim. 1995. *Population Economics*. Cambridge, MA: MIT Press.

Romer, Paul M. 1990. "Endogenous Technological Change." *Journal of Political Economy* 98:S71–S102.

Samuelson, Paul A. 1972. "A Universal Cycle?" In *The Collected Scientific Papers of P. A. Samuelson*. Vol. 3, ed. Robert Merton. Cambridge, MA: MIT Press.

———. 1976. "An Economist's Non Linear Model of Self-Generated Fertility Waves." *Population Studies* 30:243–247.

Schultz, T. Paul. 1981. *Economics of Population*. Reading, MA: Addison-Wesley.

———. 1988. "Economic Demography and Development." In *The State of Development Economics: Progress and Perspectives*, ed. Gustav Ranis and T. Paul Schultz. Oxford: Clarendon Press.

Willis, Robert J. 1973. "A New Approach to the Economic Theory of Fertility Behavior." *Journal of Political Economy* 81:S14–S64.

Chapter 2

Asmussen, S., and Hering, H. 1983. *Branching Processes*. Boston: Birkhauser.

Caswell, Hal. 1990. *Matrix Population Models: Construction, Analysis and Interpretation*. Sunderland, MA: Sinauer Associates.

Harris, Theodore E. 1963. *The Theory of Branching Processes*. Berlin: Springer.

Leslie, P. H. 1945. "On the Use of Matrices in Certain Population Mathematics." *Biometrica* 33:183–212.

———. 1948. "Some Further Notes on the Use of Matrices in Population Mathematics." *Biometrica* 35:213–245.

Lotka, Alfred J. 1939. "A Contribution to the Theory of Self-Renewing Aggregates, with Special Reference to Industrial Replacement." *Annals of Mathematical Statistics* 10:1–25.

Mode, Charles J. 1971. *Multitype Branching Processes: Theory and Application*. New York: Elsevier.

Parlett, Beresford. 1970. "Ergodic Properties of Populations. I. The One Sex Model." *Theoretical Population Biology* 1:191–207.

Preston, Samuel H. 1974. "Differential Fertility, Unwanted Fertility, and Racial Trends in Occupation Achievement." *American Sociological Review* 39:492–506.

Sykes, Z. M. 1969. "On Discrete Stable Population Theory." *Biometrics* 25: 285–293.

Chapter 3

Arthur, W. Brian. 1982. "The Ergodic Theories of Demography: A Simple Proof." *Demography* 19:439–445.

————, and McNicoll, Geoffrey. 1977. "Optimal Time Paths with Age-Dependence: A Theory of Population Policy." *Review of Economic Studies* 44:111–123.

————, and McNicoll, Geoffrey. 1978. "Samuelson, Population and Intergenerational Transfers." *International Economic Review* 19:241–246.

Coale, Ansley J. 1972. *The Growth and Structure of Human Populations: A Mathematical Approach*. Princeton, NJ: Princeton University Press.

Lam, David. 1984. "The Variance of Population Characteristics." *Population Studies* 38:117–127.

Lee, Ronald D. 1980. "Age Structure, Inter-generational Transfers, and Economic Growth: An Overview." *Revue Economique* 31:1129–1156.

————. 1994. "The Former Demography of Population Aging." In *Demography of Aging*, ed. Linda G. Martin and Samuel H. Preston. Washington DC: National Academy Press.

————, and Lapkoff, Shelley. 1988. "Inter-Generational Flows of Time and Goods: Consequences of Slowing Population Growth." *Journal of Political Economy* 96:618–651.

Lotka, Alfred J. 1939. "A Contribution to the Theory of Self-Renewing Aggregates, with Special Reference to Industrial Replacement." *Annals of Mathematical Statistics* 10:1–25.

Samuelson, Paul A. 1958. "An Exact Consumption-Loan Model of Interest With or Without the Social Contrivance of Money." *Journal of Political Economy* 66:467–482.

————. 1965. "A Catenary Turnpike Theorem Involving Consumption and the Golden Rule." *American Economic Review* 55:486–496.

Solow, Robert. 1956. "A Contribution to the Theory of Economic Growth." *Quarterly Journal of Economics* 79:65–94.

Willis, Robert J. 1988. "Life Cycles, Institutions, and Population Growth: A Theory of the Equilibrium Rate of Interest in an Overlapping Generations Model." In *Economics of Changing Age Distribution in Developed Countries*, ed. Ronald D. Lee, W. Brian Arthur, and Gary Rogers. Oxford: Clarendon Press.

CHAPTER 4

Adelman, Irma, Morley, Samuel, Schenzler, Christoph, and Warning, Watthew. 1994. "Estimating Income Mobility from Census Data." *Journal of Policy Modeling* 16:187–213.

Ahluwalia, M. S. 1976. "Inequality, Poverty and Development." *Journal of Development Economics* 3:307–342.

Anand, Sudhir, and Kanbur, S. M. R. 1993. "Inequality and Development: A Critique." *Journal of Development Economics* 41:19–43.

Atkinson, Anthony B. 1970. "On the Measurement of Inequality." *Journal of Economic Theory* 2:244–263.

————. 1981. "On Intergenerational Income Mobility in Britain." *Journal of Post Keynesian Economics* 3:194–218.

Becker, Gary S. 1960. "An Economic Analysis of Fertility." In *Demographic and Economic Change in Developed Countries*, ed. Richard Easterlin. Princeton, NJ: Princeton University Press.

Boulier, Brian. 1982. "Income Distribution and Fertility Decline: A Skeptical View." *Population and Development Review* 8:159–278.

Caswell, Hal. 1990. *Matrix Population Models: Construction, Analysis and Interpretation*. Sunderland, MA: Sinauer Associates.

Cheng, B. T., and Chu, C. Y. Cyrus. 1997. "Estimating the Mobility Matrix of Taiwan Using Pseudo Panel Data." Paper presented at the International Conference on Economics and Political Economy of Development at the Turn of the Century: In Memory of John C. H. Fei, Institute of Social Sciences and Philosophy, Taipei, Taiwan, August.

Chu, C. Y. Cyrus. 1985. "An Intergenerational Model of Bequest, Fertility, Income Distribution and Population Growth." Discussion Paper 85–79, University of Michigan Population Studies Center.

———. 1988. "An Income-Specific Stable Population Model: Theory and Applications." *Research in Population Economics* 6:337–366.

———. 1990. "An Existence Theorem on the Stationary State of Income Distribution and Population Growth." *International Economic Review* 31:171–185.

———, and Koo, Hui-wen. 1990. "Intergenerational Income-Group Mobility and Differential Fertility." *American Economic Review* 80:1125–1138.

Daley, D. J. 1968. "Stochastically Monotone Markov Chains. Zeitschrift fur Wahrscheinlichkeitstheorie und verwandte Gebiete. 10:305–317.

Danthine, J.-P., and Donaldson, John B. 1981. "Stochastic Properties of Fast vs. Slow Growing Economies." *Econometrica* 49:1007–1033.

Dasgupta, Partha. 1995. "The Population Problem: Theory and Evidence." *Journal of Economic Literature* 33:1879–1902.

DeTray, Dennis N. 1973. "Child Quality and the Demand for Children." *Journal of Political Economy* 81:S70–S95.

Futia, Carl A. 1982. "Invariant Distributions and the Limiting Behavior of Markovian Economic Models." *Econometrica* 50:377–408.

Hadar, Josef, and Russell, William R. 1969. "Rules for Ordering Uncertain Prospects." *American Economic Review* 59:25–34.

Kalmykov, G. I. 1962. "On the Partial Ordering of One-Dimensional Markov Processes." *Theory of Probability and Its Applications* 7:456–459.

Loury, Glenn C. 1981. "Intergenerational Transfers and the Distribution of Earnings." *Econometrica* 49:843–867.

Samuelson, Paul A. 1958. "An Exact Consumption-Loan Model of Interest With or Without the Social Contrivance of Money." *Journal of Political Economy* 66:467–482.

Schultz, T. Paul. 1981. *Economics of Population*. Reading, MA: Addison-Wesley.

———. 1988. "Economic Demography and Development." In *The State of Development Economics: Progress and Perspectives*, ed. Gustav Ranis and T. Paul Schultz. Oxford: Clarendon Press.

Varian, Hal R. 1992. *Microeconomic Analysis*. New York: Norton.

Willis, Robert J. 1973. "A New Approach to the Economic Theory of Fertility Behavior." *Journal of Political Economy* 81:S14–S64.

CHAPTER 5

Becker, Gary S. 1991. *A Treatise on the Family: An Enlarged Edition*. Cambridge, MA: Harvard University Press.

Blinder, Alan S. 1976. "Inequality and Mobility in the Distribution of Wealth." *Kyklos* 29:607–638.

Chu, C. Y. Cyrus. 1991. "Primogeniture." *Journal of Political Economy* 99:78–99.

———, and Lee, Ronald D. 1994. "Famine, Revolt and the Dynastic Cycle: Population Dynamics in Historic China." *Journal of Population Economics* 7:351–378.

Cole, John W., and Wolf, Eric R. 1974. *The Hidden Frontier: Ecology and Ethnicity in an Alpine Valley*. New York: Academic Press.

Freedman, Maurice. 1966. *Chinese Lineage and Society: Fukien and Kwangtung*. London: Athlone.

Galton, Francis. 1873. "Problem 4001." *Educational Times* 1:17.

Habakkuk, H. John. 1955. "Family Structure and Economic Change in Nineteenth Century Europe." *Journal of Economic History* 15:1–12.

Ho, Ping-ti. 1959. "The Examination System and Social Mobility in China, 1368–1911." In *Intermediate Society, Social Mobility and Communication*, ed. Verne F. Ray. Seattle, WA: American Ethnological Society.

———. 1962. *The Ladder of Success in Imperial China: Aspects of Social Mobility, 1368–1911*. New York: Columbia University Press.

Mode, Charles J. 1971. *Multitype Branching Processes: Theory and Application*. New York: Elsevier.

Nakane, Chie. 1967. *Kinship and Economic Organization in Rural Japan*. London: Athlone.

Pryor, Frederic L. 1973. "Simulation of the Impact of Social and Economic Institutions on the Size Distribution of Income and Wealth." *American Economic Review* 63:50–72.

Samuelson, Paul A. 1958. "An Exact Consumption-Loan Model of Interest With or Without the Social Contrivance of Money." *Journal of Political Economy* 66:467–482.

Smith, Adam. [1776] 1937. *An Inquiry to the Nature and Causes of the Wealth of Nations*. New York: Modern Library.

CHAPTER 6

Behrman, Jere, Pollak, Robert, and Taubman, Paul. 1986. "Do Parents Favor Boys?" *International Economic Review* 27:33–54.

Bennett, Neil. 1983. *Sex Selection of Children*. New York: Academic Press.

Ben-Porath, Yoram, and Welch, Finis. 1976. "Do Sex Preferences Really Matter?" *Quarterly Journal of Economics* 90:285–307.

———. 1980. "On Sex Preferences and Family Size." *Research in Population Economics* 2:387–399.

Blinder, Alan S. 1973. "A Model of Inherited Wealth." *Quarterly Journal of Economics* 87:608–626.

Caswell, Hal. 1990. *Matrix Population Models: Construction, Analysis and Interpretation*. Sunderland, MA: Sinauer Associates.

Chu, C. Y. Cyrus. 1991. "Primogeniture." *Journal of Political Economy* 99:78–99.

———, and Yu, R. 1996. "Individual Sex Preferences and Population Sex Ratio of Newborns." Discussion Paper, Department of Economics, National Taiwan University.

DeTray, Dennis. 1984. "Son Preferences in Pakistan: An Analysis of Intention vs. Behavior." *Research in Population Economics* V:185–200.

Fisher, R. A. 1958. *The Generalized Theory of Natural Selection*. 2nd ed. New York: Dover.

Hsiao, Cheng. 1986. *Analysis of Panel Data*. New York: Cambridge University Press.

James, William H. 1990. "The Hypothesized Hormonal Control of Human Sex Ratio at Birth—An Update." *Journal of Theoretical Biology* 143:555–564.

———. 1992. "The Hypothesized Hormonal Control of Mammalian Sex Ratio at Birth—A Second Update." *Journal of Theoretical Biology* 155:121–128.

———. 1995a. "What Stabilizes the Sex Ratio." *Annals of Human Genetics* 59:243–249.

——— 1995b. "Follicular Phases, Cycle Day of Conception and Sex Ratio of Offspring." *Human Reproduction* 10:2529–2533.

Leung, Sui-Fai. 1991. "A Stochastic Dynamic Analysis of Parental Sex Preferences and Fertility." *Quarterly Journal of Economics* 106:1063–1088.

———. 1994. "Will Sex Selection Reduce Fertility?" *Journal of Population Economics* 7:379–392.

Pollak, Robert A. 1986. "A Reformulation of the Two-Sex Problem," *Demography* 23:247–259.

———. 1987. "The Two-Sex Problem with Persistent Union: A Generalization of the Birth Matrix-Mating Rule Model." *Theoretical Population Biology* 32:176–187.

———. 1990. "Two-Sex Demographic Models." *Journal of Political Economy* 98:399–420.

Repetto, Robert. 1972. "Son Preference and Fertility Behavior in Developing Countries." *Studies in Family Planning* 3:70–76.

Rosenzweig, Mark. 1986. "Birth Spacing and Sibling Inequality: Asymmetric Information Within the Family." *International Economic Review* 27:55–76.

Ross, Sheldon M. 1983. *Introduction to Stochastic Dynamic Programming*. New York: Academic Press.

Williams, Robert, and Gloster, Susan. 1992. "Human Sex Ratio As It Relates to Caloric Availability." *Social Biology* 39:285–291.

Williamson, Nancy. 1976. *Sons or Daughters: A Cross-Cultural Survey of Parental Preferences*. Beverly Hills, CA: Sage.

CHAPTER 7

Beddington, J. 1974. "Age Distribution and the Stability of Simple Discrete Time Population Models." *Journal of Theoretical Biology* 47:65–74.

Caswell, Hal. 1990. *Matrix Population Models: Construction, Analysis and Interpretation*. Sunderland, MA: Sinauer Associates.

Chesnais, Jean-Claude. 1992. *The Demographic Transition: Stages, Patterns, and Economic Implications*. Oxford: Clarendon Press.

Chu, C. Y. Cyrus, and Lee, Ronald D. 1994. "Famine, Revolt and the Dynastic Cycle: Population Dynamics in Historic China." *Journal of Population Economics* 7:351–378.

———, and Lu, Huei-Chung 1997. "Predator–Prey Models with Endogenous Decisions." Mimeographed.

Coale, Ansley J. 1972. *The Growth and Structure of Human Populations: A Mathematical Approach*. Princeton, NJ: Princeton University Press.

Cohen, Joel E. 1976. "Ergodicity of Age Structure in Populations with Markovian Vital Rates. I. Countable States." *Journal of the American Statistical Association* 71:335–339.

———. 1979. "Ergodic Theorems in Demography." *Bulletin of the American Mathematical Society* 1:275–295.

Cushing, James M. 1989. "A Strong Ergodic Theorem for Some Nonlinear Matrix Models for the Dynamics of Structured Populations." *Natural Resource Modeling* 4:331–357.

Easterlin, Richard A. 1961. "The American Baby Boom in Historical Perspective." *American Economic Review* 51:860–911.

Frauenthal, James C., and Swick, Kenneth E. 1983. "Limit Cycle Oscillations of the Human Population." *Demography* 20:285–298.

Golubitsky, Martin, and Schaeffer, David G. 1985. *Singularities and Groups in Bifurcation Theory*. vol. 1. Berlin: Springer-Verlag.

Goubert, Pierre. 1965. "Recent Theories and Research in French Population Between 1500 and 1700." In *Population in History*, ed. D. V. Glass and D. E. C. Eversley. Ghicago: Aldine.

Guckenheimer, J., Oster, G., and Ipakchi, A. 1977. "The Dynamics of Density-Dependent Population Models." *Journal of Mathematical Biology* 4:101–147.

Hasting, A. 1978. "Evolutionary Stable Strategies and the Evolution of Life History Strategies. I. Density Dependent Models." *Journal of Theoretical Biology* 75:527–536.

Hirsch. Morris W., and Smale, Stephen. 1974. *Differential Equations, Dynamic Systems, and Linear Algebra*. New York: Academic Press.

Lee, Ronald D. 1974. "The Formal Dynamics of Controlled Populations and the Echo, the Boom and the Bust." *Demography* 11:563–585.

———. 1977. "Methods and Models for Analyzing Historical Series of Births, Deaths, and Marriages." In *Population Patterns in the Past*, ed. Ronald Demos Lee. New York: Academic Press.

———. 1987. "Population Dynamics of Humans and Other Animals." *Demography* 24:443–465.

Lorenz, Hans-Walter. 1989. *Nanlinear Dynamical Economics and Chaotic Motion*. Berlin: Springer-Verlag.

Lotka, Alfred J. 1925. *Elements of Physical Biology*. Baltimore: Williams and Wilkens.

Samuelson, Paul A. 1972. "A Universal Cycle?" In *The Collected Scientific Papers of P. A. Samuelson*. vol. 3, ed. Robert Merton. Cambridge, MA: MIT Press.

———. 1976. "An Economist's Non-linear Model of Self-Generated Fertility Waves." *Population Studies* 30:243–247.

Swick, Kenneth E. 1981. "Stability and Bifurcation in Age-Dependent Population Dynamics." *Theoretical Population Biology* 40:80–100.

Tuljapurkar, Shripad. 1987. "Cycles in Nonlinear Age-Structured Models. I. Renewal Equations." *Theoretical Population Biology* 32:26–41.

———. 1990. *Population Dynamics in Variable Environments*. New York: Springer-Verlag.

Usher, Michael B. 1972. "Developments in Leslie Matrix Model." In *Mathematical Models in Ecology*, ed. N. R. Jeffers. Oxford: Blackwell.

Volterra, Vito. 1931. *Leçons sur la Theorie Mathematique de la Lutte pour la Vie*. Paris: Gauthier-Villars.

Wachter, Kenneth W., and Lee, Ronald D. 1989. "U.S. Birth and Limit Cycle Models." *Demography* 26:99–115.

CHAPTER 8

Arthur, W. Brian. 1989. "Competing Technologies, Increasing Returns, and Lock-In by Historical Events." *Economic Journal* 99:116–131.

Benjamini, Y., and Maital, S. 1985. "Optimal Tax Evasion and Optimal Tax Evasion Policy: Behavioral Aspects." In *The Economics of the Shadow Economy*, ed. W. Gaetner and A. Wenig. Berlin: Springer-Verlag.

Boldrin, M. 1988. "Persistent Oscillations and Chaos in Economic Models: Notes for a Survey." In *The Economy as an Evolutionary Complex System*, ed. P. W. Anderson, K. J. Arrow, and D. Pines. New York: Addison-Wesley.

Chu, C. Y. Cyrus. 1990. "A Model of Income Tax Evasion with Venal Tax Officials." *Public Finance* 45:392–408.

———. 1993. "Oscillatory vs. Stationary Enforcement of Law." *International Review of Law and Economics* 13:303–315.

Cooter, Robert D., and Ulen, Thomas. 1988. *Law and Economics*. London: Scott, Foresman.

David, Paul. 1988. "Path-Dependence: Putting the Past into the Future of Economics." Stanford Institute for Mathematical Studies in the Social Science (Economic Science) Technical Report 533, August.

Gordon, J. P. F. 1989. "Individual Morality and Reputation Costs as Deterrents to Tax Evasion." *European Economic Review* 33:797–805.

Hardin, Garrett. 1968. "The Tragedy of the Commons." *Science* 162:1243–1248.

Jones, Robert. 1976. "The Origin and Development of a Medium of Exchange." *Journal of Political Economy* 84:757–776.

Lui, Francis T. 1986. "A Dynamic Model of Corruption Deterrence." *Journal of Public Economics* 31:215–236.

Schelling, Thomas. 1978. *Micromotives and Macrobehavior*. New York: Norton.

Schlicht, E. 1985. "The Shadow Economy and Morals: A Note." In *The Economics of the Shadow Economy*, ed. W. Gaetner and A. Wenig. Berlin: Springer-Verlag.

Theil, Henry. 1971. *Principles of Econometrics*. New York: Wiley.

Wilson, John Q. 1983. *Thinking about Crime*. New York: Basic Books.

CHAPTER 9

Chang, S.-L. 1983. *History of Chinese Peasant Revolution*. Peking: People's Publisher (in Chinese).

Chao, K. 1986. *Man and Land in Chinese History: An Economic Analysis*. Stanford, CA: Stanford University Press.

Chao, Wen-lin, and Hsieh, Shu-chun. 1988. *History of Chinese Population*. Peking: People's Publisher (in Chinese).

Chu, C. Y. Cyrus, and Lee, Ronald D. 1994. "Famine, Revolt and the Dynastic Cycle: Population Dynamics in Historic China." *Journal of Population Economics* 7:351–378.

———. 1997. "Corrigendum." *Journal of Population Economics* 10, in press.

Chu, Ko-chen. 1973. "A Preliminary Study of the Climate Fluctuations During the Last 5,000 years in China." *Scientia Sinica* 16:226–256.

von Clausewitz, C. 1976. *On War*, ed. and trans. M. Howard and P. Paret. Princeton, NJ: Princeton University Press.

Durand, John D. 1960. "The Population Statistics of China, A.D. 2–1953." *Population Studies* 13:209–257.

Hartwell, Robert. 1982. "The Demographic, Political, and Social Transformation of China, 750–1550." *Harvard Journal of Asiatic Studies* 42:365–442.

Ho, Ping-ti. 1959. *Studies on the Population of China: 1368–1953.* Cambridge, MA: Harvard University Press.

Kelsey, David. 1988. "The Economics of Chaos or the Chaos of Economics." *Oxford Economic Papers* 40:1–31.

Kuan, T.-K. 1983. "Demographic Changes Between the Warring States Period and the Early Han." *Bulletin of the Institute of History and Philosophy* 54:64–108.

Lee, Ronald D. 1987. "Population Dynamics of Humans and Other Animals." *Demography* 24:443–465.

———, and Galloway, Patrick R. 1985. "Some Possibilities for the Analysis of Aggregate Historical Demographic Data From China." Paper presented at the Workshop on Qing Population History, California Institute of Technology, Pasadena, CA.

Maddala, G. S. 1983. *Limited Dependent and Qualitative Variables in Econometrics.* Cambridge: Cambridge University Press.

Ranis, Gustav, and Fei, John C. H. 1961. "A Theory of Economic Development." *American Economic Review* 51:533–558.

Samuelson Paul A. 1958. "An Exact Consumption-Loan Model of Interest With or Without the Social Contrivance of Money." *Journal of Political Economy* 66:467–482.

Usher, Dan. 1989. "The Dynastic Cycle and the Stationary State." *American Economic Review* 79:1031–1044.

Wright, A. F. 1965. "Comments on Early Chinese Views." In *The Pattern of Chinese History*, ed. John Meskill. Lexington, MA: Heath.

CHAPTER 10

Berger, Mark C. 1983. "Changes in Labor Force Composition and Male Earnings: A Production Approach." *Journal of Human Resources* 17:177–196.

Berndt, Ernst R. 1991. *The Practice of Econometrics: Classic and Contemporary.* New York: Addison-Wesley.

Bonneuil, Noël. 1989. "Conjoncture et Structure dans le Comportement de Fecondite." *Population* 1:135–157.

———. 1990. "Turbulent Dynamics in a XVIIth Century Population." *Mathematical Population Studies* 2:289–311.

———. 1992. "Attractors and Confiners in Demography." *Annals of Operations Research* 37:17–32.

Chesnais, Jean-Claude. 1992. *The Demographic Transition: Stages, Patterns, and Economic Implications.* Oxford: Clarendon Press.

Chu, C. Y. Cyrus, and Lu, Huei-chung. 1995. "Toward a General Analysis of Endogenous Easterlin Cycles." *Journal of Population Economics* 8:35–57.

Connelly, Rachel. 1986. "A Framework for Analyzing the Impact of Cohort Size on Education and Labor Earning." *Journal of Human Resources* 21:543–562.

Day, Richard H., Kim, K.-H., and Macunovich, D. 1989. "Complex Demoeconomic Dynamics." *Journal of Population Economics* 2:139–159.

Diewert, W. Erwin. 1974. "Applications of Duality Theory." In *Frontiers of Quantitative Economics*. Vol. 2, ed. Michael Intriligator and David Kendrick. Amsterdam: North-Holland.

Easterlin, Richard A. 1961. "The American Baby Boom in Historical Perspective." *American Economic Review* 51:860–911.

———. 1980. *Birth and Fortune*. 2nd ed. Chicago: University of Chicago Press.

Feichtinger, Gustav, and Dockner, Engelbert J. 1990. "Capital Accumulation, Endogenous Population Growth, and Easterlin Cycles." *Journal of Population Economics* 3:73–87.

———, and Sorger, Gerhard. 1989. "Self-Generated Fertility Waves in a Nonlinear Continuous Overlapping Generations Model." *Journal of Population Economics* 2:267–280.

Frauenthal, James C. 1975. "A Dynamical Model for Human Population Growth." *Theoretical Population Biology* 8:64–73.

———, and Swick, Kenneth E. 1983. "Limit Cycle Oscillations of the Human Population." *Demography* 20:285–298.

Freeman, Richard. 1979. "The Effect of Demographic Factors on Age-Earnings Profiles." *Journal Human Resources* 14:289–318.

Keyfitz, Nathan. 1972. "Population Waves." In *Population Dynamics*, ed. T. N. E. Greville. New York: Academic Press.

Lau, Lawrence J. 1986. "Functional Forms in Econometric Model Building." In *Handbook of Econometrics*. Vol. 3, ed. Zvi Griliches and Michael D. Intriligator. Amsterdam: North-Holland.

Lee, Ronald D. 1974. "The Formal Dynamics of Controlled Populations and the Echo, the Boom and the Bust." *Demography* 11:563–585.

———. 1978. "Causes and Consequences of Age Structure Fluctuations: The Easterlin Hypothesis." *Proceedings of Conference on Economic and Demographic Change: Issues for the 1980s*. Vol. 1:405–418.

Lorenz, Hans Walter. 1989. *Nonlinear Dynamical Economics and Chaotic Motion*. Berlin: Springer-Verlag.

Pesaran, M. Hashem, and Deaton, Angus S. 1978. "Testing Non-nested Non-linear Regression Models." *Econometrica* 46:677–694.

Samuelson, Paul A. 1976. "An Economist's Non-Linear Model of Self-Generated Fertility Waves." *Population Studies* 30:243–247.

Swick, Kenneth E. 1981a. "Stability and Bifurcation in Age-Dependent Population Dynamics." *Theoretical Population Biology* 40:80–100.

———. 1981b. "A Nonlinear Model for Human Population Dynamics." *SIAM Journal of Applied Mathematics* 40:266–278.

Tuljapurkar, Shripad. 1987. "Cycles in Nonlinear Age-Structured Models. I. Renewal Equations." *Theoretical Population Biology* 32:26–41.

Varian, Hal R. 1984. *Microeconomic Analysis*. 2nd ed. New York: Norton.

Wachter, Kenneth W. 1991. "Elusive Cycles: Are There Dynamically Possible Lee–Easterlin Models for U.S. Births?" *Population Studies* 45:109–135.

———, and Lee, Ronald D. 1989. "U.S. Birth and Limit Cycle Models." *Demography* 26:99–115.

Ward, Michael D., and Butz, William P. 1980. "Completed Fertility and Its Timing." *Journal of Political Economy* 88:917–940.

CHAPTER 11

Barro, Robert J. 1974. "Are Government Bonds Net Wealth?" *Journal of Political Economy* 81:1095–1117.

Becker, Gary S., Murphy, Kevin M., and Tamura, Robert. 1990. "Human Capital, Fertility and Economic Growth." *Journal of Political Economy* 98:S12–S37.

Bishop, John A., Chow, K. V., and Formby, John P. 1994. "Testing for Marginal Distributions with Lorenz and Concentration Curves." *International Economic Review* 35:479–488.

Black, Duncan. 1958. *The Theory of Committees and Elections*. Cambridge: Cambridge University Press.

Boadway, Robin W., and Wildasin, David E. 1989. "A Median Voter Model of Social Security." *International Economic Review* 30:307–328.

Browning, E. K. 1975. "Why the Social Insurance Budget Is So Large in a Democratic Society." *Economic Inquiry* 13:373–388.

Chesnais, Jean-Claude. 1992. *The Demographic Transition: Stages, Patterns, and Economic Implications*. Oxford: Clarendon Press.

Chu, C. Y. Cyrus, and Jiang, Lily. 1997. "Demographic Transition, Family Structure, and Income Inequality," *Review of Economics and Statistics* 79:665–669.

Deaton, Angus S., and Paxson, Christina H. 1997. "The Effects of Economic and Population Growth on National Saving and Inequality." *Demography* 34:97–114.

Ehrlich, Issac, and Lui, Francis T. 1991. "Inter-Generational Trade, Longevity, and Economic Growth." *Journal of Political Economy* 99:1029–1059.

Feldstein, Martin S. 1974. "Social Security, Induced Retirement, and Aggregate Capital Formation." *Journal of Political Economy* 82:905–927.

Fei, John C. H., Ranis, Gustav, and Kuo, Shirley W. Y. 1979. *Growth with Equity: The Taiwan Case*. Oxford: Oxford University Press.

Higgins, Matthew, and Williamson, Jeffrey G. 1997. "Age Structure Dynamics in Asia and Dependence on Foreign Capital." *Population and Development Review* 23:261–293.

Hu, Sheng-cheng. 1982. "Social Security, Majority Voting Equilibrium and Dynamic Efficiency." *International Economic Review* 23:269–287.

Kuznets, Simon. 1965. "Demographic and Economic Change in Developed Countries," in Economic Growth and Structure: Selected Essays, ed. by Simon Kuznets. N.Y.: W. W. Norton.

Lee, Ronald D. 1994a. "Population Age Structure, Inter-Generational Transfer, and Wealth." *Journal of Human Resources* 29:1027–1063.

———. 1994b. "The Formal Demography of Population Aging, Transfers and the Economic Life Cycle." In *Demography of Aging*, ed. Linda G. Martin and Samuel S. Preston. Washington DC: National Academy Press.

Leff, N. H. 1969. "Dependency Rates and Savings Rates." *American Economic Review* 59:886–895.

Lewis, F. D. 1983. "Fertility and Savings in the United States: 1830–1900." *Journal of Political Economy* 91:825–839.

Mankiw, N. Gregory, Romer, D., and Weil, David N. 1992. "A Contribution to the Empirics of Economic Growth." *Quarterly Journal of Economics* 107:407–437.

Mason, Andrew. 1987. "National Saving Rates and Population Growth: A New Model and New Evidence." In *Population Growth and Economic Development: Issues and Evidence*, ed. D. Gale Johnson and Ronald D. Lee. Madison, WI: University of Wisconsin Press.

Neher, P. A. 1971. "Peasants, Procreation and Pensions." *American Economic Review* 61:380–389.

Nerlove, Marc. 1996. "Reflections on Agricultural Development, Population Growth, and the Environment." In *Current Issues in Economic Development: An Asian Perspective*, ed. M. G. Quibria and J. Malcolm Dowling. New York: Oxford University Press.

———, and Raut, Lakshmi K. 1997. "Growth Models with Endogenous Population: A General Framework." In *Handbook of Population and Family Economics,* ed. M. R. Rosenzweig and O. Stark. Amsterdam: North-Holland.

Solow, Robert. 1956. "A Contribution to the Theory of Economic Growth," *Quarterly Journal of Economics* 79:65–94.

Stark, Oded, Taylor, Edward, and Yitzhaki, Shlomo. 1986. "Remittances and Inequality," *Economic Journal* 96:722–740.

Tabellini, Guido. 1990. "A Positive Theory of Social Security." Working paper #3272, National Bureau of Economic Research.

CHAPTER 12

Arthur, Brian W. 1984. "The Analysis of Linkages in Demographic Theory." *Demography* 21:109–128.

Atkinson, Anthony B. 1970. "On the Measurement of Inequality." *Journal of Economic Theory* 2:244–263.

Chu, C. Y. Cyrus. 1997. "Age Distribution Dynamics During Demographic Transition." *Demography* 34:551–563.

———, and Koo, Hui-wen. 1990. "Intergeneration Income-Group Mobility and Differential Fertility." *American Economic Review* 80:1125–1138.

Coale, Ansley J. 1957. "How the Age Distribution of Human Population is Determined." *Cold Spring Harbor Symposia on Quantitative Biology* 22:83–89.

———. 1972. *The Growth and Structure of Human Populations*. Princeton, NJ: Princeton University Press.

Fishburn, Peter C. 1980. "Stochastic Dominance and Moments of Distributions." *Mathematics of Operations Research* 3:295–311.

Foster, James E., Greer, J., and Thorbecke, E. 1984. "Decomposable Poverty Measures." *Econometrica* 52:761–766.

———, and Shorrocks, Anthony F. 1988. "Poverty Orderings." *Econometrica* 56:173–177.

Hadar, Josef, and Russell, William R. 1969. "Rules for Ordering Uncertain Prospects." *American Economic Review* 59:25–34.

Kart, Cary S. 1994. *The Reality of Aging: An Introduction to Gerontology*. Boston: Allyn & Bacon.

Keyfitz, Nathan. 1988. "Fertility, Age Distribution and Intergenerational Relations." In *Economics of Changing Age Distribution in Developed Countries*, ed. R. D. Lee, W. B. Arthur, and G. Rogers. Oxford: Clarendon Press.

Lam, David. 1984. "The Variance of Population Characteristics." *Population Studies* 38:117–127.

Lee, Ronald D. 1980. "Age Structure, Intergenerational Transfers, and Economic Growth: An Overview." *Revue Economique* 31:1129–1156.

———. 1994. "The Formal Demography of Population Aging." In *Demography of Aging*, ed. Linda G. Martin and Samuel H. Preston. Washington DC: National Academy Press.

———, and Lapkoff, Shirley. 1988. "Intergenerational Flows of Time and Goods: Consequences of Slowing Population Growth." *Journal of Political Economy* 96:618–651.

Manton, K. G., Stallard, E., and Singer, B. H. 1994. "Methods for Projecting the Future Size and Health Status of the U.S. Elderly Population." In *Studies in the Economics of Aging*, ed. David A. Wise. Chicago: University of Chicago Press.

Mason, Andrew. 1988. "Saving, Economic Growth, and Demographic Change." *Population and Development Review* 14:113–144.

Preston, Samuel H. 1982. "Relations Between Individual Life Cycles and Population Characteristics." *American Sociological Review* 47:253–264.

Sen, A. K. 1976. "Poverty: An Ordinal Approach to Measurement." *Econometrica* 44:219–231.

Stolnitz, G. J. 1992. *Demographic Causes and Economic Consequences of Population Aging: Europe and America*, United Nations Population Fund, Economics Studies No. 3. New York: United Nations.

Willis, Robert. 1988. "Life Cycles, Institutions, and Population Growth: A Theory of the Equilibrium Rate of Interest in an Overlapping Generations Model." In *Economics of Changing Age Distribution in Developed Countries*, ed. Ronald D. Lee, W. Brian Arthur, and G. Rogers. Oxford: Clarendon Press.

CHAPTER 13

Arrow, Kenneth J. 1962. "The Economic Implications of Learning by Doing," *Review of Economic Studies* 24:155–173.

Backus, David K., Kehoe, Patrick J., and Kehoe, Timothy J. 1992. "In Search of Scale Effect in Trade and Growth." *Journal of Economic Theory* 58:377–409.

Barro, Robert J., and Sala-i-Martin, Xavier. 1995. *Economic Growth*. New York: McGraw-Hill.

Bonneuil, Noël. 1994. "Malthus, Boserup and Population Viability." *Mathematical Population Studies* 5:107–119.

Boserup, Ester. 1966. *The Conditions of Agricultural Growth: The Economics of Agrarian Change Under Population Pressure*. Chicago: Aldine Publishing.

———. 1981. *Population and Technological Change*. Chicago: University of Chicago Press.

Chu, C. Y. Cyrus. 1997. "Population Density and Infrastructure Development." *Review of Development Economics*, in press.

———, and Tsai, Y. 1995. "Productivity, Investment in Infrastructure, and Population Size." Paper presented at the Conference on Increasing Returns and Economic Analysis, Monash University, Australia, September.

Ethier, Wilfred J. 1982. "National and International Returns to Scale in the Modern Theory of International Trade." *American Economic Review* 72:389–405.

Fogel, Robert W. 1964. *Railroads and American Economic Growth: Essays in Econometric History*. Baltimore: Johns Hopkins Press.

Goodfriend, Marvin, and McDermott, John. 1995. "Early Development." *American Economic Review* 85:116–133.

Jones, E. L., and Woolf, S. J. 1969. *Agrarian Change and Economic Development*. London: Methuen.

Kremer, Michael. 1993. "Population Growth and Technological Change: One Million B.C. to 1990." *Quarterly Journal of Economics* 108:681–716.

Kuznets, Simon. 1960. "Population Change and Aggregate Output." In Universities-National Bureau of Economic Research, *Demographic and Economic Change in Developed Countries*. Princeton, NJ: Princeton University Press.

Lee, Ronald D. 1986. "Malthus and Boserup: A Dynamic Synthesis." In *The State of Population Theory: Forward from Malthus*, ed. David Coleman and David Schofield. Oxford: Basil Blackwell.

———.1988. "Induced Population Growth and Induced Technological Progress: Their Interaction in the Acceleration Stage." *Mathematical Population Studies* 1:265–288.

Ng, Yew-Kwang. 1986. "On the Welfare Economics of Population Control." *Population and Development Review* 12:247–266.

Pryor, Frederic L., and Maurer, Stephen B. 1982. "On Induced Economic Change in Pre-Capitalist Society." *Journal of Development Economics* 10:325–353.

Rivera-Batiz, L. A., and Romer, Paul M. 1991. "Economic Integration and Economic Growth." *Quarterly Journal of Economics* 106:531–555.

Romer, Paul M. 1990. "Endogenous Technological Change." *Journal of Political Economy* 98:S71–S102.

———.1994. "The Origin of Endogenous Growth." *Journal of Economic Perspectives* 8:3–22.

Simon, Julian. 1977. *The Economics of Population Growth*. Princeton, NJ: Princeton University Press.

———.1981. *The Ultimate Resource*. Princeton, NJ: Princeton University Press.

Solow, Robert M. 1956. "A Contribution to the Theory of Economic Growth." *Quarterly Journal of Economics* 70:65–94.

Yang, Xiaokai, and Ng, Yew-Kwang. 1993. *Specialization and Economic Organization*. Amsterdam: North-Holland.

CHAPTER 14

Arrow, Kenneth, et al. 1995. "Economic Growth, Carrying Capacity, and the Environment." *Science* 268:520–521.

Arthur, W. Brian. 1989. "Competing Technologies, Increasing Returns, and Lock-In by Historical Events." *Economic Journal* 99:116–131.

Chu, C. Y. Cyrus. 1997. "Population Density and Infrastructure Development." *Review of Development Economics* 1:294–304.

———, and Tai, Chin. 1997. "Economic Development, Ecological Change, and Population Dynamics." Mimeographed.

———, and Tsai, Y. 1995. "Productivity, Investment in Infrastructure, and Population Size." Paper presented at the Conference on Increasing Returns and Economic Analysis, Monash University, Australia.

Dobzhansky, Theodosius. 1961. "Man and the Natural Selection." *American Scientist* 49:285–299.

Goodfriend, Marvin, and McDermott, John. 1995. "Early Development." *American Economic Review* 85:116–133.

Gould, Jay. 1977. *Ever Since Darwin—Reflections in Natural History*. New York: Norton.

Hammer, M., Jansson, A., Jansson, B-O. 1993. "Diversity Change and Sustainability: Implications for Fisheries." *Ambio* 22:97–105.

Hardin, Garrett. 1968. "The Tragedy of the Commons." *Science* 162:1243–1248.

Harvey, Brian, and Hallet, J. D. 1977. *Environment and Society: An Introductory Analysis*. Cambridge, MA: MIT Press.

Kremer, Michael. 1993. "Population Growth and Technological Change: One Million B.C. to 1990." *Quarterly Journal of Economics* 108:681–716.

Meadows, D. H., Meadows, D. L., and Radners, Jorgen. 1992. *Beyond the Limits*. Post Mills, VT: Chelsea Green.

Nerlove, Marc. 1991. "Population and Environment: A Parable of Firewood and Other Tales." *American Journal of Agricultural Economics* 73:1335–1347.

————. 1993. "Procreation, Fishing and Hunting: Renewable Resources and Dynamic Planar Systems." *American Journal of Agricultural Economics* 75:59–71.

Ng, Yew-Kwang. 1995. "Toward Welfare Biology: Evolutionary Economics of Animal Consciousness and Suffering." *Biology and Philosophy* 10:255–285.

Romer, Paul M. 1990. "Endogenous Technological Change." *Journal of Political Economy* 98:S71–S102.

Shaw, Jane S., and Stroup, Richard L. 1990. "Global Warming and Ozone Depletion." In *Economics and the Environment: A Reconciliation*, ed. Walter Block. Vancouver, B.C.: Fraser Institute.

Smith, Fraser. 1996. "Biological Diversity, Ecosystem Stability, and Economic Development." *Ecological Economics* 16:191–203.

Swanson, Timothy M. 1995. "Uniformity in Development and the Decline of Biological Diversity." In *The Economics and Ecology of Biodiversity Decline*, ed. T. M. Swanson. New York: Cambridge University Press.

Yang, Xiaokai, and Ng, Yew-Kwang. 1993. *Specialization and Economic Organization*. Amsterdam: North-Holland.

CHAPTER 15

Chu, C. Y. Cyrus, and Tsai, Yiru. 1997. "Fertility Decline, and Pension Systems: An Equilibrium Analysis." National Taiwan University. Mimeographed.

Fogel, Robert W. 1994. "Economic Growth, Population Theory, and Physiology: The Bearing of Long-Term Processes on the Making of Economic Policy." *American Economic Review* 84:369–395.

Samuelson, Paul A. 1976. "An Economist's Non-Linear Model of Self-Generated Fertility Waves." *Population Studies* 30:243–247.

Simon, Julian L. 1981. *The Ultimate Resource*. Princeton, NJ: Princeton University Press.

Author Index

Subject Index